Teaching Mathematics
Using Popular Culture

Teaching Mathematics Using Popular Culture

Strategies for Common Core Instruction from Film and Television

ELANA REISER

McFarland & Company, Inc., Publishers
Jefferson, North Carolina

Library of Congress Cataloguing-in-Publication Data

Reiser, Elana, 1979–
     Teaching mathematics using popular culture : strategies for common
core instruction from film and television / Elana Reiser.
          p.   cm.
     Includes bibliographical references and index.

     ISBN 978-0-7864-7706-7 (softcover : acid free paper) ∞
     ISBN 978-1-4766-2122-7 (ebook)

     1. Mathematics—Study and teaching.   2. Mathematics—
Psychological aspects.   3. Mathematics in mass media.   4. Popular
culture.   I. Title.
     QA11.R426 2015
     510.71'073—dc23   2015035342

British Library cataloguing data are available

On the cover: *inset* Jake Gyllenhaal in *October Sky*, 1999; *background* boys
watching rocket launch, *October Sky*, 1999 (both images Photofest)

Printed in the United States of America

McFarland & Company, Inc., Publishers
  Box 611, Jefferson, North Carolina 28640
    www.mcfarlandpub.com

Acknowledgments

I'd like to thank my husband Justin for his endless patience in thoughtful editing, giving suggestions, and being somebody to bounce ideas off of.

I'd also like to thank my parents for encouraging me to write a book and making me think it was possible through their own accomplishments and published books.

Many thanks to my students and former students at St. Joseph's College for being so enthusiastic, especially to James Fanning for all the help with pictures, and to Kristi Burns, Julianne Miller, and Ashley Schreck for helping me find examples to use.

Finally, thank you to my family for their help and encouragement. This includes Michael and Sofia for all their help with the pictures, Rachel for being my hand model, and John, Lisa, and Florian.

Language and Content Advisory

Several of the movies and television shows given as examples in this book contain bad language and/or inappropriate scenes. For the most part the clips containing math are not affected by these, but there are some cases where curses are audible. It is advisable to watch all clips beforehand and decide if they are appropriate to show in your classroom.

Table of Contents

Solutions Explained

Most of the activities in Chapters Two through Seven are explained in detail and solutions are given. There are, however, some activities that are not worked out in full detail, for various reasons. For a selected number of these, the solutions are provided in Appendix B.

Preface

This book explores contemporary movies and television shows that contain mathematical elements. This book also shows how math teachers can use popular media to boost student motivation. The primary purpose of using media in the mathematics classroom is to garner student interest, which one hopes can translate into attention and then interest in mathematics. This adds a new method to an educator's teaching techniques, allowing for an additional way to reach students in a subject that is notorious for being difficult. The examples in this book show that math is relevant to a student's life by highlighting real-world scenarios involving math played out by familiar characters. This book hopes to make it clear that math practitioners can better serve their students by using student interests in popular media to increase student motivation.

This book provides a rationale, based on research and experience, for using popular media in the mathematics classroom, as well as examples of how to use such media. This is an important topic because student motivation in mathematics is an integral component of student success, and using popular media in the classroom is one way of motivating students. The popular media discussed in this book includes films and television shows. The book is organized based on the subject strands of the Common Core State Standards Initiative. This allows teachers to go to the specific chapter that they need to get examples for the class that they are teaching rather than having to search through the book. The Common Core Standards were initiated at the state level as a way for the states in the United States to have a shared set of standards in English and mathematics. This should help ensure that no matter what state a child lives in, he or she is getting the same level of education. The standards were designed to prepare students for entering college and competing in a global economy.

The film and television examples included in this book are the result of an exhaustive search I conducted with the help of friends and family. Online resources listing math in movies and television shows were used to locate additional clips.[1] I tried to view each movie and television show in its entirety in order to understand the clip's context. To do this I rented them from my library or watched them online through Hulu and Netflix. Most clips are available on YouTube. Once I had a description of the math content, I created an activity to go along with it. Activities were generated in various ways. Some activities I had already done in my own classroom. Some followed easily from the clip, such as when a math problem was given in the clip. Others were adapted from lessons I have been taught or have otherwise encountered.

The first chapter of this book includes a history of how visual media is used in the mathematics classroom and a discussion of why visual media serves as a student motivator. The second chapter briefly goes over what the Common Core Standards in mathematics are and explains how popular media can be used in conjunction with them. Each of the next six chapters discusses how to use popular media in each of the high school Common Core Standards' subject strands. These strands include number and quantity, algebra, functions, modeling, geometry, and statistics and probability. Within each strand, I describe the clip and provide examples of how to use it in a classroom. Then, the example is built into an activity that introduces, reviews, or builds upon a mathematical topic. There is also a description of how each example fits with the Common Core Standards for Mathematical Practice (problem solving, reasoning, constructing arguments, modeling, using appropriate tools, precision, structure, and repeated reasoning). These chapters are not meant to provide full lesson plans to teachers. Teachers can incorporate the suggestions for activities however they feel works best with their curriculum. The final chapter provides suggestions on how students can look for examples of mathematics in popular media on their own, independent of the classroom. Other ideas for uses outside the classroom are also discussed, such as home schooling, tutoring, and self-study.

The primary target audience for this book consists of two groups. The first group consists of mathematics teachers who are interested in alternative methods of teaching. The second group consists of mathematics teachers interested in incorporating technology into their classrooms. Additionally, college-level professors of education will be able to use this book in their classrooms with pre-service mathematics teachers. This book will also be of interest to libraries (public and school-based) as a reference book for mathematics teachers. Parents will also be interested in this book as a way to teach their children mathematics outside of the classroom. This book will be valuable for home schooling and tutoring, and other activities that occur outside of school, precisely because it follows an approved curriculum.

The idea for this book originated when I was writing a personal essay on what influenced me to become interested in mathematics as a female (the stereotype is still commonly held that males are better in math than females). Writing this essay caused me to reflect on my past and think about not only how I became interested in math, but also how I stayed interested in math. I had some of the typical influences, such as great math teachers and natural ability. However, one unexpected influence I recalled at this time was watching one of my favorite television shows, called *Byrds of Paradise*. I remember one scene where the teenage son was studying for a math test and had to memorize the quadratic formula. He kept repeating, "Negative b plus or minus the square root of b squared minus $4ac$ over $2a$." I got excited because I also had just learned the quadratic formula. Seeing the connection between what I was learning in the classroom and what I was watching on television perpetuated my interest in math. The show is not available on DVD so it is not included as an example in this book.

This memory inspired me to include clips from movies and television shows in some of my college-level math classes. I showed problem-solving to a class of non–math majors using *Die Hard: With a Vengeance* (see Chapter Five). It was great to see them get excited while figuring out the problem presented in the movie. After they figured it out, one student said she had seen the movie many times but it was not until then that she actually had understood how they solved the problem. I have also used clips from *The Price Is Right* and *Who Wants to Be a Millionaire* (see Chapter Seven) in my probability and statistics class. Students were extraordinarily engaged in these lessons and enjoyed them.

Over the years I have written a few articles on this topic, including one for the Mathematical Association of America (MAA) and one for the National Council for Teachers of Mathematics (NCTM) 2011 yearbook. I have also presented this topic to mathematics teachers and scholars at the NCTM annual conference in 2008 and at the MAA annual conference in 2009. Through these presentations I have seen how receptive math teachers are to this topic, and that inspired me to explore it further in the form of this book.

Introduction: The Theory of Visual Media in the Mathematics Classroom

Garnering student interest in mathematics is a long-documented battle. One part of the puzzle of getting students interested in mathematics is motivation. Martin Ford defines motivation as having three dimensions: goals, emotions, and self-efficacy.[1] Goals are described as either intrinsic or extrinsic. Intrinsic motivational goals include learning for the sake of learning. Students with this type of motivation want to do well because they enjoy the learning process. Extrinsic motivation is learning to get a reward or to avoid a punishment. This can include praise or criticism from a parent or teacher, grades, or a monetary reward. Emotions are defined as how interested a student is in the topic. Self-efficacy is how confident students are in their ability. If the task appears to be too difficult, then students will not be motivated to attempt it.

Middelton and Spanias found that students who are intrinsically motivated do better and understand the material they are learning more thoroughly.[2] Intrinsic motivation has also been found to lead to creativity and high-quality learning.[3] In one study, intrinsic motivation was found to be a better predictor of mathematical achievement than intelligence quotient (IQ).[4] Extrinsic motivation has been found to have negative effects on learning, including student anxiety and lower creativity.[5] Additionally, the expectation of a reward weakens the intrinsic desire to learn.[6]

The emotional aspect of motivation involves students' interest levels. Deci and Ryan found that there is a correlation between intrinsic motivation and self-reports of interest.[7] It makes sense that students are more likely to be motivated if they are interested in a topic and enjoy it.[8] If our challenge

as teachers is, as Deitte and Howe suggest, to motivate students to feel respon-
sible for their educational development, we need to understand what drives
them. "This goal," Deitte and Howe continue, "is most effectively accom-
plished if students convince themselves that mathematics is interesting and
useful."[9]

From birth, people are naturally "active, inquisitive, curious, and playful
creatures, displaying a ubiquitous readiness to learn and explore, and they
do not require extraneous incentives to do so."[10] Researchers have found that
in the lower elementary grades students are generally very motivated to learn
mathematics.[11] As they get older, students become less motivated because by
the middle grades they start to view themselves as either being good or bad
at math.[12] Once a student classifies math as an interest he or she will likely
become engaged in it, regardless of the specific activity. Once a student classifies math as a non-interest he or she will likely not become engaged, regardless of the specific activity.[13] While student motivation is fairly stable, it is
possible to increase it through instructional design.[14]

Since we know it is possible to increase motivation and that intrinsic
motivation is the more desirable type of motivation, the goal becomes to find
a way for students to be intrinsically motivated in mathematics. One way
found to increase intrinsic motivation is for teachers to choose activities that
stimulate, provide student control, and correlate with students' interests.[15]
The degree of stimulation is affected by how challenging a problem is and
how curious the student is about it. For there to be student control, the student
must have free choice in how to solve the problem, and it shouldn't be too
difficult. Similarly, Devlin suggests making math "cool" so that it becomes
something that students want to practice and master.[16]

We will now focus on increasing student interest as a method of increasing intrinsic motivation. One way to do this is by introducing or reviewing
a topic using movies or television. In recent years an increasing number of
television shows and movies have incorporated mathematical topics into their
scripts and, by doing so, offer the idea that math is both interesting and func-
tional. Culturally, students of all ages have a deep interest in movies and television. This interest can serve as a motivator for learning math. Beckmann,
Thompson, and Austin echo this statement, further explaining, "If we can
draw the mathematics out of the movies and literature that students find
engaging, then we can make mathematics more meaningful and interesting
to students."[17] Given that students are more interested in learning when the
topic is relevant to them, popular culture provides a necessary means for student engagement. Chappell and Thompson state that including popular
media in the classroom can increase motivation as well as connect math to

the students' lives and surroundings.[18] Using clips from movies and television shows is one way math teachers can use entertainment as a means of increasing student interest, in order to boost student motivation.

Another reason to use clips from movies and television shows in the classroom is that they provide a meaningful context for students. This has been shown in various studies. In one such study students learned probability.[19] The examples given to the students were either abstract, set in an educational context, or set in a medical context. Some of the students in the study were education majors, while others were nursing majors. Overall, it was found that the students given the examples set in a context (educational or medical) did better than the students given abstract examples. Additionally, it was found that students did the best when they were provided examples that had a meaningful context. In other words, the education students did best when given problems set in an education setting and the nursing students did best when given problems set in a medical setting.

In the Jasper Project at Vanderbilt University, educators used this research along with movies to provide students a meaningful context in which to learn mathematics.[20] Problems taken from popular movies were used as a basis for mathematics lessons. For example, in *Raiders of the Lost Ark*, Indiana Jones replaces a golden idol with a bag of sand. Students are asked to guess the weight of the sand and the idol. Through questions like this they are introduced to the concept of density in a meaningful context. The Jasper Project has since grown to be a collection of short videos about a boy named Jasper. These videos foster the development of mathematical problem-solving skills. Research on the Jasper Project has shown that students in classes that learn using meaningful contexts are more adept at complex problem-solving than students from traditionally taught classrooms.

There are a number of examples of movies and television shows being used in the mathematics classroom. Here we will discuss some media-driven activities along with feedback, if available, on how successful they have been.

Greenwald and Nestler give examples of how to use clips from *The Simpsons* in the math classroom. One example shows Bart's teacher telling a joke using calculus. They have an activity to go along with this clip and assign it to students taking Calculus I. Students were impressed the joke was featured in the show.[21] Another activity using a different clip is given on the first day of precalculus as an ice-breaker.[22] Greenwald and Nestler also discuss an activity on three dimensions and say that it serves as a great motivator, helping students feel comfortable with the topic while engaging them and encouraging them to be creative.[23] A last example uses a clip showing two girls playing jump rope and singing a rhyme about pi where they list some of the digits. This example helps visual learners as well as auditory learners.[24] Greenwald and Nestler like to use clips from *The Simpsons* because students start by laughing at the jokes; this helps lower math anxiety and allows an avenue for further mathematical study. "Most students find it interesting, entertaining, and creative."[25] This observed feedback concurs with what the literature says: the use of examples that students are interested in leads to engagement and creativity, which are both benefits of intrinsic motivation.

Butterworth and Coe discuss using *The Price Is Right* as a way of bringing fun and excitement into the classroom. They suggest that this television show helps make math more accessible and less abstract to weaker students. They also state that using the show will help students become interested in the calculations involved in the games because they are curious about the outcomes of the games.[26] Additionally, "students take ownership of the problems they solve and gain confidence in their own mathematical abilities."[27] Butterworth and Coe do caution that teachers wanting to use the games featured in *The Price Is Right* should work out solutions ahead of time, because some games are very easy to analyze while others are extremely difficult. Naresh and Royce also use *The Price Is Right* in the classroom. They have students play a computer simulation of the game Plinko and then have students design their own Plinko board.[28] They found that using this activity effectively engaged the students. Again, the results of these studies show that using television shows in the classroom leads to an increase in motivation.

Project Look Sharp, based at Ithaca College, "develops and provides lesson plans, media materials, training, and support for the effective integration of media literacy with critical thinking into classroom curricula at all education levels."[29] They do not have a math category, but they do provide lessons from the sciences. One example discussed by Scheibe involves the movie *Antz*. Students in a science class spent two weeks studying ants and other insects, and then they went to a viewing of the movie *Antz*.[30] Students made lists of how the ants in the movie were portrayed correctly and how they were portrayed incorrectly. This led to a class discussion on why the ants were portrayed the way they were. Teachers found that this activity increased student interest and led to a deeper understanding of the material. Tests reflected that students did best on the questions based on the class discussion of ants. Additionally, the tests showed that students retained the material covered in the movie six months later.[31]

Maillet uses the math featured in *Numb3rs* in his classroom. He shares many activities based on this television show on his blog. He states that using these activities in his classroom made students more excited about coming to class, which led to an increase in attendance. Also, one class went from a 56 percent pass rate on the Regents exam to a 91 percent pass rate.[32] Hopkins uses the "Six Degrees of Kevin Bacon" game to teach graph theory. Students are enthusiastic about this activity and become engaged.[33]

The above examples of mathematics featured in popular media being applied to the classroom provided feedback on how students responded to popular media's usage as a teaching tool. All of the feedback says the same thing: students become more engaged in the material, like its usage in the classroom, and are more motivated to learn. This agrees with the literature on the subject. There are many other examples of classroom use of math in popular media that do not provide feedback on student responses. Some of these are included below in order to provide a fuller picture of the different types of clips that have been used in the classroom setting.

The Numbers Behind Numb3rs describes some of the mathematical techniques that law enforcement officials use to help solve crimes. Many of the examples were featured in *Numb3rs*. For example, in the very first episode Charlie helps his brother solve a serial-killer case using a mathematical model that could locate the killer's location based on where his murders took place. Charlie's solution was based on real-life police officer and mathematician Kim Rossmo, who developed a formula that narrows down the search radius.[34]

Chappell and Thompson wrote a book that uses popular media to engage middle-school students in various activities relating mathematics to culture. For example, in one activity the authors use the plot from *The Pursuit of Happyness* to have students graph piecewise functions.[35]

Many lesson plans are provided on the *Teach with Movies* Web site. This site includes many subject areas. The math examples include lessons from *Donald in Mathmagic Land, Contact,* and *Stand and Deliver.*[36] Chartier uses the math behind the special effects in *Star Wars* as an application in his mathematics classes.[37] DeRose, Pixar's research lead, gave a TED-Ed lesson on how math is involved in creating Pixar characters.[38] Munz, Hudea, Imad, and Smith use zombie movies such as *Night of the Living Dead* to set up a model for zombie behavior.[39]

A collection of essays edited by Jessica K. Sklar and Elizabeth S. Sklar provides examples in which math intersects with popular culture. These include the numbers and equations featured in Lost,[40] using the *Matrix* trilogy to introduce mathematical topics such as computer graphics, Markov Chains, and network theory,[41] and math-savvy gamblers in *Rain Man, 21, The Hangover,* and *Numb3rs.*[42]

The bulk of this book is dedicated to giving examples of mathematics from movies and television shows. The examples that follow show how math can be made relevant to a student's life by highlighting its application in real-world scenarios dramatized by popular media. These chapters also illustrate math's pervasive presence in popular entertainment to help pique student interest.

Chapter One

Common Core State Standards Initiative

The Common Core State Standards (CCSS) developed in response to several concurrent factors in American education. Students in lower socioeconomic statuses and English language learners had not been performing as well as their peers. As a way of overcoming this, the Common Core State Standards Initiative (CCSSI) takes the same approach as "No Child Left Behind," but the standards everyone is held to are higher.

The reason that these standards are higher is that the United States is now competing in a global marketplace ... and losing. As Thomas L. Friedman says, the world is flat.[1] As a result of the development of new technologies, people in countries such as China and India are now competing for jobs that used to go to Americans. International mathematics examinations for high school students such as the Program for International Student Assessment (PISA) show that the United States is lagging in mathematics literacy behind countries such as Korea, Finland, and Japan.[2] The standards from these top-performing countries were used to create the CCSS.[3]

In addition to America's poor overall mathematical literacy, many high school graduates are not prepared for college or their careers. According to the National Center for Education Statistics, in the 2007–2008 school year 20 percent of first-year students took remedial courses.[4] These are high school level courses that are taught in college because students are not prepared to take a college level course. Data on the skills needed for college and the workplace were also taken into consideration as the CCSS were developed.[5]

Prior to the CCSS, when each state had its own standards, some states, such as Massachusetts, had consistently high standards. On the other hand, some states, such as Tennessee, had consistently lower standards.[6] Imagine a child educated in Tennessee who moves to Massachusetts. The child is likely not to be prepared to join a class of his peers. But with the CCSS this is no longer a problem. If all states share common standards then moving from state to state will not be as disruptive to a child's education.

A big criticism of mathematics education in the United States is that it is "a mile wide and an inch deep," meaning we cover a lot of topics but none of them in depth. As a reaction to this, the CCSS reduce the number of topics students cover while going into more depth on the topics that are covered.

It is with these considerations in mind that the CCSS were developed. The CCSS are meant to be higher standards and more concise than the standards states currently have. This way, the topics can be covered at a deeper level while focusing on critical thinking and problem solving skills.

There are two types of CCSS standards: the Standards for Mathematical Practice and the Grade Level Standards.[7] The Standards for Mathematical Practice span all of kindergarten through twelfth grade. The Grade Level Standards specify topics that should be covered grade by grade for kindergarten through eighth grade. For high school, the standards are split into topics rather than grades since students will be going through classes at different paces. These standards are lists of what topics students need to know. They do not provide a curriculum or suggest a way to teach the topics. The curriculum is left to the individual states to decide. For example, in New York the high school curriculum is split into Algebra I, Geometry, Algebra II, and Precalculus classes. The method of teaching the topics is left to the schools or individual teachers. As the standards state, the topic list within each grade or subject does not need to be covered in the same order as it is described in the standards.

There are eight Standards for Mathematical Practice. These standards are listed and briefly explained below:

1. Make sense of problems and persevere in solving them.
   Students must think about the problem before blindly trying to solve it. Students must be able to use multiple approaches when solving a problem. For example, if they are asked to solve a system of linear equations they should be able to solve them algebraically as well as graphically. Students should also be able to check their answers to see that they make sense.
2. Reason abstractly and quantitatively.
   While solving a problem students should first think about what the solution will look like. Then they should be able to solve the problem, explain what their solution means, and reflect on their thinking.
3. Construct viable arguments and critique the reasoning of others.

Students learn to construct mathematical proofs and understand proofs constructed by others. This is a progressive standard. In younger grades students should be able to see patterns and then make conjectures from these patterns. As students get older they should be able to think about proofs more abstractly.

4. Model with mathematics.

   Students learn to use the mathematics that they have studied in other fields and in real-world problems.

5. Use appropriate tools strategically.

   Students learn when and how to use technology appropriately so that it enhances their mathematical skills. Students should also learn how to interpret the results given by technology.

6. Attend to precision.

   Students learn to be clear about their mathematical work so that other people can understand it. For example, if a student introduces a letter into a proof they will state what that letter is representing. Rather than just saying an even number is 2n, they will specify that n is an integer.

7. Look for and make use of structure.

   Students look for patterns that commonly occur and use them to their advantage when solving problems. For example, students may realize that adding numbers in any order will produce the same result and then make a conjecture that $x + y = y + x$.

8. Look for and express regularity in repeated reasoning.

   If students notice that they are doing the same calculation many times, they should try to develop an algorithm to generalize it.

The high school level mathematics standards topics are number and quantity, algebra, functions, modeling, geometry, and statistics and probability. Number and quantity involves the real number line, complex numbers, and vectors. Algebra topics include polynomial and rational functions, and creating and solving equations and inequalities. Function topics include the definition and properties of functions including linear, quadratic, exponential, and trigonometric functions. Modeling is the practice of using mathematics in real-world problems and can involve any mathematical discipline. Geometry topics include triangle properties, proving geometric theorems, making constructions, similarity, trigonometry ratios, circle theorems, conic sections, and measurement, such as computing the area and volume of various shapes. Statistics and probability topics include being able to summarize, represent, and interpret data; perform experiments and use statistics to analyze them; perform conditional probability calculations; and understand expected value.

Since one goal of the CCSSI is to change the practice of mathematics in the United States being taught "a mile wide and an inch deep," there will be more time to spend on each topic in order for students to fully understand it. With this extra time, teachers can use creative methods of teaching in addition to traditional methods. Using this book as a guide, teachers can use popular media, which motivates students and garners their attention, to delve deeper into a topic.

Another goal of the CCSSI is to increase college and career readiness. Many of the activities in this book provide examples of critical thinking, problem solving, and creativity that will benefit any student going on to take college level courses and/or join the workforce. If the student goes on to become a mathematics major, these skills prepare that student for the rigor of higher level, proof-based mathematics. Even if the student does not pursue a degree in mathematics or the sciences, skills such as critical thinking and problem-solving are beneficial in any subject area, as well as in any workplace.

Another major goal of the CCSSI is to connect the mathematics learned in the classroom to real-world examples. Through the use of popular movies and television shows, students see the mathematics they are learning in the classroom used in the real world. Just to name a few uses, examples in later chapters use mathematics to solve crimes, measure mountains, and model behaviors.

The next six chapters are categorized by the six high-school-level standards: number and quantity, algebra, functions, modeling, geometry, and statistics and probability. Each chapter provides a series of activities that can be used in conjunction with movie or television show clips. Each example includes an introduction to the topic being discussed, a description of what happens in the media clip, and one or more activities that can be used in the classroom based on that clip. Following each activity is a description of the Standard(s) for Mathematical Practice that it satisfies.

CHAPTER TWO

Number and Quantity

What is the best number? Maybe 25 is best. It is an odd number and a square number because it can be written as 5^2. It is also the smallest square that can be written as the sum of two squares ($3^2 + 4^2$). It is curious because $25^2 = 625$, which ends in the original number, 25. It is powerful because for every prime number p that divides 25, p^2 also divides 25 (5 is the only prime that divides 25, and 5^2, which equals 25, also divides 25).

Asking students what the best number is leads to many interesting answers. In their answers, teachers can tell how much students understand about numbers and how much they are interested in them. Students can be creative with numbers. They can be used as the basis for a poem or joke. Students can have fun with numbers by proving different properties about them, using them to send secret messages, or playing games with them. Students can find uses for numbers in everyday life, such as for calculating tips or measuring objects. Numbers can be haunting. For example, students can learn about the numbers that people obsess over, such as 13, 7, and 666.

This chapter includes topics involving the different number sets (integers, rationals, reals, and complex numbers) and manipulations of them. These manipulations include evaluating exponents, measurement, and vectors.

Fermat's Last Theorem

After students learn the Pythagorean Theorem, there is an interesting extension they can be shown. Fermat's Last Theorem states that if $n > 2$ then $x^n + y^n = z^n$ has no integer solutions for x, y, and z, other than zero. Fermat made this conjecture in 1637 but did not provide a proof. He wrote it in the margin of a paper and said that the proof was too long to write there. He never gave the proof, and many mathematicians throughout history have worked on it, including Euler, Dirichlet, and Lagrange. However, it was not until 1995 that Andrew Wiles, a professor at Princeton, was able to complete the proof. It was 125 pages long and used methods that were unknown during Fermat's time. It is still unknown whether Fermat actually did have a proof, but it is widely believed that he did not.

In an episode of *Star Trek: The Next Generation* (season 2, episode 12), Captain Picard explains what Fermat's Last Theorem is. He summarizes the story told above, but since this episode was aired in 1989, the proof had not been solved.

Fermat's Last Theorem also makes an appearance in *Bedazzled*. One of the characters is the Devil. In one scene she is shown teaching a class and assigns them Fermat's Last Theorem for homework.

In an episode of *The Simpsons* (season 7, episode 6), Homer stumbles into a three-dimensional world, and the equation $1782^{12} + 1841^{12} = 1922^{12}$ can be seen in the background at one point. The values are not actually equal; they agree up to nine digits but then are different. Plugging the left side into many calculators will give $2.54121025861 \times 10^{39}$ while the right side gives $2.54121025931 \times 10^{39}$.

In another episode of *The Simpsons* (season 10, episode 2), Homer decides to become an inventor, and in one scene he writes the equation $3987^{12} + 4365^{12} = 4472^{12}$ on a chalkboard. These values agree up to 10 digits. Plugging the left side into many calculators will give $6.39766563497 \times 10^{43}$ while the right side gives $6.39766563485 \times 10^{43}$.

Prior knowledge needed:

Students need to know how to evaluate exponents.

Classroom use:

1. Have students try to find integer solutions to $x^3 + y^3 = z^3$. Ask some students to share their strategies for trying to find a solution. After they are unsuccessful ask if they think there are any solutions.
2. Show clips from *The Simpsons* and have students plug the values into a calculator to see if they are equal.
3. Tell students the story about Fermat's Last Theorem and show the clip from *Star Trek: The Next Generation*.

Connection to Common Core:

Students make sense of Fermat's Last Theorem by trying it for the $n = 3$ case rather than starting with the general case. Students attend to precision when they notice that the equations given in these clips do not work out correctly.

Prime Numbers

A prime number is defined as any natural number greater than 1 that has only 1 and itself as its positive divisors. A popular way to figure out which numbers are prime is to use the Sieve of Eratosthenes. In this method the numbers 1 through 100 are listed out. The number 100 is the typical stopping point, although any number can be used. According to the definition of a prime number we know 1 is not prime, so it can be crossed out. Next, the 2 can be circled since this is the first prime number. Then every even number can be crossed off because it will have 2 as a divisor. The 3 can also be circled, as it is the next prime number. Likewise, cross off any multiple of 3. Continue with this process until all numbers are either crossed off or circled. The circled numbers are all prime numbers between 1 and 100. A nice trick to know is that the numbers to check for multiples will never surpass the square root of the highest value on the list. In this example the square root of 100 is 10, so only the multiples of 2 through 10 need to be checked.

Prime numbers can be seen in various movies. In *Contact* an alien race transmits blueprints for an interstellar vehicle. A team of astronomers receive them while searching for alien life. The transmission comes in the form of sounds that correspond to numbers. The first numbers they get are 2, 3, 5, and 7. Eleanor realizes that they are all prime numbers.

Another example occurs in the movie *Cube*. A group of five people find themselves in a cube-shaped room with hatches on the floor, the ceiling, and each wall. Each hatch leads to another cube-shaped room. Some of the cubes have traps in them that could kill someone. The rooms are numbered with nine digits written as three groups of three digits. At one point Leaven realizes that the rooms that don't have any three-digit prime numbers are safe.

A third example is in *The Mirror Has Two Faces*. Rose gives Greg cufflinks made of dice that have prime numbers on them.

PRIOR KNOWLEDGE NEEDED:

Students need to know how to find multiples of a number.

CLASSROOM USE:

1. Go over the definition of a prime number and go over some examples.
2. Show one or more of these clips.

3. Explain how the Sieve of Eratosthenes works and have students go through it to get all the primes between 1 and 100 (see Appendix B).
4. Have students explain why the Sieve leaves only the prime numbers.

Connection to Common Core:

In this activity, students makes sense of the problem when they figure out how to find the prime numbers between 1 and 100.

Germain Primes

In *Proof* Hal and Catherine are discussing female mathematicians, and Catherine brings up Sophie Germain. They discuss Germain primes and the property that if a Germain prime is doubled and 1 is added, it gives another Germain prime. They give the example that 2 is prime, double plus 1 is 5, which is also prime. Catherine mentions that $92305 \times 2^{16998} + 1$ is the biggest known Germain prime. At the time the movie was filmed in 2005 this was the largest known Germain prime, but larger Germain primes have been found since then.

If students are familiar with this movie, or the play that it was based on, they may find it interesting to see the similarities between Catherine and Sophie Germain. Both are self-taught in the field of mathematics and are not known in the field. Another similarity is that they are both women in a male-dominated field. Germain entered a contest run by the Paris Academy of Sciences. The first two times she entered anonymously because she didn't want the judges to know she was female. It wasn't until the third year that she entered in her own name and won the prize. Unfortunately, she was unable to attend the prize ceremony because she was female.[1] Catherine was in a similar situation. She claims to have written a complicated and difficult to understand mathematical proof that some people believe she is not capable of.

Sophie Germain is also used as the basis for Lisa's character in an episode of *The Simpsons* (season 17, episode 19). Springfield Elementary School gets a new principal who thinks that females should be taught mathematics with more emotion. She asks the females how numbers make them feel. This leads to the creation of separate schools for boys and girls. Lisa is sick of this new math, so she dresses up as a boy and sneaks into the boys' math class. Similarly, Germain wanted to attend a school in Paris that only allowed men to enroll. Germain was able to get lecture notes and send comments to a tutor at the school. The only catch was that she had to pretend to be male.

One reason why Germain primes are useful is that Sophie Germain was able to prove that Fermat's Last Theorem held true for Germain primes. This means that if p is a Germain prime, then there are no non-zero integer solutions for x, y, and z in the equation $x^p + y^p = z^p$.

PRIOR KNOWLEDGE NEEDED:

Students should know what a prime number is for this activity.

CLASSROOM USE:

1. Show students the clip from *Proof*. The example of 2 and 5 was shown, so students should be able to understand from watching it what a Germain prime is, but further clarification can be given if needed.
2. Have students work in pairs to try to come up with all single- and double-digit Germain primes. The solutions are 2, 3, 5, 11, 23, 29, 41, 53, 83, and 89.
3. For extra credit students can watch this episode of *The Simpsons* and explain or write a paper on how Lisa is similar to Sophie Germain.

CONNECTION TO COMMON CORE:

In this activity students make sense of problems and persevere in solving them. They have to first think about what the single- and double-digit prime numbers are and then figure out how to check if these are Germain primes.

Mental Math

With the easy availability of calculators and computers to perform calculations, mental math is often not taught in the classroom. Mental math can be empowering and can lead to better test scores.[2] Even if a calculator is available, students need mental math skills in order to make sure the calculator gives them a reasonable answer.[3] Teachers can find books and web sites that teach mental math.[4]

In the movie *Matilda*, Matilda has a gift for quickly adding and multiplying numbers in her head, which she exhibits in several scenes. In one such scene, Matilda's dad asks his son to document the prices for which he has sold several used cars and to add them using pen and paper. Matilda is able to sum the numbers in her head faster than her brother can by hand. In another scene from this movie, Matilda is in a classroom, and the teacher gives a multiplication problem while the students answer aloud together. The teacher starts with simple examples such as 2 times 4, but then she jokingly asks 13 times 379. Matilda immediately says the answer.

Another character who is good at mental math is Malcolm from the television series *Malcolm in the Middle*. In one episode (season 1, episode 8),

Malcolm and his family attend a class picnic that features a talent show. The picnic is not going well, but then Malcolm steps in to do his act. He asks to see some credit cards, and two fathers show theirs. Malcolm looks at the cards and recites the numbers. He then says that adding the individual digits on each card gives 74 and 66, and multiplying those numbers gives 4,884. The square of 4884 is 23,853,456. The square root of 4,884 is 69.885, and the square root of that is 8.3597. He then takes requests from the audience to perform other mental calculations.

At a doctor's office in the movie *Rain Man* the doctor asks Ray to do calculations in his head: multiply 312×123 and $4,343 \times 1,234$, and find the square root of 2,130. Ray is able to answer them all correctly. In another scene at a diner the waitress drops toothpicks on the floor and after just looking at them for a few seconds Ray says there are 82. He is correct.

In the first episode of *Lost* we see a plane that has crashed onto an island. One of the survivors, Sayid, repairs the plane's transceiver. He hears a radio broadcast coming from the island. The words are in French and they are followed by a number that tells how many times the message has been broadcast. After hearing the message Sayid figures out in his head that 17,294,535 iterations of the thirty-second message means that it has been broadcasting for sixteen years and five months.

In an episode of *White Collar* (season 1, episode 1), Neal is good at doing calculations in his head. A bond was stolen that has a $1,000 face value with 9 percent interest compounded over 64 years. Neal said it comes to $248,000, and his colleagues using a calculator confirm his answer. Since we have the answer we can figure out how many times the interest is compounded per year. The compound interest formula is $A = P(1 + r/n)^{nt}$ where A is the final amount, P is the principal amount, r is the interest rate, t is the number of years, and n is the number of times compounded per year. In this case we know P is 1,000, r is .09, and t is 64. Letting $n = 1$ gives an A value of $248,482.53.

An online game called *Break Apart* teaches students a good mental trick for addition.[5] The idea is to break the second number up into what will sum with the first number to make 10 and what is left over. For example, to sum 8 and 6, the 6 gets broken into $2 + 4$ since 2 will add to the 8 to make 10. Finding the sum then becomes easy because it becomes 10 plus what was left over. In this case there was a 4 left over, so $8 + 6 = 10 + 4 = 14$.

In another online game called *Kakooma*, students can get practice doing mental arithmetic.[6] Each puzzle consists of a bunch of mini-puzzles. In the mini-puzzles students have to click on the number that is the sum of two other numbers present. For example, one mini-puzzle could have the values

3, 7, 13, and 4. The correct answer is 7 since 3 and 4 sum to 7. Once each mini-puzzle is solved, it turns into a larger puzzle of the same type.

PRIOR KNOWLEDGE NEEDED:

The only prior knowledge needed is numeral multiplication and addition.

CLASSROOM USE:

1. Show one or more of these clips.
2. Show students one mental math trick for multiplying by 11. For example, to find 1784 × 11 think of it as 1784 × (10 + 1). First compute 1784 × 10 = 17840. Then sum 17840 + 1784 = 19624.
3. Ask students to come up with another mental math trick for multiplying by a number other than 11 or for adding numbers quickly.
4. Have students play the online games mentioned earlier to get practice with mental addition. Both games are timed, so it is easy to have a class tournament.

CONNECTION TO COMMON CORE:

Students reason quantitatively when playing *Break Apart* by understanding how to split the second number correctly.

Taxicab Numbers

In *Fever Pitch* Ben brings four students from his honors geometry class to visit Lindsey, who is a mathematician, in order to show his students a role model who makes practical use of mathematics. Lindsey asks the students if anyone notices numbers in things like addresses and license plates. Lindsey also asks the students if they have tried adding different numbers up or re-arranging numbers to make interesting patterns.

An example of interesting number patterns occurs in the television show *Futurama*. The number 1,729 was used in several scenes where a random number was needed. One of the characters named Bender is a robot. He receives a Christmas card from his mother in which he is identified as son #1729 (season 2, episode 8). In another episode (season 1, episode 4) there is a spaceship called BP-1729. A different episode (season 5, episode 10) shows parallel universe #1729. One reason 1,729 is interesting is that it is the smallest integer that can be expressed in two different ways as the sum of two cubes (of positive integers): $1^3 + 12^3 = 1 + 1728$ and $9^3 + 10^3 = 729 + 1000$.

This type of number first became famous because one mathematician, G.H. Hardy, was visiting another mathematician, Srinivasa Ramanujan. The cab that he took was numbered 1729. Hardy remarked that it was a rather dull number, but Ramanujan said it was a very interesting number for the reason above. That is why it became known as a taxicab number. The nth taxicab number is a number that can be expressed n distinct ways as the sum of two cubes. The first taxicab number is 2 because it can be written as $1^3 + 1^3$. The second taxicab number is 1729. Thus far only the first six taxicab numbers are known. The remaining ones are 87,539,319, 6,963,472,309,248, 48,988,659,276,962,496, and 24,153,319,581,254,312,065,344.

PRIOR KNOWLEDGE NEEDED:

Students must know how to evaluate exponents.

CLASSROOM USE:

1. Explain what a taxicab number is and show clips from *Futurama* that feature these numbers.
2. In groups, have students come up with other examples of special numbers by making up their own rules. Have each group share their numbers with the class.

CONNECTION TO COMMON CORE:

Students attend to precision when explaining their number rules.

Pascal's Triangle

Pascal's Triangle can be constructed by starting row zero with a number 1. Row one has two 1s. Each subsequent row will have a 1 on each side, and each middle number is the sum of the two above it. Here is Pascal's Triangle up to row four:

$$
\begin{array}{c}
1 \\
1 \quad 1 \\
1 \quad 2 \quad 1 \\
1 \quad 3 \quad 3 \quad 1 \\
1 \quad 4 \quad 6 \quad 4 \quad 1
\end{array}
$$

Math teachers love this triangle because there are so many patterns that can be spotted in it. Because of the abundance of patterns it can be used in many different ways. A few of the more basic patterns include:

The counting numbers (in bold) and the triangle numbers (highlighted):

$$1$$
$$1 \; \mathbf{1}$$
$$1 \; \mathbf{2} \; 1$$
$$1 \; \mathbf{3} \; 3 \; 1$$
$$1 \; \mathbf{4} \; 6 \; 4 \; 1$$
$$1 \; \mathbf{5} \; 10 \; 10 \; 5 \; 1$$
$$1 \; \mathbf{6} \; 15 \; 20 \; 15 \; 6 \; 1$$
$$1 \; \mathbf{7} \; 21 \; 35 \; 35 \; 21 \; 7 \; 1$$

Summing up each row gives powers of 2:

$$1$$
$$1 + 1 = 2$$
$$1 + 2 + 1 = 4 = 2^2$$
$$1 + 3 + 3 + 1 = 8 = 2^3$$
$$1 + 4 + 6 + 4 + 1 = 16 = 2^4$$

Getting more advanced, if the first non-one entry in a row is a prime number, then all of the other non-one numbers in that row are divisible by it. As an example, look at row seven. The number 7 divides 21 and 35. Another pattern is that row n gives the coefficients of the binomial expansion of $(x + y)^n$. For example, $(x + y)^4 = 1x^4 + 4x^3y + 6x^2y^2 + 4xy^3 + 1y^4$.

In an episode of *Scorpion* (season 1, episode 7), Walter is trying to have a man who he believes was kidnapped get in contact with him. This man is a borderline genius, so Walter sets up Pascal's Triangle where, if all of the odd numbers are deleted, the

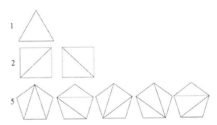

Fig. 1. Geometric representation of Catalan Numbers.

numbers remaining form an address for an online bulletin board where he can be reached.

Advanced students can use Pascal's Triangle to list the Catalan Numbers. Catalan Numbers are a sequence of numbers that define the number of ways a polygon can be partitioned into triangles using the polygon's diagonals. A three-sided polygon already is a triangle, so there is only one way. A square has two ways and a pentagon has five ways. Keeping with this pattern, the Catalan Numbers are 1, 2, 5, 14, 42, 132, 429,.... The nth Catalan Number can be calculated by the formula $\frac{(2n)!}{(n+1)!n!}$. One way to see the Catalan Numbers in

Pascal's Triangle is by looking down the center column. Only rows with an odd number of elements will have this center element. Take the center element and subtract the number immediately to its right. In row two, 2 - 1 = 1 is calculated. In row four, 6 - 4 = 2 is calculated.

In *The Carrie Diaries* (season 1, episode 10), Mouse is talking to Stacey, an alum of her high school who goes to Harvard. Stacey says that she loves Pascal's Triangle, especially the rows with the Catalan Numbers, and Mouse said that she got a shiver just now when Stacey said that.

Prior knowledge needed:

Students need to know whatever number patterns they will be finding in Pascal's Triangle. They also need to know the definition of a polygon and its diagonals.

Classroom use:

1. Show the two clips and ask if anyone has seen Pascal's Triangle before.
2. Give students a picture of Pascal's Triangle partially filled in and have them figure out a pattern they can use to fill in the remaining spots.
3. As a class, ask students to brainstorm to come up with a list of different types of numbers that they know, such as triangle numbers, square numbers, Fibonacci numbers, etc.
4. In groups, ask students to find any of the number types on the list (or any other patterns) within Pascal's Triangle.
5. Explain what a Catalan Number is. Show the example for a square and see if students can figure out the correct amount of partitions for a pentagon.
6. Ask students to find the Catalan Numbers in Pascal's Triangle. One way was given above, but there are other ways to get these numbers.

Connection to Common Core:

In this activity students look for and make use of structure as they analyze the patterns in Pascal's Triangle.

Fibonacci Numbers

Fibonacci posed the following brain-teaser in his book *Liber Abaci* in 1202:

How Many Pairs of Rabbits
are Created by One Pair in One Year.

A certain man had one pair of rabbits together in a certain enclosed place, and one wishes to know how many are created from the pair in one year when it is the nature of them in a single month to bear another pair, and in the second month those born to bear also.[7]

This is the same as saying that each month a pair of rabbits bears another pair of rabbits with a one-month incubation period.

Let us take a closer look at this situation. In the first month there are no offspring. In the following month the first pair has two offspring. The next month the first pair again has two offspring but the second pair does not, and it keeps going like this. The sequence that is produced is 1, 1, 2, 3, 5, 8, 13,.... The first 1s are considered initial conditions, and then the previous two numbers are summed to get the following number. The numbers in this sequence are called the Fibonacci numbers. The Fibonacci numbers are defined recursively in this method, meaning that in order to get a specific value in the sequence one needs to know all of the previous terms. In general terms, the recursive formula is $F_n = F_{n-1} + F_{n-2}$. The Fibonacci numbers also have a closed form, $F_n = \frac{(1+\sqrt{5})^n - (1-\sqrt{5})^n}{2^n\sqrt{5}}$, meaning that one would not have to know all the previous terms. For example, the twelfth Fibonacci number is $\frac{(1+\sqrt{5})^{12} - (1-\sqrt{5})^{12}}{2^{12}\sqrt{5}} = 144$. The only problem with the closed form is that it is a lot more complicated than the recursive form.

There are many interesting things that can be done with the Fibonacci numbers. Here are just a few of them:

1. Fibonacci Sum Calculation

   To find the sum of the first n Fibonacci numbers, students can rearrange the recursive formula to notice that $2-1 = 1$, $3-2 = 1$, $5-3 = 2$, $8-5 = 3$, and in general, $F_n = F_{n+2} - F_{n+1}$. List out these equations so that the left side will sum to the first n Fibonacci numbers.

   $F_1 = F_3 - F_2$
   $F_2 = F_4 - F_3$
   $F_3 = F_5 - F_4$
   $+ \ldots$
   $F_{n-1} = F_{n+1} - F_n$
   $F_n = F_{n+2} - F_{n+1}$

   sum of first n Fibonacci numbers $= F_{n+2} - F_2 = F_{n+2} - 1$

   For example, the sum of the first five Fibonacci numbers is $1 + 1 + 2 + 3 + 5 = 12$. Using the formula just derived, the sum of the first five Fibonacci numbers is $F_{5+2} - 1 = F_7 - 1 = 13 - 1 = 12$.

2. Ratio of Fibonacci Numbers

   Students can also look at $\lim_{n \to \infty} \frac{F_n}{F_{n-1}}$. As n increases, this ratio gets closer to the Golden Ratio, also known as phi (Φ). Phi's exact value is $\frac{1+\sqrt{5}}{2}$, which is approximately 1.618.

$\frac{1}{1} = 1, \frac{2}{1} = 2, \frac{3}{2} = 1.5, \frac{5}{3} = 1.67, \frac{8}{5} = 1.6, \frac{13}{8} = 1.625, \frac{21}{13} = 1.615, \frac{34}{21} = 1.619, \frac{55}{34} = 1.6176$, etc. This is true because $\lim_{n\to\infty} \frac{F_n}{F_{n-1}} = \lim_{n\to\infty} \frac{F_{n-1}+F_{n-2}}{F_{n-1}} = \lim_{n\to\infty} 1 + \frac{F_{n-2}}{F_{n-1}} = 1 + \lim_{n\to\infty} \frac{F_{n-2}}{F_{n-1}}$. Then $\lim_{n\to\infty} \frac{F_n}{F_{n-1}}$ and $\lim_{n\to\infty} \frac{F_{n-2}}{F_{n-1}}$ are both equal to the same value, since the ratios are both a Fibonacci number divided by the previous Fibonacci number and we are interested in increasingly larger values of n. Since they are both equal to the same value, let's call that value x. Then the equation becomes: $x = 1 + \frac{1}{x}$. Rearranging this leads to: $x^2 - x - 1 = 0$. Then solving this using the quadratic formula gives the positive solution of $x = \frac{1+\sqrt{5}}{2}$. This is the same value as phi.

3. Pascal's Triangle

    Students who have seen Pascal's Triangle may recognize the Fibonacci numbers as the sums of the diagonals.

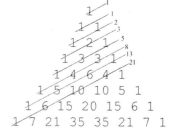

    The Fibonacci numbers are featured in many movies and television shows. In *The Da Vinci Code* the French police ask the main character, Robert Langdon, to look at the crime scene where the curator of the Louvre has died. There is a secret message written in invisible ink near him. It reads:

Fig. 2. The Fibonacci numbers in Pascal's Triangle.

13–3–2–21–1–1–8–5
O, Draconian devil!
Oh, lame saint!

    While the message at first appears cryptic, Langdon realizes the numbers are a mixed-up version of the Fibonacci numbers. He rearranges the words and gets "Leonardo Da Vinci the Mona Lisa." This leads Langdon to the *Mona Lisa* painting, which contains the next clue in solving the murder.

    The Fibonacci numbers are also featured in the movie *21*. The first eight Fibonacci numbers are on a birthday cake written in icing, and there are twenty-one candles on the cake. Twenty-one is the ninth Fibonacci number.

    In the television show *Psych* (season 7, episode 9), Sean is trying to remember his old phone number, and Gus says it is 555–0135. When Sean questions why he knows that, Gus says it is part of the Fibonacci sequence. The number 5,550,135 itself is not a Fibonacci number. It is not clear what Gus meant when he said this, but one way to think of it is that 55, 5, and 13 are all Fibonacci numbers.

Fibonacci is mentioned in an episode of *Go On* (season 1, episode 12), when Ryan is a guest on Bob Costas' television show. Costas decides to branch out from talking about sports and tries to engage Ryan in a discussion on Fibonacci. He gives facts about Leonardo Fibonacci, including that he was a mathematician born in 1170 in Pisa and he died in 1240 in Pisa. Costas then asks for Ryan's thoughts on the Fibonacci sequence: is it a divine numerical progression or a cruel illusion of order out of chaos?

In an episode of *Criminal Minds* (season 4, episode 8), a serial killer uses the Fibonacci numbers to choose the number of victims and their locations. The killer comes to the FBI agents and says that he has committed seven perfect murders, but there are five more victims that can still be saved. Through profiling, the FBI agents figure out who the previous seven victims were and notice that they are all strikingly beautiful. They also look at the Virginia cities that these victims were abducted from and notice that 1 woman was abducted from Richmond, 1 from Dinwiddie, 2 from Gloucester Point, 3 from Saluda, and that the 5 that are still alive are from Loretta. The agents recognize these as Fibonacci numbers. Previously the audience had seen that the killer wore a necklace showing the geometric representation of the Fibonacci numbers with the golden spiral. The agents superimposed a picture of the Golden Ratio onto a map of Virginia and were able to see where the final group of 5 victims was located.

The reason that the victims were so beautiful is that their faces were in proportion with the Golden Ratio, phi. Humans see symmetry and proportionality as beauty.[8] The closer these calculations are to phi, the more beautiful a person is perceived as being. One measurement is to take the length of the face divided by the width of the face. One of the FBI agents said that many people we find attractive have bodies and/or faces that are proportionally close to that ratio. Another clue given earlier was at an abduction that took place at a nursery school. There the killer had arranged toys in the shape of the Greek letter phi.

In *Mr. Magorium's Wonder Emporium*, Henry goes for a job interview to be the new accountant, and Mr. Magorium asks him to name the eleventh to sixteenth integers in the Fibonacci Sequence. Henry correctly answers 89, 144, 233, 377, and 610. Mr. Magorium then asks if we really need the number four, and Henry answers, if you like squares you do.

In *Touch* (season 1, episode 1), Jake is a mute eleven-year-old who communicates through numbers. The series opens with Jake saying the ratio between two consecutive Fibonacci numbers is always 1:1.618 (as discussed earlier). He also says that patterns are in plain sight if you know where to look. Things most people see as chaos actually follow a set of laws, such as galaxies, planets, and seashells. Later, another character named Arthur Teller talks about the Fibonacci Sequence and how it appears in nature.

In an episode of *Fringe* (season 1, episode 2), Walter recites the Fibonacci numbers to try to help him go to sleep.

PRIOR KNOWLEDGE NEEDED:

Prior knowledge for this activity will depend on what Fibonacci properties the students look at. The activity can be done at a low level with just knowledge of addition, up to a higher level with knowledge of limits.

CLASSROOM USE:

1. Show some of the Fibonacci number clips mentioned above.
2. Ask students to work in pairs to derive a formula for the Fibonacci numbers.
3. Once they get the recursive formula, ask students to create their own sequence similar to the Fibonacci numbers, but start with two different initial values. Have students name their sequence and find any interesting properties it has. Depending on the class level, teachers can first go over properties of the Fibonacci numbers such as those listed above. Students will probably be interested to find that even though their sequence starts with different initial values, dividing the successive terms will still result in an approximation to the Golden Ratio. For example, if the initial values chosen are 2 and 4, then the ratios look like this: $\frac{2}{4} = .5, \frac{6}{4} = 1.5, \frac{10}{6} = 1.67, \frac{16}{10} = 1.6,$ $\frac{26}{10} = 1.625, \frac{42}{26} = 1.615,$ etc. The reason this works is that the proof for this Fibonacci property did not use the starting values at all. Therefore, the result holds true for different starting values as long as they follow the same recursive pattern as the Fibonacci numbers.

CONNECTION TO COMMON CORE:

Students look for and express regularity in repeated reasoning as they search for properties for their numbers.

Cryptography

The scene from *The Da Vinci Code* with the secret code, mentioned earlier, can also be used as an introduction to cryptography. Cryptography is a way to encode and decode information. A simple kind of cryptography is the Caesar Cipher. This allows for coding and decoding messages by assigning letters to their number equivalent, such as a = 1, b = 2, etc. The Caesar Cipher is named after Julius Caesar because he used it to send secret messages to soldiers. Now we have ciphers that are a lot more complicated, and they have a myriad of uses. For example, when a purchase is made online, the credit card number is encrypted because the purchaser does not want anyone to see the actual credit card number.

There are many different ciphers in actual use. Some ciphers are relatively simple to decode, while others are quite difficult. An easy one for students to start with lists letters in alphabetical order in one column and in another column lists letters in alphabetical order but starting at a random letter. For example, if the second column starts with "n," the cipher would change "a" to "n," "b" to "m," "c" to "o," etc. Another similar idea would be to have the second column be in a mixed up order. A slightly more complicated cipher is called the Vigenère cipher. This cipher uses a key. This is a chosen word that is public knowledge. To encrypt a message using the Vigenère cipher it would be helpful to have a table that lists the letters of the alphabet across the top and along the side. Within the table, the first row has the letters A through Z. The second row starts at B, goes through Z, and adds the A at the end. The remaining rows work similarly. A Vigenère table is shown here:

	A	B	C	D	E	F	G	H	I	J	K	L	M	N	O	P	Q	R	S	T	U	V	W	X	Y	Z
A	A	B	C	D	E	F	G	H	I	J	K	L	M	N	O	P	Q	R	S	T	U	V	W	X	Y	Z
B	B	C	D	E	F	G	H	I	J	K	L	M	N	O	P	Q	R	S	T	U	V	W	X	Y	Z	A
C	C	D	E	F	G	H	I	J	K	L	M	N	O	P	Q	R	S	T	U	V	W	X	Y	Z	A	B
D	D	E	F	G	H	I	J	K	L	M	N	O	P	Q	R	S	T	U	V	W	X	Y	Z	A	B	C
E	E	F	G	H	I	J	K	L	M	N	O	P	Q	R	S	T	U	V	W	X	Y	Z	A	B	C	D
F	F	G	H	I	J	K	L	M	N	O	P	Q	R	S	T	U	V	W	X	Y	Z	A	B	C	D	E
G	G	H	I	J	K	L	M	N	O	P	Q	R	S	T	U	V	W	X	Y	Z	A	B	C	D	E	F
H	H	I	J	K	L	M	N	O	P	Q	R	S	T	U	V	W	X	Y	Z	A	B	C	D	E	F	G
I	I	J	K	L	M	N	O	P	Q	R	S	T	U	V	W	X	Y	Z	A	B	C	D	E	F	G	H
J	J	K	L	M	N	O	P	Q	R	S	T	U	V	W	X	Y	Z	A	B	C	D	E	F	G	H	I
K	K	L	M	N	O	P	Q	R	S	T	U	V	W	X	Y	Z	A	B	C	D	E	F	G	H	I	J
L	L	M	N	O	P	Q	R	S	T	U	V	W	X	Y	Z	A	B	C	D	E	F	G	H	I	J	K
M	M	N	O	P	Q	R	S	T	U	V	W	X	Y	Z	A	B	C	D	E	F	G	H	I	J	K	L
N	N	O	P	Q	R	S	T	U	V	W	X	Y	Z	A	B	C	D	E	F	G	H	I	J	K	L	M
O	O	P	Q	R	S	T	U	V	W	X	Y	Z	A	B	C	D	E	F	G	H	I	J	K	L	M	N
P	P	Q	R	S	T	U	V	W	X	Y	Z	A	B	C	D	E	F	G	H	I	J	K	L	M	N	O
Q	Q	R	S	T	U	V	W	X	Y	Z	A	B	C	D	E	F	G	H	I	J	K	L	M	N	O	P
R	R	S	T	U	V	W	X	Y	Z	A	B	C	D	E	F	G	H	I	J	K	L	M	N	O	P	Q
S	S	T	U	V	W	X	Y	Z	A	B	C	D	E	F	G	H	I	J	K	L	M	N	O	P	Q	R

To decode a letter look at the column of the letter and the row of the corresponding letter in the key. For example, if the key is "key" and the word to encode is "math" start with the column with "m" and the row with "k." This yields a "w." Repeat this process for the remaining letters. When the key is shorter than the word, it gets repeated as many times as necessary. In this case there is only one extra letter so the key becomes "keyk." Using this method the decoded word is "werr." Decryption works the same way. Since the key is known look at the row with "k" and find the "w" within it. Tracing that back to the column heading yields the "m."

Another example of cryptography is seen in *Gossip Girl* (season 5, episode 22). Blair and Chuck have a stolen date book that is written in code and they are trying to figure out how to decode it. Blair says that it is not classic Caesar code and then proceeds to take out a cipher code. She mentions using it in the third grade because she suspected her mother was reading her diary. Blair ends up figuring out a way to decode it by noticing that the first Saturday of every month has the same appointment. They figure out what appointment it is and from that they get the rest.

Prior knowledge needed:

The ciphers shown here require almost no mathematical knowledge. If students are able to read a table they will be able to do this activity. More difficult ciphers can be shown to students if a higher difficulty level is desired.[9]

Classroom use:

1. Show one or both of these clips to introduce the idea of cryptography.
2. Show students how the Caesar Cipher works and discuss why it would not be a good cipher to use to keep a message secret. Students should quickly realize that is very easy to crack. Also introduce different ciphers such as those shown earlier.
3. Have the students work in pairs to create a cipher of their own and work out some examples of messages encoded using this cipher.
4. Each pair can then switch their messages in encoded and decoded form with another pair. Using these examples, have students try to figure out what the cipher was.

Connection to Common Core:

Students make sense of problems when they make up their own cipher and persevere at solving problems when they try to figure out another group's cipher.

Polar Graphs

In an episode of *Wizards of Waverly Place* (season 2, episode 1), Alex competes in a quiz bowl. In the first question in the competition the contestants are asked what the polar coordinates of the point with Cartesian coordinates (0, 3) are. Alex rings in and answers $(3, \frac{\pi}{2})$.

Students may be more interested in learning about polar coordinates and equations if they understand why it is sometimes more helpful to use this form over the well-known Cartesian form. Looking at the gridlines along with the x and y axes plus the circles that form the polar grids, students can see that equations that have straight lines in them are better suited for the Cartesian plane, while equations that have circular shapes in them are better suited for the polar system. For example, a vertical line in Cartesian form is written as $x = 4$. That same line written in polar form would be $r = \frac{4}{\cos\theta}$. Clearly the Cartesian form is nicer looking and easier to understand. However, an example of an equation of a circle in Cartesian form is $x^2 + y^2 = 4$. That same circle written in polar form is $r = 2$. This time the polar form is nicer looking and easier to understand.

PRIOR KNOWLEDGE NEEDED:

For this activity students should know trigonometry and the Pythagorean Theorem.

CLASSROOM USE:

1. Show students pictures of the two graphing systems and ask them what types of graphs are better suited for which system. Have them come up with a hypothesis for whether the equation of a line is simpler in Cartesian or polar, and likewise for the equation of a circle.
2. Plot a point in the Cartesian plane and ask students to draw lines representing the x and y distance of the point. Then have them add in the remaining line to form a right triangle and label that side r for radius. Finally, have them label the angle formed by x and r as θ.
3. Ask students to use their knowledge of right-triangle trigonometry to figure out some relationships between x and y to r and θ. They should get equations such as $x^2 + y^2 = r^2$, $y = r\sin\theta$, $x = r\cos\theta$, and $\tan = y/x$.
4. Show this clip to students and have them go through the steps to check Alex's answer.
5. Give students additional problems to practice going back and forth between polar and rectangular forms.
6. Now ask students to test their hypothesis by writing out the equations of a line and a circle in rectangular form and then translating them to polar form.

CONNECTION TO COMMON CORE:

In this activity students construct viable arguments when they make a conjecture and then prove or disprove it.

Mathematical Poems

In the movie *Harold and Kumar Escape from Guantanamo Bay*, Kumar recites a poem entitled *The Square Root of 3* to try to win back his ex-girlfriend Vanessa.

I'm sure that I will always be
A lonely number like root three

The three is all that's good and right,
Why must my three keep out of sight
Beneath the vicious square root sign,
I wish instead I were a nine

For nine could thwart this evil trick,
with just some quick arithmetic

I know I'll never see the sun, as 1.7321
Such is my reality, a sad irrationality

When hark! What is this I see,
Another square root of a three

As quietly co-waltzing by,
Together now we multiply
To form a number we prefer,
Rejoicing as an integer

We break free from our mortal bonds
With the wave of magic wands

Our square root signs become unglued
Your love for me has been renewed

In an episode of *A Different World* (season 3, episode 57), Dwayne Wayne must write a poem for his class. Dwayne is a mathematician and is only taking this poetry class as a requirement. He reads Shakespeare for inspiration but falls asleep while reading *Hamlet*. Shakespeare visits Dwayne in a dream and tells him to write about something he is passionate about. Dwayne writes a poem about his love for mathematics.

This would be a good assignment to coordinate with a colleague in the English department while students are studying poetry. It can also be given as an extra credit assignment.

PRIOR KNOWLEDGE NEEDED:

Students should know the structure of the type of poem they will be writing.

CLASSROOM USE:

1. Show clips of each poem being recited.
2. Have students write a poem about mathematics. A specific type of poem can be assigned. A haiku might be the easiest type to start with. A haiku is three lines long. The first line has five syllables, the second line has seven, and the last line has five. Here is an example haiku:

> Thinking about math
> While writing some poetry
> Joins arts and science

CONNECTION TO COMMON CORE:

Students attend to precision by taking a mathematical topic and then explaining it in the form of a poem.

Cross Product

In an episode of *Head of the Class* (season 3, episode 6), Arvid's father teaches a math class. He tells the following math joke: What do you get when you cross an elephant with a grape? The answer is elephant, grape, sine theta. Students can also find other mathematical jokes online.[10]

PRIOR KNOWLEDGE NEEDED:

To understand this joke, students should already know the cross product formula.

CLASSROOM USE:

1. Show students this clip after they have learned the cross product formula $\|\vec{a} \times \vec{b}\| = \|\vec{a}\|\|\vec{b}\| \sin\theta$.
2. As an extra credit assignment, students can make up a joke on a topic they have learned in class. The class can vote on the funniest joke.

CONNECTION TO COMMON CORE:

Students attend to precision by taking a mathematical topic and explaining it in the form of a joke.

Memorizing v. Understanding

An episode of *Modern Family* (season 4, episode 2) brings up a very important question in mathematics education: do students merely memorize math or do they understand it? There should be a balance between the two. Some memorization needs to take place, such as multiplying single-digit numbers. Otherwise, problems would take too long. In fact, research shows that many skills, including critical thinking, require the knowledge of facts.[11] On the other hand, lack of understanding means that students will not be able to do similar problems or more advanced problems. In *Modern Family* Cameron asks his daughter Lily what the square root of 64 is, and she replies 8. Lily's cousin Luke then asks Lily what the square root of plate is and she also replies 8, thereby demonstrating that she only knows this one square root.

PRIOR KNOWLEDGE NEEDED:

No specific prior knowledge is needed.

CLASSROOM USE:

1. Show students this clip and ask them to think about whether it is better for them to memorize or understand math.
2. Have students list topics from their current math class that require some memorization as well as some topics that they are better off understanding how to do.

CONNECTION TO COMMON CORE:

Students make sense of problems by deciding when memorization is appropriate and when it is better to understand the problem.

Calculations

On an episode of *The Big Bang Theory* (season 6, episode 4), Leonard and Sheldon play a series of games against Penny and Amy. It starts with Pictionary, but when the girls keep winning, the guys try to come up with a game that they can win. In one game Penny and Sheldon spin around for one minute with their heads on a *Star Wars* light saber and then go to whiteboards to do a long division problem. They have to divide 851 by 23. Sheldon gets so dizzy that Penny ends up winning.

Another calculation occurs in the movie *Twilight*. Bella tells Edward that he has to give her some answers and Edward says, "Yes, no, to get to the other side, 1.77245." Bella says that she does not want to know the square root of pi.

In an episode of *Seinfeld* (season 9, episode 15), Jerry gives his father Morty an electronic Wizard organizer. Even though the organizer can be used for many complicated things, Morty is most excited to use it to calculate tips. Morty calculates a 12.4 percent tip and gets $4.366666. He decides to round down.

In an episode of *Suburgatory* (season 2, episode 4), Dallas compares her boyfriend to going to the Cirque Du Soleil show *Zumanity*. She says take the experience of going to *Zumanity*, multiply by 20, divide by 3, raise it to the tenth power, add 9, subtract 2, and add back 1.

In an episode of *Modern Family* (season 4, episode 18), Claire and Cameron are remodeling a house so that they can sell it for more than they bought it for. Whenever Claire doesn't want to buy something that Cameron wants, she uses math to confuse him. In one scene Claire says that they can't buy the fixtures Cameron wants because they are 23 percent, or $982, over the budget, and the room they would be in is only 12 percent of the house's 1,462 square feet. Claire says to compensate for this difference they would need to spend less on flooring and then she throws some more numbers out that don't really mean anything but are meant to confuse Cameron. Cameron quickly says that's fine as long as the fixtures they buy are pretty.

In *School of Rock*, Dewey fills in for his roommate as a substitute teacher and gets the class into playing music. One afternoon the principal stops by and wants to observe so Dewey sings a song about math and asks the students math problems. He starts with 3 - 4 is -1. He then sings 6 times a billion is 6 billion and asks 54 is 45 more than what? One of the students named Marta says 9, Dewey says 8, and Marta says no it is 9.

In *Brooklyn Nine-Nine* (season 1, episode 12), Jake wants to catch the Pontiac Bandit, who is known to have stolen 230 Pontiacs and has left no evidence. Diaz caught an identity thief who has information that could help Jake find the Pontiac Bandit. In return for this information, the criminal wants to cut a deal to have all his charges dropped. When they are speaking with the captain to try to decide whether to take the deal, Diaz says that she has been searching for the identity thief for a month. Jake says he has been searching for the Pontiac Bandit for eight years and asks if she knows how many months that is. Diaz says 96 while Jake says 80 40 6 months. The captain asks if Jake needs a math tutor.

In an episode of *House M.D.* (season 5, episode 19), House is trying to make sure a patient who can only move his eyes understands what is going on. House asks him what the square root of nine is and the patient blinks three times.

A similar situation occurs in the movie *Bingo*. Chuckie is working on his math homework and he asks Bingo what the square root of nine is. Bingo barks three times.

In an episode of *That '70s Show* (season 5, episode 8), Kelso brings Eric's math teacher over to Eric's house as his Thanksgiving date. When Eric asks how he could do this, Kelso says that she won't quiz him, but just in case she does, the square root of zero is zero.

In *The Internship*, students are put into teams to compete for an internship at Google. One of the competitions is to come up with an app. One night Lyle's team goes out drinking and Lyle hits it off with Saffron. On the way home he wants to text her, but his teammates want to make sure he is not drunk so they quiz him by asking him what 17 squared is. He answers 289 but says they need a harder question to be able to tell. They ask him what the square root of 17 is and he says it might be 4.23. He was pretty close; it is actually approximately 4.123. This helps the team think of their idea for their app that will make people answer a quiz question before they are allowed to send a text or call somebody when possibly drunk.

An episode of *Scorpion* (season 1, episode 2) opens with a classroom scene in which a teacher has the numbers 105, 212, 988, 703, 556, and 902 written on the board. He asks which of these can be divided by four. Walter says that they all can be. When the teacher says that 703 is not divisible by four, Walter replies that 703 divided by 4 is 175.75. He says that they all can be divided by four, just with a remainder.

While these are low-level topics, they can provide a light-hearted way to show students that knowing how to do math is useful.

Prior knowledge needed:

Necessary knowledge is dependent on what calculation each student chooses.

Classroom use:

1. Show students any of these clips.
2. Give students a certain amount of time, such as a week, to find a situation in their own life where they have to do a math calculation.
3. Have each student share their experience with the class.

Connection to Common Core:

Students are modeling with mathematics by applying math to everyday life.

Measurement

In the movie *This Is Spinal Tap* the band wants an 18-foot replica of Stonehenge onstage while they play a song about Stonehenge. Unfortunately the person who gives the specs to the artist building the replica does not know the difference between feet and inches and, as a result, the band gets a tiny version.

In an episode of *Modern Family* (season 5, episode 5), Gloria and Haley discuss the size of Gloria's earrings. Haley thinks that Gloria's hoop earrings are too small, and Gloria says that she has earrings in the same color but one meter bigger. Haley says that is like a foot, and Manny says it is actually like a yard. Gloria suggests maybe they are a millimeter bigger, and Manny asks if she means a centimeter. Finally Gloria and Haley go upstairs to look at the earrings.

PRIOR KNOWLEDGE NEEDED:

Students should have some familiarity with measuring objects.

CLASSROOM USE:
1. Show one or both of these clips.
2. Ask students to make a list of objects that are normally measured in inches and another list of objects that are normally measured in feet. Students can also list objects measured in millimeters and objects measured in meters.

CONNECTION TO COMMON CORE:

Students make sense of problems when they decide what type of measurement to use.

Summing Integers

It was said that Gauss' elementary school teacher gave his class the busy work of summing the first 100 numbers. Gauss outsmarted his teacher because he figured out how to sum these values by listing the numbers forwards and under that listing the numbers backwards.

100	99	98	...	3	2	1
1	2	3	...	98	99	100

Each column sums to 101. He had 100 such sums, which yields 101(100), but then the numbers were listed twice so he had to divide by 2. This gives the sum as $[101(100)]/ 2 = 5{,}050$. The same kind of argument can be used to find the sum of the first n integers. Listing the numbers out 1, 2, 3,..., $n - 1$, n on top and then as n, $n - 1$,..., 3, 2, 1 makes each column sum to $n + 1$. There are n copies of these sums, which gives $n(n + 1)$. Then we listed each number twice so the final sum becomes $\frac{n(n+1)}{2}$. This tells us that $\sum_{i=1}^{n} i = \frac{n(n+1)}{2}$.

In an episode of *Person of Interest* (season 2, episode 11), a substitute teacher named Mr. Swift teaches a math class and sees that they are doing addition. One of the students explains that as a punishment they have to add all the numbers from 1 to 100. The teacher says that Guass was assigned the same thing and he found a way around it. He asked the class if they had any ideas on how he did it. When nobody knows the answer, Mr. Swift gives them a hint by writing $100(100 + 1)$ on the blackboard. The bell rings before he can explain any further. The teacher is then shown talking on the phone inquiring about one of the students in his class who spent the whole class doodling in his notebook. Mr. Swift takes a paper that the student threw in the trash can and its says $\frac{100(100+1)}{2} = 50(101) = 5{,}050$.

PRIOR KNOWLEDGE NEEDED:

For this activity students just need to know basic arithmetic.

CLASSROOM USE:

1. Show this clip to students.
2. Ask students to explain the solution written on the discarded paper.
3. Have students generalize the solution for summing the integers from one to n.

CONNECTION TO COMMON CORE:

Students construct viable arguments when they generalize the solution for summing n integers.

Numerology

Number mystics use numbers as tools for understanding the world while numerologists apply mysticism to people and things.[12] Numerology is reported to have been made popular by the Pythagoreans. The Pythagoras School was also like a religion. Some of the rules they followed were to not eat beans, not to pick up what had fallen, and not to look in a mirror beside a light.[13] A main belief of the school was that "all is number," meaning they applied attributes to the numbers. For example, they considered odd numbers masculine and even numbers feminine. Pythagoreans studied the properties of numbers and looked at special types of numbers such as square numbers and triangle numbers.

Square numbers take the form of an integer squared. Square numbers can be represented geometrically in the shape of a square. Figure 3 shows the first five square numbers.

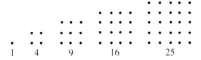

Fig. 3. Geometric representations of square numbers.

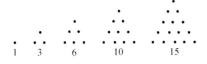

Fig. 4. Geometric representations of triangle numbers.

The triangle numbers are numbers that take the shape of a triangle. Figure 4 shows the first five triangle numbers.

An easy way to define a triangle number is recursively. Start with the first triangle number, $t_1 = 1$, and notice that the next one takes the previous and adds 2: $t_2 = t_1 + 2$. The third triangle number takes the previous and adds 3: $t_3 = t_2 + 3$. In general, this leads to $t_n = t_{n-1} + n$.

There are a couple different ways to find a closed formula. Lower-level students can look at it geometrically by taking two copies of the nth triangle

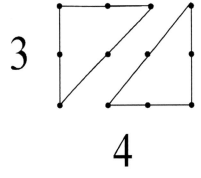

Fig. 5. Geometric representation of two copies of the third triangle number.

number and counting the dots. Here are some examples. The first example (fig. 5) takes two copies of the third triangle number tilted in such a way that they form a rectangle with a length of 4 and a width of 3. This gives a total of 3(4) = $n(n + 1) = 12$ dots.

The second example (fig. 6) takes two copies of the fourth triangle num-

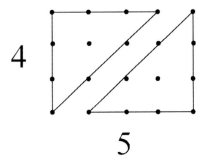

Fig. 6. Geometric representation of two copies of the fourth triangle number.

ber. Similarly, the rectangle formed has a length of 5 and a width of 4 giving $4(5) = n(n + 1) = 20$ dots.

In general, $2t_n = n(n + 1)$, and dividing both sides by 2 gives the closed form $t_n = \frac{n(n+1)}{2}$. Higher-level students can notice that the nth triangle number is equal to $1 + 2 + 3 + \cdots + n$ and either prove by induction or use Gauss' trick to get $t_n = \frac{n(n+1)}{2}$.

Modern numerology involves Birth Path Numbers and Life Path Numbers. A Birth Path Number represents one's destiny. To calculate a Birth Path Number, sum the numbers in a birthday. The digits keep getting added until a single-digit answer is obtained. For example, the date August 27, 1983, translates to $8 + 2 + 7 + 1 + 9 + 8 + 3 = 38 = 3 + 8 = 11 = 1 + 1 = 2$. A Life Path Number represents one's personality type. Calculating a Life Path Number is similar to calculating a Birth Path Number. For each letter in a person's name, the corresponding number is obtained from the following table:

1	2	3	4	5	6	7	8	9
A	B	C	D	E	F	G	H	I
J	K	L	M	N	O	P	Q	R
S	T	U	V	W	X	Y	Z	

For example, the name Steve Smith becomes $1 + 2 + 5 + 4 + 5 + 1 + 4 + 9 + 2 + 8 = 41 = 4 + 1 = 5$.

While there is no set interpretation for what these numbers mean, following is one possible brief overview for each number.[14]

1 = leader
2 = mediator
3 = sociable and friendly
4 = hard-working
5 = freedom lover
6 = peace lover
7 = deep thinker
8 = business-minded
9 = teacher

Nowadays numerology is regarded in a similar manner as astrology. There is no proof that numerology is accurate.[15] Critics of numerology say that people are good at recognizing patterns, even patterns that do not exist. See the "Texas Sharpshooter Fallacy" in Chapter Eight for an explanation of why this happens.

In the movie *The Number 23*, the main character, Walter, is reading a book about a man who becomes obsessed with the number 23. Walter starts to believe that the book is written about him and also becomes obsessed with the number 23. The movie gives many instances of names and dates summing to 23. Here are some examples:

Walter's birthday is February 3.

Walter was born at 11:12 PM, and 11 + 12 = 23.

Walter's driver's license is d3730510. Count the "d" as a 4 since it is the fourth letter of the alphabet and then sum these values to get 4 + 3 + 7 + 3 + 0 + 5 + 1 + 0 = 23.

Walter met his wife on September 14, and 9 + 14 = 23.

Walter married his wife on October 13, and 10 + 13 = 23.

Walter lives at house number 1814, and 1 + 8 = 9 + 14 = 23.

Walter visits a doctor who says that since Walter is looking for the number 23, he is finding it.

The movie *Pi* has a similar situation involving the number 216. Max becomes obsessed when his computer gets a virus and prints out a 216-digit number. His mentor basically says the same thing as the doctor in *The Number 23*, that once you start looking for a number you start finding it everywhere. The mentor also says that as soon as you discard scientific rigor you are no longer a mathematician, you are a numerologist.

PRIOR KNOWLEDGE NEEDED:

Activity #1: Only knowledge of basic arithmetic is needed.

Activity #2: Students need to know algebra.

CLASSROOM USE:

Activity #1 for lower-level students:

1. Show these clips to students.
2. Have students calculate their Birth Path and Life Path Numbers and see how they compare to the chart.

Activity #2 for higher-level students:

1. Show clips to students and go over the definitions for square and triangle numbers.
2. Have students prove various properties of square and triangle numbers such as:

- Prove: $s_n = t_n + t_{n-1}$

$$t_n + t_{n-1} = \frac{n(n+1)}{2} + \frac{(n-1)(n)}{2} = \frac{n[n+1+n-1]}{2} = \frac{n(2n)}{2} = n^2 = s_n$$

- Show $n^2 + 2n + 1$ is a square number

$$n^2+2n+1=(n+1)(n+1)=(n+1)^2 =(\text{integer})^2$$

- Show $2n^2 + n$ is a triangle number

$$(2n^2+n)\frac{2}{2} = \frac{4n^2+2n}{2} = \frac{2n(2n+1)}{2} = t_{2n}$$

- Prove $9t_n + 1$ is a triangle number

$$9t_n + 1 = 9\frac{n(n+1)}{2} + 1 = \frac{9n(n+1)+2}{2} = \frac{9n^2+9n+2}{2} = \frac{(3n+1)(3n+2)}{2} = t_{3n+1}$$

- Prove $t_{2n+4} + 2n^2 + 3n - 1$ is a square number

$$t_{2n+4} +2n^2 +3n -1= \frac{(2n+4)(2n+5)}{2} +2n^2 +3n -1 = \frac{2(n+2)(2n+5)}{2} +2n^2 + 3n - 1$$

$$= (n + 2)(2n + 5) + 2n^2 + 3n - 1 = 2n^2 + 15n + 10 + 2n^2 + 3n - 1 = 4n^2 +$$

$$18n + 9 = (2n + 3)(2n + 3) = (2n + 3)^2 = s_{2n+3}$$

CONNECTION TO COMMON CORE:

Students construct viable arguments when they prove various properties of triangle and square numbers.

The Perfect Number

On an episode of *The Big Bang Theory* (season 4, episode 7), Sheldon says that the perfect number is 73 because 73 is the twenty-first prime number. The mirror of 73 is 37, which is the twelfth prime number. 12's mirror is 21. The product of 7 and 3 is 21. The digits 7 and 3 joined make 73. Also, in binary, 73 is a palindrome, 1001001.

PRIOR KNOWLEDGE NEEDED:

Prior knowledge depends on what properties the students come up with. Useful topics for them to know are prime numbers, triangle numbers, square numbers, perfect numbers, etc.

CLASSROOM USE:

Activity #1

1. Show students this clip.
2. In pairs or groups have students pick their favorite number and come up with as many facts about it as they can.

Activity #2[16]

PRIOR KNOWLEDGE NEEDED:

Students should know addition and the definition of a palindrome.

This activity further explores palindromes. The Palindrome Conjecture states that any number can be turned into a palindrome by adding the number to its mirror a certain amount of times. For example, take the number 36: 36 + 63 = 99, which is a palindrome. An example that takes three steps is the number 86: 86 + 68 = 154 + 451 = 605 + 506 = 1111, which is a palindrome. This is still a conjecture because it has not been either proven or disproven yet. Within the first 100,000 natural numbers, only 251 of them do not give a palindrome in 23 or fewer steps.[17] However, there are known numbers such as 196 and 887 that do not seem to work.

1. Show students the clip and explain the Palindrome Conjecture.
2. Have students get into groups and give each group a sheet that has the numbers 1 through 100 on it so that each number is in a box. Also give each group seven different colored markers or crayons.
3. Ask students to figure out how many steps it takes to make each number into a palindrome. Have students color each box that starts as a palindrome the same color, each number that takes one step to become a palindrome the same color, etc. Have them try to find patterns so that they don't have to actually do 100 calculations. The completed sheet looks like this:

1	2	3	4	5	6	7	8	9	10
11	12	13	14	15	16	17	18	19	20
21	22	23	24	25	26	27	28	29	30
31	32	33	34	35	36	37	38	39	40
41	42	43	44	45	46	47	48	49	50
51	52	53	54	55	56	57	58	59	60
61	62	63	64	65	66	67	68	69	70
71	72	73	74	75	76	77	78	79	80
81	82	83	84	85	86	87	88	89	90
91	92	93	94	95	96	97	98	99	100

Palindrome	
1 step	
2 steps	
3 steps	
4 steps	
6 steps	
24 steps	

4. Have students explain any patterns they find. Some of the patterns that students may notice include:

- A two-digit number and its mirror will be the same color because on the first step of adding the two together, both will result in the same sum. For example, 87 and 78 will both be 165 on the first sum, either by adding 87 + 78 or 78 + 87.
- Any multiple of 10 will take 1 step because the mirror starts with zero and the second digit (the third digit in the case of 100) is the same as the first digit in the original number. If x represents a digit then x0 has a mirror of 0x. Adding these terms gives x0 + 0x = xx, which is a palindrome.
- Many of the lower numbers take two steps because adding the mirror results in a two-digit number that has the same value in the ones and tens positions. For example, 21 + 12 will give 2 + 1 in the tens position and 1 + 2 in the ones position, both resulting in 3. This continues to work down the first column until the number 91. Adding 91 to 19 results in a three-digit number and is no longer a palindrome. Going to the second column, the same idea holds until the number 82. Again, at this point 82 + 28 is no longer a two-digit number. Each following column works the same way, just stopping one spot earlier. The multiples of 11 already are palindromes so there is no need to add the mirror, although they remain palindromes if the mirror was added.

CONNECTION TO COMMON CORE:

Students look for and make use of structure by finding patterns within the table. Students attend to precision when they explain the patterns they find.

Hexadecimal

In an episode of *The Simpsons* (season 7, episode 6), Homer has stepped through a portal into a three-dimensional world. As he travels through the portal, Homer encounters a sequence of numbers and letters: 46 72 69 6E 6B 20 72 75 6C 65 73 21. This sequence is written in hexadecimal (base 16) notation. If each number is converted to decimal (base 10) notation then the code corresponds to ASCII values and the message can be translated to read, "Frink rules!" For example, 46 corresponds to $\underline{4}\ 16^1 + \underline{6}\ 16^0 = 64 + 6 = 70$ in decimal notation. Using an ASCII table shows that 70 is the code for the letter "f." Hexadecimal notation is used in computer science.

One popular application of hexadecimal notation is in representing HTML colors. Computers store HTML colors by remembering the amount of red, green, and blue in the color. Since computers store everything in binary, the number of different shades per primary color has to be a power of two. HTML's designers chose 2^8, allowing for 256 shades of each primary color. Since 16^2 is 256, this decision was well suited for hexadecimal representation. The number 16^2 allows for a two-digit hexadecimal number ranging from 00 to FF, with decimal equivalents from 0 to 255. The number 00 represents the lack of a primary color's presence. The number FF represents full saturation of the primary color. Since F is the equivalent of 15 in hexadecimal, FF is equivalent to $15 \cdot 16^1 + 15 \cdot 16^0 = 240 + 15 = 255$ in decimal notation.

The color black has no saturation. Therefore, black has zeros in all its positions (000000). White has full saturation of each color, so it has the value FF (255) for each color (FFFFFF). To create a shade of red, green, or blue, the corresponding position has a positive value while the remaining positions are zeros. For example, the darkest red would be written as 010000 and the lightest red would be FF0000.

Shades of gray have equivalent red, green, and blue values. Black is the darkest shade of gray, so the spectrum starts with 000000 and ends with white (FFFFFF), the lightest shade of gray. For example, one of the middle shades of gray has all color values of 120 in decimal notation. Since $120 = 112 + 8 = 7 \cdot 16^1 + 8 \cdot 16^0$, 78 is the corresponding hexadecimal notation. Thus, this gray is written as 787878. All other colors can be obtained as a mixture of red, green, and blue. For example, purple is a mixture of red and blue, so one shade of purple can be written as FF00FF.

PRIOR KNOWLEDGE NEEDED:

The only prior knowledge needed is multiplication and addition.

CLASSROOM USE:

1. Show students the clip and tell them it contains a secret message that they have to decode.
2. Explain how we represent numbers in base 10. For example, show that 123 is really $100 + 20 + 3 = 1 \cdot 10^2 + 2 \cdot 10^1 + 3 \cdot 10^0$. Ask students to think about representing numbers with a base of 16. Have students think of how many digits there would be and what the digits would look like. Using letters after the number 9 should be a natural extension once they realize there have to be 16 digits.
3. Practice some conversions from decimal to hexadecimal and from hexadecimal to decimal. These examples can be teacher generated and led, or

students can work in groups to come up with the algorithms themselves, depending on the amount of time allotted to spend on this activity and the skill level of the students.

4. Give students an ASCII table and have them decode the message shown in the clip from *The Simpsons*.

5. To further this activity, students can be introduced to HTML's usage of hexadecimal for rendering color. Once they understand the basic idea, students can use a Web site such as this[18] to view sample HTML. An example of the sample code given includes the background color and text color, written as <body bgcolor = "#ffffcc" text = "#000000">. Students can choose a color to display, figure out the hexadecimal notation, and then change these values to check their answer.

Connection to Common Core:

Students look for and make use of structure when they come up with formulas for changing between hexadecimal and decimal notation. In the extension activity, students model with mathematics as they apply hexadecimal notation to a real-world example.

Other Bases

In *Entrapment* Gin is an insurance investigator who is undercover posing as a criminal in order to catch a thief. She has a plan with the thief to steal billions of dollars from a bank using a computer program. Gin needs to accumulate an extra 10 seconds to accomplish this, so she sets up a device that steals 1/10th of a second every minute from 11PM to midnight. Unfortunately, minutes use base 60. For one hour Gin will steal 1/10th of a second every minute. There are 60 minutes in an hour, so she steals 60(1/10) = 6 seconds. If there were 100 minutes in an hour then her plan would have worked correctly. This mistake was unnoticed by makers of the film.

In *Babylon 5* the Mimbari aliens use a base of 11 when counting. This is because they count with their fingers and their head. In real life, some people argue that we should use a base of 12 when counting rather than a base of 10. They suggest that we could use 10 fingers along with 2 feet. These "dozenals" think base 12 is easier to work with because 12 has 4 factors (not counting 1 and itself) while 10 only has 2.[19]

Prior knowledge needed:

Students just need to know basic arithmetic skills.

CLASSROOM USE:

1. Show students the *Entrapment* clip and have them figure out if her plan will work.
2. If students have done the previous hexadecimal activity then they will already be familiar with how to change bases. If they have not, show students how to go from decimal to binary and from binary to decimal with a few examples.
3. Tell students about the "dozenals," who think that we should count in base 12. The Dozenal Society of America publishes a duodecimal bulletin that is available on their Web site.[20] In each bulletin there are examples showing why base 12 is better than base 10. Pick one or two of these examples to share with students.
4. Ask students to change numbers between base 10 and base 12.

CONNECTION TO COMMON CORE:

In this activity students look for and make use of structure when they figure out how to convert numbers to different bases.

Multiplication by Nines

In *Stand and Deliver*, Jaime is a new math teacher. On the second day of class he asks a student if he knows the times tables. Jaime then shows him a

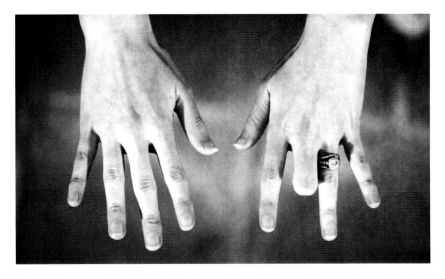

Fig. 7. Multiplying by nine: hand trick for 9 times 3 (photo Michael J. Epstein).

hand trick to multiply a number from one to ten by nine. He shows them $9 \cdot 3$ and $6 \cdot 9$. To do this trick, start will all ten fingers up. Then take the number nine is multiplied by, and hold its finger down. The number of fingers showing before the finger held down is the tens digit of the answer. The number of fingers showing after the held down finger is the ones digit of the answer. For example, to find nine times three hold the third finger (middle finger) down. Then there are two fingers before the middle finger and seven fingers after. This indicates that nine times three is twenty-seven. The reason this trick works is that the digits in a multiple of nine will sum to nine. This is always true for multiplying nine by one through ten. For larger numbers the rule still holds as long as you keep going until a single digit is obtained. For example, nine times eleven is ninety-nine. Then nine plus nine equals eighteen and one plus eight equals nine.

Prior knowledge needed:

Not much prior knowledge is needed. Students just need to know how to multiply by nine.

Classroom use:

1. Show students this clip and have them figure out the multiplication trick. In groups have them write out the steps to use it.
2. Students can then practice some multiplication-by-nine examples.
3. Optional: A more advanced student may be able to read through this article[21] on the topic and figure out the proof for why this multiplication trick works (see Appendix B).

Connection to Common Core:

In this activity students use appropriate tools strategically when they use their hands to aid in multiplication. Students also have to attend to precision when they write out the steps for doing this trick.

Fractions

In the 1980s it was proven that Americans, as a whole, are not good with fractions. The fast food company A&W released a hamburger to compete with McDonald's Quarter Pounder. The A&W burger had one-third of a pound of meat, cost less than the Quarter Pounder, and was preferred in taste tests. Despite all of this, people snubbed the burger. Focus groups revealed the reason: Americans thought that a third was less than a quarter and therefore thought the A&W burger was too expensive.[22]

A similar misunderstanding occurs in *Small Time Crooks*. A group of criminals dig underground to try to rob a bank. In one scene they discuss cutting one of the wives in on the stolen money. Benny suggests that she gets a partial share. Denny says they each get a fourth while the wife gets a third. Luckily Benny does understand fractions, and he points out that she would be getting more than they would.

PRIOR KNOWLEDGE NEEDED:

Students should know what fractions are.

CLASSROOM USE:

1. Give students a list of fractions and ask them to arrange the numbers from smallest to largest.
2. Ask some students to explain their answers.
3. Show this clip to students.
4. Ask them to explain why one-third is bigger than one-fourth.

CONNECTION TO COMMON CORE:

In this activity students reason abstractly and quantitatively when they solve the problem of arranging the numbers and then explain their reasoning to others.

Imaginary Numbers

The first mention of the imaginary numbers occurred in 50 AD by Heron of Alexandria. Heron was trying to compute the volume of a pyramid but was coming up with a negative number under a square root, and so he gave up.[23] In the 1500s Gerolamo Cardan was one of the Italian mathematicians working on solving cubic and quartic equations. He realized that negative numbers sometimes appeared under the square root in the solutions but didn't really understand them.[24] Another Italian mathematician named Rafael Bombelli was the first to give the rules for addition, subtraction, and multiplication of imaginary numbers.[25] Descartes gave them the name imaginary numbers because he said that they were imagined roots to a polynomial that don't correspond to a real quantity.[26]

There are several movies and televisions shows that mention the imaginary numbers. In an episode of *Robot Chicken* (season 4, episode 13), a teacher is shown writing on the blackboard that the square root of negative one is the imaginary number *i*. One student who understands this has his head explode.

Another student says he doesn't get it, but after a second he says now he gets it and then his head explodes too.

In *Proof*, Hal's band, which is composed of all math nerds, has a song called "i" where they play nothing for 3 minutes.

In *Superbad*, one scene takes place in a math class where the teacher is talking about imaginary numbers. He says that i is the square root of negative one and i^2 is equal to negative one.

Prior knowledge needed:

In this activity student should know how to work with exponents and how to multiply binomials.

Classroom use:

1. Show students these clips.
2. Have students calculate i^n for n equaling an integer greater than or equal to zero.
3. Ask students to explain why the answers repeat themselves.
4. Next, show students that the standard form for a complex number is $a + bi$, with a being the real part and bi being the imaginary part. Show them how to add two complex numbers by adding the real parts together and adding the imaginary parts together. Then, have students go through a few examples of adding complex numbers.
5. Ask students to find examples where two complex numbers sum to a real number and where two complex numbers sum to a strictly imaginary number. Then ask them to find a general rule for when these will both occur. To sum to a real number, the imaginary parts would have to cancel each other out yielding $(a + bi) + (c - bi) = (a + c)$. To sum to an imaginary number, the real parts would have to cancel each other out yielding $(a + bi) + (-a + ci) = (b + c)i$.
6. Then go through the process for multiplying two complex numbers. This should not be too difficult, since students should be familiar with multiplying binomials. In general, $(a + bi)(c + di) = ac + adi + bci + bdi^2 = (ac - bd) + (ad + bc)i$.
7. Ask students to find examples where two complex numbers multiply to a real number. Also have them find examples where two complex numbers multiply to a strictly imaginary number. Then ask them to find a general rule for when these both will occur. To multiply to a real number, the imaginary parts would have to cancel each other, meaning $ad + bc = 0$, or $ad = -bc$. For example, multiplying $(3 - i)(6 + 2i)$ yields $18 + 6i - 6i - 2i^2 =$

18 + 2 = 20. We knew this would work because $ad = 3(2) = 6$ and $-bc =$ $-(-1)(6) = 6$. To multiply to an imaginary number the real parts would have to cancel each other out, meaning $ac - bd = 0$, or $ac = bd$. For example, multiplying $(4 + 2i)(3 + 6i)$ yields $12 + 24i + 6i + 12i^2 = 12 + 30i - 12 = 30i$. We knew this would work because $ac = 4(3) = 12$ and $bd = (2)(6) = 12$.

CONNECTION TO COMMON CORE:

In this activity students construct viable arguments when they find the general rules for adding and multiplying two complex numbers to get a purely real number or a purely imaginary number.

Finding the Day of the Week

In *Forrest Gump*, Forrest says that Jenny died on a Saturday. Her gravestone has the date March 22, 1982, on it. This was actually a Monday. In an episode of *Scorpion* (season 1, episode 5), Walter is trying to get a code from an old friend. The friend keeps giving him numbers that are not the code but have significance in their relationship. One such number is 1,199. Walter says that 1,199 days ago it was May 20 on a Thursday when they discussed the quantum mechanics of time travel.

Figuring out the day of the week for a given date is a good way for students to practice using the quotient-remainder theorem. Here is an example problem: On a Monday, a friend says he will meet you in 30 days. What day of the week will it be? There are 7 days in a week, so $30 = 7(4) + 2$. Since today is Monday, in 30 days it will be Wednesday.

PRIOR KNOWLEDGE NEEDED:

For this activity students just need to know basic arithmetic rules.

CLASSROOM USE:

1. Show the clips from *Forrest Gump* showing Forrest saying that Jenny died on a Saturday and then the date on the tombstone.
2. Ask students to figure out if Forrest gave the correct day. Give students some information such as that March 22, 1981, was a Sunday and 1982 was not a leap year. They can write 365 as $7(52) + 1$ to show that it will be one day later, a Monday.
3. Give students additional problems to solve such as these:
   a. If today is Tuesday, what day of the week will it be 1,000 days from today? (See Appendix B.)

b. If today is Friday, then what day will it be a year from today (if this year and next year are not leap years)? (See Appendix B.)

c. Jan 1, 2000 was a Saturday and 2000 was a leap year. What day of the week will Jan 1, 2050 be? (See Appendix B.)

Connection to Common Core:

In this activity students need to make sense of the problem and persevere in solving it.

Math Bloopers

In *Glee* (season 2, episode 17), Mr. Schuster tries to convince the glee club to sell saltwater taffy to raise money so the club can go to nationals. The taffy is 25 cents each and they have to raise $5,000 to go to nationals. Based on this, Mr. Schuster says they will have to sell 20,000 pieces of taffy. He writes on the board 5,000 .25 = 20,000. What Mr. Schuster said, was correct but unfortunately he wrote the problem out incorrectly. He should have written $.25x = 5000$ and then $x = 20,000$. He really wanted to divide 5000 by .25 rather than multiply.

In *Abbott and Costello: In the Navy*, Costello bakes 28 doughnuts and claims that each of the 7 officers will get thirteen of them because 7 goes into 28 thirteen times. When asked to prove this, he writes on the chalkboard 7 divided by 28. The 7 doesn't go into 2, so he moves to the 8 in the ones spot. Seven goes into 8 one time. This 1 gets written on top and 1 times 7 is 7. Then 28 minus 7 gives 21. Seven goes into 21 three times. This 3 gets written on top, giving an answer of 13. Then the officer tells him to check his answer by multiplying and writes 13 over 7. Then 7 times 3 is 21. Next, 7 times 1 is 7; add those and you get 28. Next he says to put down 13 seven times to add them up. He adds up all the threes to get 21 and then adds the ones to get 28 total.

In *Arrested Development* (season 1, episode 18), Maeby's nana usually sends checks for her birthday, but Maeby's mother kept the checks for herself. Once Maeby learns this she agrees to split the present 55–55.

In *The Wonder Years* (season 3, episode 2), Mr. Collins writes two sets on the board: $A = \{-1, -2, -3, -4,...\}$ and $B = \{1, 2, 3, 4,...\}$. Mr. Collins says that these two sets together make up the set of rational numbers. Too bad they are actually the set of integers minus the zero.

In *Super Mario Brothers*, Spike has just gone through an "evolution machine," and he asks his friend Ignatius if he knows the square root of 26,481.

When Iggy doesn't know, Spike says it is 191. The square root of 26,481 is actually approximately 162.73. This error most likely occurred because the square of 191 is 36,481.

In the original *Star Trek* (season 1, episode 20), Captain Kirk says that they can increase the capability of an object to hear sounds by 1^4 power.

In an episode of *The Daily Show* (season 16, episode 11), Jon Stewart reports that Detroit might have to close down half of its public schools. The reporter is shown saying that classroom size will go from 32 students to 62 students.

PRIOR KNOWLEDGE NEEDED:

Prior knowledge will vary depending on which examples are used, but most of them use only basic computations.

CLASSROOM USE:

Show any of these clips and have students correct the mathematics in them.

CONNECTION TO COMMON CORE:

In this activity students make sense of problems and persevere in solving them, as they have to find the error in each clip and make the appropriate corrections.

CHAPTER THREE

Algebra

Algebra is an exciting topic, as evidenced by Bart Simpson. In an episode of *The Simpsons* (season 14, episode 7), Bart has to write a paper on World War I. While trying to work on his paper Bart looks around his room for distractions. He sees a book called *Advanced Algebra* and says, "Ooh, algebra! I'll just do a few equations."

The algebra topic includes algebraic expressions, equations, and inequalities. It also includes using these in word problems to represent modeling. In this chapter students will guess celebrities' ages, relate algebra to cars, basketball, baseball, and gigolos, and see how long it takes to paint a fence.

Mr. Collins

In *The Wonder Years* (season 3, episode 2), Kevin's new math teacher, Mr. Collins, appears to be a no-nonsense, uncaring teacher who lives for math. Kevin is upset that he got a D on a quiz, so he vents to Paul that half the class didn't understood what an absolute value is. Paul says it is the value of the number without regard to the sign. Mr. Collins suggests Kevin comes for extra help after school, but when Kevin sees the losers who attend the extra help he decides not to go inside. As a result, Kevin hands in a test completely blank. He tells Mr. Collins not to bother grading it because he has no idea what he's doing and he failed it. Mr. Collins says this is good because it means that Kevin is ready to start learning. Later, Mr. Collins goes over the multiplicative inverse: for every nonzero a there is a real number $\frac{1}{a}$ such that a times $\frac{1}{a}$ equals 1. He asks Kevin to simplify a quotient. Kevin initially answers one-fifth, but after Mr. Collins says this is incorrect, Kevin correctly answers negative one-fifth.

In another episode (season 3, episode 9), Kevin starts to like Mr. Collins. Kevin thinks he is fair and respects his teacher. Kevin even calls him a hero because Mr. Collins inspires Kevin to do his best. His best at this point is a C. Some of Kevin's classmates start to cheat on the quizzes because Mr. Collins takes the quizzes straight from the textbook, and one of the students acquired a solution manual. Kevin thinks that Mr. Collins will easily catch these students cheating, but they go undetected. Since Mr. Collins grades on a curve, Kevin gets a D on this quiz. He thinks this is unfair, so he begins to cheat on the quizzes too. Kevin keeps getting higher scores on the quizzes until he reaches a 96. Mr. Collins suggests that Kevin joins the honors math class. In one class they go over completing the square, and Kevin is completely lost. It turns out that Mr. Collins did not take the unit test from the book, and all of the students who were cheating got an F on this test, which counted for 50 percent of their grade. Kevin realizes that Mr. Collins had known what was going on the whole time and had saved Kevin by moving him into the honors class. Kevin also realizes that if he hadn't started cheating then, with the curve, he would have earned a B on the unit test.

In another episode (season 3, episode 20), Mr. Collins shows the class how to divide polynomials. Kevin gets the answer correct but misses the remainder. Kevin asks Mr. Collins how he is doing in the class, hoping to get some accolades. Instead, Mr. Collins suggests that they study together for the midterm because he thinks Kevin is capable of getting an A. They work together every day after school, and Kevin enjoys spending time with Mr. Collins. One day Mr. Collins has to go to an appointment and tells Kevin that he will be unable to meet again before the test. Kevin gets upset and says, "I thought you were my friend." Mr. Collins says he is Kevin's teacher, not his friend. On the day of the midterm Kevin is so upset with Mr. Collins that he doesn't answer any of the questions and instead writes things like "factor this!" and "who cares" as the answers. The following Monday we learn that Mr. Collins had been ill and had passed away over the weekend. The replacement teacher later tells Kevin that all of the midterms had been graded, but Kevin's was missing. Mr. Collins had left a blank test with Kevin's name on it so Kevin was able to re-take the midterm. When Kevin hands his test in, the teacher says Kevin's grade is an A.

In addition to the actual math mentioned, the episodes with Mr. Collins also provide a good example of Kevin's relationship with his math teacher and show how Mr. Collins earns his respect. Kevin even gets jealous when Mr. Collins writes on Paul's quiz, "Good job, Paul."

Activity #1: Absolute Value

PRIOR KNOWLEDGE NEEDED:

Students only need to know how to subtract positive integers for this activity.

CLASSROOM USE:

1. Show students a series of pictures of celebrities one at a time and ask them to guess each one's age to the nearest year. Students should draw a chart with the following headings: name, age guess, actual age, and difference between guess and actual age. Show the first picture, give students a few seconds to make a guess, and then reveal the correct age. Repeat this process for other celebrities and have students fill in their charts as the pictures are being shown. At the end students can sum the last column to see who won with the lowest total deviation value. (See Appendix B.)
2. Ask students to discuss with a partner how their answers differed. Did it matter to their total difference if they guessed too high or too low? For example, if an actor is 56 and one student guessed 58 while another guessed 54, is one student a better guesser than the other (meaning does one student have a lower total differential)? (See Appendix B.)
3. Show students the clip from episode 2 where Paul gives a definition of absolute value.
4. Ask students to put the definition in their own words and tie everything together to make sure students understand what absolute value is.

CONNECTION TO COMMON CORE:

Students model with mathematics when they relate the idea of absolute value to a real world problem.

Activity #2: Completing the Square

PRIOR KNOWLEDGE NEEDED:

Students should be familiar with second-degree polynomials and know how to square a term of the form $(x \pm a)$.

CLASSROOM USE:

1. Ask students which of these is easier to graph and why: $x^2 - 4x + 7$ or $(x - 2)^2 + 3$.
2. After some class discussion, make sure that students understand why the

second expression is easier. Also, ensure that students can take the graph of x^2 and apply transformations to get $(x - 2)^2 + 3$. Additionally, make sure that they realize that the two expressions are equivalent. If the students don't bring this up, have them multiply out the second expression to see that it turns into the first.

3. Give students a list of equations similar to the ones below and ask them to find the missing numbers and signs:

$$(x + \_)^2 = x^2 + 2x + \_$$

$$(x - \_)^2 = x^2 - 6x + \_$$

$$(x \_\_)^2 = x^2 + x \_\_$$

$$(x \_\_)^2 = x^2 - \frac{3}{2}x \_\_$$

$$(x \_\_)^2 = x^2 - \frac{4}{3}x \_\_$$

$$(x \_\_)^2 = x^2 + \frac{5}{3}x \_\_ . \text{ (See Appendix B.)}$$

4. Ask students to explain any patterns they find. They should realize that the sign between the squared term and the x term on the right will match the sign on the left. Also, the coefficient of the x term will be double the constant term on the left, and the constant term on the right will be the constant term on the left, squared. In other words, they are showing that $(x \pm a)^2 = x^2 \pm 2ax + a^2$.

5. Next, have students fill in the blanks to eventually get a squared term on the left:

$$x^2 - 8x + 17 = 0$$

$$x^2 - 8x + \_\_ = -17\_\_$$

$$(x \_\_)^2 = \_\_ . \text{ (See Appendix B.)}$$

6. After making sure students understand how this example works, have them try other examples without giving them all of the intermediate steps. Students can manipulate the following equations to get a squared term on the left: $x^2 - 10x + 23 = 0$ and $x^2 + \frac{2}{3}x - \frac{10}{9} = 0$. (See Appendix B.)

7. At this point, students can be told that the method they just used is called completing the square. Have students come up with a list of steps they need to follow in order to complete the square. Based on how the steps were broken up, their steps should look something like this: First, bring the constant term over to the right side. Then, get a new constant term by taking the

coefficient of the x term, dividing it by 2, and then squaring it. Add this new constant to both sides of the equation. Finally, write the left side as a squared term.

8. Show students the clip from episode 9 of *The Wonder Years* where they discuss completing the square.

CONNECTION TO COMMON CORE:

In this activity students look for and make use of structure when they find the missing numbers and signs in step 3 and then apply the result in step 7.

Activity #3: Dividing Polynomials

PRIOR KNOWLEDGE NEEDED:

Students should know how to do long division with integers. Students should also have familiarity with polynomials and multiplying polynomials.

CLASSROOM USE:

1. Ask students in pairs to write out an algorithm for dividing two numbers using long division. They can use 626 divided by 5 as an example (or choose their own values). One possible answer is to see how many times the 5 goes into 6. It goes in 1 time. Then multiply the 5 times 1 to get 5 and subtract that from the 6. This leaves a 1. Bring down the remaining 26 and we are left with 126. The steps are to divide, multiply, and subtract. Then repeat these steps until the remainder is a value less than the divisor (which is 5 in this example).

2. Ask each pair to trade with another pair to make sure that their algorithms make sense and can be followed.

3. Next, give students two polynomials to divide using the algorithm they wrote. An easy example to start with is something like $x^2 + 5x + 2$ divided by x. They can see how many times the x goes into x^2 to get x (divide), multiply that answer by the x to get x^2 (multiply), and subtract the original x^2 minus the x^2 from the multiply step to get 0 (subtract). Next they will bring down the remaining $5x$ + 2 and repeat the process. They can see how many times the x goes into $5x$ to get 5 (divide), multiply that answer by the x to get $5x$ (multiply), and subtract the original $5x$ minus the $5x$ from the multiply step to get 0 (subtract). At this point x can't divide into 2, so the remainder becomes $\frac{2}{x}$.

$$\begin{array}{r} 1 \\ 5\,\overline{)\,626} \\ \underline{5} \\ 126 \end{array}$$

Fig. 8. Long division example.

One difference between dividing integers and dividing polynomials is that students will need to keep the plus or minus sign between the values in their answers; i.e., the solution will look like $x + 5 + \frac{2}{x}$ and not $x5$ with remainder $\frac{2}{x}$.

4. Show students the clip from episode 20 of *The Wonder Years* so they can see an example of long division.

CONNECTION TO COMMON CORE:

In this activity students attend to precision when they write out the long division algorithm so that other students are able to understand it. Students also look for and make use of structure when they generalize the long division algorithm for integers to work for polynomials.

Square Roots Are Radical

In an episode of *Friday Night Lights* (season 1, episode 20), Tyra is in the library studying for an algebra test. Landry asks how she is doing, and Tyra says she wishes she could build a time machine to go back and shoot whoever invented algebra. Landry says that is a catch 22 because Tyra would need to know algebra in order to build the time machine. Later they are having a study session and are solving a problem together. They end up with $\sqrt{x} = 7$, and Landry asks how Tyra can get rid of the pesky square root. She says to square both sides, resulting in an x value of 49.

In one of the episodes of *The Wonder Years* described earlier (season 3, episode 9), Mr. Collins teaches the class how to solve equations with a single radical. He goes through the solution to $\sqrt{x} + 3 = x + 1$.

PRIOR KNOWLEDGE NEEDED:

Students should know how to solve algebraic equations with one variable.

CLASSROOM USE:

1. Show these clips as an introduction to the topic of solving equations with square roots. Show the *Friday Night Lights* clip first, because it shows students how to get rid of the square root when solving for x. Then show the clip from *The Wonder Years*, because it shows students learning how to solve a multi-step equation with a square root.

2. Ask each student to make up their own equation that has a square root in it and write the solution to it.

3. Have all students switch problems with a neighbor and have each student solve the problem they receive.
4. Then, have students switch back and have the first student check the second student's work.
5. Finally, have the student pairs meet together to discuss the two problems and explain any corrections that were made.

Connection to Common Core:

In this activity students critique the reasoning of others when they check another student's work.

Equation of a Line

In *Thirteen*, Tracy is secretly getting her tongue pierced. She is shown calling her mom to say that she is at the library. Tracy asks her mom if she knows the difference between point slope form and slope intercept form. Presumably her mom says no; Tracy says that's why she needs to be at the library—because they have tutors who can help her.

Students are more familiar with the slope intercept form of a line, but it will be helpful for them to see that the point slope form is also valid and, in some cases, easier to figure out. To see where the point slope form comes from, students can start with the definition for slope as m = change in y over change in x. This corresponds to $m = \frac{y-y_1}{x-x_1}$. Moving the denominator over gives us $(y-y_1) = m(x - x_1)$, which is the point slope form.

Students can show that the two forms are equivalent by starting with $(y-y_1) = m(x - x_1)$. In the $y = mx + b$ form we call b the y intercept. Therefore, the y-intercept point can be written as $(0, b)$. Plugging this point into the point slope form yields $(y - b) = m(x - 0) = mx$. Solving for y gives us $y = mx + b$, the slope intercept form.

Prior knowledge needed:

In this activity students should be familiar with the equation of a line. They should also know the definition of the slope of a line and how to manipulate algebraic equations.

Classroom use:

1. Show this clip to students.
2. Ask students what the equation of a line is. Show students the point slope form if nobody brings it up. Then show students how the formula is derived.

Make sure they are clear on what all of the letters represent in both equations.
3. Have students prove that the two equations are equivalent.

CONNECTION TO COMMON CORE:

Students construct viable arguments when they prove that the two forms for the equation of a line are equivalent.

Where Does the 1 Go?

In *I.Q.*, Catherine is the niece of Albert Einstein. She is engaged to a psychologist that Einstein thinks is not suited for her. Einstein coaches a mechanic named Edward in physics so that Catherine will think he is smart enough to date. Edward ends up giving a talk on cold fusion, and Catherine questions one of the formulas he used. Einstein and his friends make hand motions for Edward to say: $x = 1 + w^3$ over pi. For the last part they take an ice cube and then put that on top of a piece of pie. It is unclear whether they mean the formula to be $x = 1 + \frac{w^3}{\pi}$ or $x = \frac{1+w^3}{\pi}$. It is difficult to know which is correct because it appears that this is not a real formula, or at least the correct one in question. Catherine asks Edward about de Broglie's formulas, which are a set of equations that relate wavelength to momentum and frequency to the total energy of a particle. The first equation is $\lambda = \frac{h}{p}$, where λ represents wavelength, h is Planck's constant, and p represents momentum. The second equation is $f = \frac{E}{h}$, where f is the frequency, E is the total energy, and h is Planck's constant.

PRIOR KNOWLEDGE NEEDED:

Students should know how to graph equations on a graphing calculator.

CLASSROOM USE:

1. Show this clip to students.
2. Ask students to use a graphing calculator to graph both $x = \frac{1+w^3}{\pi}$ and $x = 1 + \frac{w^3}{\pi}$ and to describe the differences between the two equations (see Appendix B).

CONNECTION TO COMMON CORE:

In this activity students use appropriate tools strategically when they use the graphing calculator to see what these equations look like.

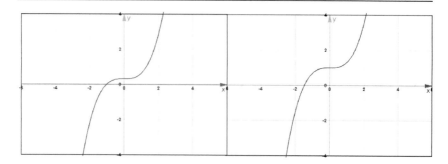

Fig. 9. Graphs of the two cubic equations.

Find the Target

In an episode of *Numb3rs* (season 3, episode 7), there are a series of blackouts caused by attacks on electrical substations. Charlie maps out what areas of downtown Los Angeles were affected by each blackout and sees where the three areas overlap. This gives him a fairly large region, so Charlie also looks at the regions that would have been affected if other substations had been attacked. From this Charlie is able to narrow down the targeted region to a few blocks, and the FBI agents figure out that the criminals are trying to break into a prison to kill someone who plans to testify against them.

PRIOR KNOWLEDGE NEEDED:

For this activity students should know how to plot linear inequalities.

CLASSROOM USE:

1. Show this clip to students.
2. Have students work in groups on the following problems. Each group will need three graph paper transparency sheets, a red, blue, and green marker, and a handout.
3. Plot the following four inequalities and shade the region enclosed by all four in red: $y \leq 4$, $y \geq 2x - 5$, $y \leq 3x + 8$, and $y \geq \frac{1}{3}x - 3$.
4. Plot the following four inequalities and shade the region enclosed by all four in blue: $y \leq 2$, $y \geq -2$, $y \leq \frac{3}{4}x + 2$, and $y \leq \frac{3}{4}x + 2$.
5. Plot the following four inequalities and shade the region enclosed by all four in green: $y \leq \frac{1}{4}x + 2$, $y \geq \frac{1}{4}x - 5$, $y \leq 2x + 6$, and $y \geq 2x - 3$.
6. Place all three transparency sheets on top of each other and over the given map. Locate a possible target for the blackouts. (See Appendix B.)

CONNECTION TO COMMON CORE:

In this activity students model with mathematics when they apply their knowledge of linear inequalities to solving a crime.

Mean Girl Math

During one scene in *Mean Girls*, Cady is sitting with the most popular girls in the school at lunch. Regina is reading a food label that lists 120 calories and 48 calories from fat. She asks what percent that is. Cady answers 40 percent and explains that since $48/120 = x/100$ she can cross-multiply and get the value of x.

Later on Cady has to join the Mathletes to get extra credit for failing math. Cady is failing math because she pretended to be dumb in order to make a boy think she needed help so he would tutor her. During the Illinois state championship meet, various math questions are asked. A couple of the questions involve algebra. One question states two facts about two numbers. First, twice the larger of the two numbers is three more than five times the smaller. Second, the sum of four times the larger and three times the smaller is 71. The contestants are asked to find the two numbers. The correct answers are given as 14 and 5. This question is not too difficult because it involves two simultaneous equations. Translating the two facts into equations gives $2x = 3 + 5y$ and $4x + 3y = 71$, with x representing the larger of the two numbers. One way to solve these equations is to multiply the first one by 2 to get $4x = 6 + 10y$. Substituting this into the second equation gives $6 + 10y + 3y = 71$. Solving this equation for y yields 5, and plugging the y value of 5 back into one of the equations gives x a value of 14. This is the same answer the contestant gave.

Another question the host asks is to find an odd three-digit number whose digits add up to 12. The digits are all different and the difference between the first two digits equals the difference between.... The host does not get to finish the question because one of the contestants rings in and gives the answer of 741. This problem is a little more challenging. First, let's assume that the host was going to finish his sentence saying that the difference between the first two digits is equal to the difference between the second two digits. If we let the digits in the three digit number be represented by x, y, and z then we are given $x + y + z = 12$, and x does not equal y does not equal z. We also know that the number is odd, so z has to be 1, 3, 5, 7 or 9. For each of these z values we can figure out what $x + y$ would have to equal. For example, if z is 1 then $x + y = 11$. This gives us eight possible three-digit numbers:

291, 921, 381, 831, 471, 741, 561, and 651. Figuring out the remaining possibilities using the other values of z along with our givens yields a total of 24 three-digit numbers. Using the final given, that the difference of the first two equals the difference of the second two, leaves us with 741, 543, 345, and 147. The contestant's answer of 741 is on this list, but from just these givens there are three other possible answers. Because the host got cut off we don't know if he was planning to give additional information.

PRIOR KNOWLEDGE NEEDED:

Students need to know how to solve algebraic equations, how to solve simultaneous equations, and what odd numbers are.

CLASSROOM USE:

1. Show the first clip where Cady calculates the percentage of fat calories in her food.
2. Ask students to work the problem out themselves and explain how they got their answer.
3. Show the clip from the Mathletes competition.
4. Have students work out the first problem and explain their solution.
5. For the second problem let students assume that the host was going to finish his sentence by saying that the difference of the first two digits is the same as the difference between the second two digits. Ask them to check that 741 is a correct solution. Then ask students if this is the only correct solution and to explain why or why not.

CONNECTION TO COMMON CORE:

In this activity students reason abstractly and quantitatively as they figure out all of the possible solutions to the second Mathletes problem.

More Mathletes

Another math competition takes place in *Little Man Tate*. In the competition the contestants had to find a number that meets these rules: First, when the number is divided by the product of its digits, the quotient is three. Second, adding 18 to the number gives the original number but with its digits reversed. The answer given in the movie is 24. Assuming that the number has two digits we can write it as $a + 10b$, where a is the ones digit and b is the tens digit. The problem translates to $\frac{a+10b}{ab} = 3$ and $a + 10b + 18 = b + 10a$. Adding like terms in the second equation gives us $9b = 9a - 18$, which reduces to $b = a - 2$. This can be plugged into the first equation to get $\frac{a+10(a-2)}{a(a-2)} = 3$. After multiplying out the numerator and denominator and then adding like terms, we end up with $3a^2 - 17a + 20 = 0$. This factors into $(3a - 5)(a - 4)$. Since a and b represent digits, they have to be integer values. Setting $3a - 5$ equal to zero leads to $a = \frac{5}{3}$. Since this is not an integer, the solution can be rejected. Setting $a - 4$ equal to zero leads to the solution $a = 4$. Then $b = a - 2 = 4 - 2 = 2$ and $a + 10b = 4 + 10(2) = 24$.

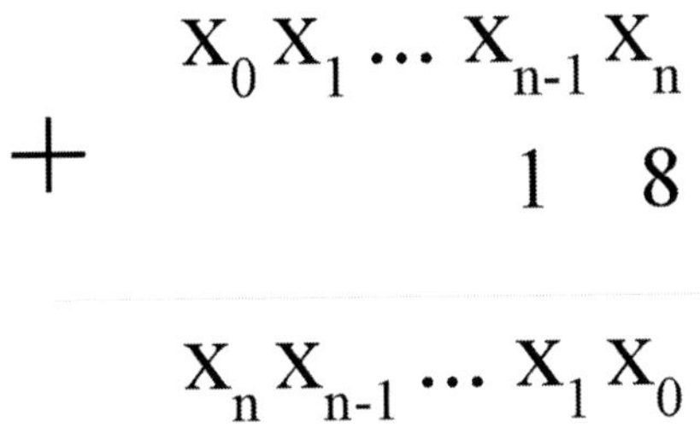

We can see why there will not be any solutions with more than two digits using the second rule. The rule tells us that

$x_0x_1...x_{n-1}x_n + 18 = x_nx_{n-1}...x_1x_0$,

with the digits of the number being $x_0, x_1, ..., x_{n-1},$ and x_n. The second rule tells us that looking at the two extremes is all that is necessary to show this will

$$\begin{array}{r} X_0\ X_1\ \cdots\ X_{n-1}\ X_n \\ +\qquad\qquad\quad 1\quad 8 \\ \hline \end{array}$$

$$X_n\ X_{n-1}\ \cdots\ X_1\ X_0$$

Fig. 10. Addition of digits.

never work. Adding the ones digits could give us $x_n + 8 = x_0$ (if x_n is a 0 or 1). If x_n is greater than 1, then $x_n + 8 > 9$, which means that a 1 will be carried over to the next column and $x_n + 8 = 10 + x_0$. This reduces to $x_n = 2 + x_0$. In the highest position either $x_0 = x_n$ (if nothing was carried over from the addition in the previous position) or $x_0 + 1 = x_n$. Note that the most that can be carried over is 1, because the highest value for the digits is 9 and nothing additional is being added to them after the tens position. Additionally, we cannot have a case where $x_0 + 1$ is more than 9, because if it were, the number would gain an extra digit and there is no way it could equal its reverse when 18 is added. We will first look at the case where $x_n + 8 = x_0$ and $x_0 = x_n$. This leads to $0 = 8$, which will never happen. The other three cases lead to similar situations, ruling out all possible cases. Therefore, the property never holds true. The reason why this argument doesn't hold for the two-digit case is that the tens-column possibilities are either $x_0 + 1 = x_n$ or $x_0 + 2 = x_n$. It is the second equation that gives a solution with $x_n = 2 + x_0$. Putting these together leads to $2 + x_0 = 2 + x_0$, which is true.

Another interesting problem given in this movie is to find a number whose cube plus five times its square minus 42 times the number and 40 has a zero remainder. The problem corresponds to solving the equation $x^3 + 5x^2 - (42x + 40) = 0$. One way to factor this cubic expression is to use long division, dividing it by x minus one of the factors of 40. The only one that works is $x - 5$. Going through the long division gives us $x^3 + 5x^2 - (42x + 40) = (x - 5)(x^2 + 10x + 8)$. At this point we can easily see that $x = 5$ will be a solution when the first factor is set equal to zero. This is the solution given in the movie. To factor $x^2 + 10x + 8$ we can use the quadratic formula and get. There are, in fact, three solutions, but 5 is the only integer solution. However, it is not specified in the reading of the problem that they are only looking for an integer solution.

PRIOR KNOWLEDGE NEEDED:

In this activity students should understand base 10 notation, be able to manipulate algebraic expressions, know long division, and know how to use the quadratic formula.

CLASSROOM USE:

1. Show students the clip for the first problem.
2. Have students check that 24 is a solution to this problem.
3. Ask students to prove that there are no solutions with more than two digits, giving guidance as needed.
4. Show students the clip for the second problem.
5. Have students check that 5 is a solution to this problem.
6. Ask students to find other solutions.

CONNECTION TO COMMON CORE:

Students construct viable arguments when they prove that the first problem has no solutions greater than two digits.

In Other Words

Since algebra is abstract in nature, one popular method of helping students understand it is to put it in terms they can relate to. The following examples use cars, basketball, baseball, and gigolos.

In an episode of *Veronica Mars* (season 2, episode 21), Cassidy is tutoring Eli in math in exchange for getting his car fixed. Cassidy tries to put the math in terms Eli can understand by relating it to spark plugs and cans of oil.

In *Big*, Josh helps the son of his girlfriend's friend learn algebra. He starts off with an example of a basketball player scoring ten points in the first quarter. He then asks how many points the player is going to score in the whole game. The kid says that's easy; he will score 40 points. Josh says that's algebra. One quarter is to 10 points just as 4 is to y or x or whatever it is you're looking for.

In *Everybody Hates Chris* (season 2, episode 21), Chris is usually an average student, except when it comes to algebra. When his teacher asks Chris to solve $-9x + 1 = -80$, he guesses 89. Another student answers correctly, saying x is 9. Chris' teacher urges him to get better at algebra so that the class can win a school competition for pizza. Chris asks his mom for a tutor, but his mom can't imagine one exists in their Brooklyn neighborhood. The scene flashes to a guy on the street teaching a group of kids. If there are 6 units and 12 tenants in a building with x = number of units with televisions and y = the people who are at work now, how many TVs can they steal? After a failed attempt with his mom tutoring, Chris asks his grandmother for help. She uses baseball as a way to help him learn algebra. In one example she says that in yesterday's game, Daryl Strawberry batted 500 with 6 at-bats; how many hits did he get? Chris lets a equal the number of at-bats, b equal the batting average, and h equal the number of hits. He expresses the batting average as .5. Since batting average is equal to the number of hits divided by the number of at-bats, Chris writes this as $.5 = h$ over 6. He then multiplies both sides of the equation by 6, giving the number of hits as 3. Chris eventually learns algebra, but on the day of the test he fills out the test answers incorrectly. He answers question 1 in the spot for question 2 and ends up getting every question wrong, so his class doesn't get pizza.

In *Stand and Deliver*, the students read this problem from the board: Juan has five times as many girlfriends as Pedro. Carlos has one girlfriend less than Pedro. If the total number of girlfriends between them is 20, how many does each gigolo have? One student says that if Juan is x and Carlos is y then Pedro is $x + y$. Another student says $5x$ = Juan's girlfriends and Carlos has $x - 5$ girlfriends. Finally a student answers correctly with $x + 5x + x - 1 = 20$, so $x = 3$.

PRIOR KNOWLEDGE NEEDED:

In this activity students should know how to solve algebraic equations.

CLASSROOM USE:

1. Show these clips to students.
2. In groups ask students to come up with an application for algebra using a sport or activity that they enjoy. They should make up several algebra problems using their activity.
3. Have groups switch problems and solve the new problems they receive.

CONNECTION TO COMMON CORE:

Students model with mathematics as they use algebra to create and solve problems that relate to a real-world situation.

Word Problems, Part 1

In the movie *Little Big League*, Billy, a 12-year-old baseball team owner, is studying math when one of the players comes into his office. The player says it helps him to write problems down, so they go to a big chalkboard. Billy reads the problem: If Joe can paint a house in 3 hours and Sam can paint the same house in 5 hours, then how many hours does it take for both of them to paint the house? After hearing it is a word problem the player calls over other players for help. Soon the whole team is working on it. One guy suggests the answer is 5 times 3, but he is shot down. Another player says the answer is 5 + 3, or 8. A third player says that's not right because there are two of them, so divide the 8 by 2 to get 4 hours. Finally a player steps forward and says the answer is 5 times 3 divided by 5 plus 3, which gives 1 and 7/8.

One way to solve this problem is to change the rates for Joe and Sam into hourly rates. Joe takes three hours to paint one house so he can paint 1/3 of a house in one hour. Similarly, Sam can paint 1/5 of a house in one hour. Adding these together gives a combined hourly rate of 1/3 + 1/5 = 8/15. This means that Joe and Sam together can paint 8/15 of a house in one hour. But we want to know how many hours it takes to paint one house, so solve 8/15 x = 1 to give 15/8, or 1 7/8. The method that the baseball player used is a little different but gives the same answer. To see why his solution also works, we can show that the two methods are equivalent. To generalize our method let's say that Sam can paint 1/m of a house in an hour and Joe can paint 1/n of a house in an hour. Then their combined hourly rate is $\frac{1}{m} + \frac{1}{n} = \frac{n+m}{nm}$. Next we want to solve the equation $\frac{n+m}{nm} x = 1$. This gives us $\frac{nm}{n+m}$. The player's solution was to multiply the number of hours it takes for Sam to paint one house (m) by the number of hours it takes Joe to paint one house (n) and divide that by the sum of those two values. This is equivalent to the equation $\frac{nm}{n+m}$.

Prior knowledge needed:

Students need to know how to solve for unknowns and need to have some practice solving word problems.

Classroom use:

1. Show this clip to students.
2. Ask students to think of other ways to solve this problem.
3. After some students share their solutions, ask them to prove that their method is equivalent to the baseball player's method.
4. Ask students to create a general solution to the problem that works if there are three painters (see Appendix B).

Students make sense of this problem and persevere at solving it when they find multiple solutions. Students also look for and express regularity in repeated reasoning when they generalize the problem from two people to three people.

Word Problems, Part 2

In an episode of *Family Guy*, Peter says there's nothing that kids learn in school that they can't learn in the streets. Then there is a flash to a scene with two kids on the street. One wants to know where Louie is because it is 3 o'clock. The other says Louie left his house at 2:15 and travels a distance of 6.2 miles at a rate of 5 miles per hour and asks what time he will arrive. The other says it depends if he stops to see his ho. And the first guy says that's what we call a variable. Louie travels 5 miles per 1 hour, which corresponds to 6.2 miles in 1.24 hours. 1.24 hours converts to 74.4 minutes. This means he left at 2:15 and it will take him 74.4 minutes. Assuming Louie does not make any stops, he should arrive at 3:29 and 24 seconds.

In an episode of *2 Broke Girls* (season 2, episode 23), Caroline appears on Piers Morgan's television show along with Ms. Rosenthall, an ex-employee of Caroline's father who was given a million-dollar advance to write a book about him. Caroline thinks Ms. Rosenthall is telling a bunch of lies since she lied on her resume. Caroline asks her a math question to test her because she claimed to have a degree in finance. Caroline asks, if a train carrying 27 passengers leaves Grand Central station at 9 AM and travels 800 miles to Chicago and arrives at 5 PM, then how fast was the train traveling? Piers correctly answers 100 miles an hour and then admits to being a mathlete.

In *The Santa Claus 3*, the elves' teacher asks, if a reindeer leaves Ellsberg flying west at 20 miles per hour, and another reindeer flies east travelling at 50 miles per hour, how many hours does it take for them to be 210 miles apart? In 1 hour the reindeers will be 70 miles apart, so it takes 3 hours for them to be 210 miles apart.

On an episode of *The Office* (season 9, episode 4), Dwight closes the building to do repairs, so he has everyone work on board a bus. They decide to take a road trip to get pies. The pie shop closes at 5. When Kevin hears this he worries that they won't make it in time. It is 20 minutes till 5 and the pie shop is 13 miles away. Kevin, who is usually dim-witted, can do math when pies are involved. He says that at 55 mph that gives them only 5 minutes to spare. The others are amazed that he can do these calculations in his head, so they ask him how many 19,154 pies divided by 61 pies is. Kevin says 314 pies. When they change it to salads he is back to his usual self.

In an episode of *Who's the Boss* (season 4, episode 17), Tony is studying for a college entrance exam. Angela asks him the following math question: There is a jar of red and green jellybeans. The ratio of red jellybeans to green jellybeans is 5:3. If the jar contains a total of 160 jellybeans, how many of them are red? Tony gets it wrong, but Tony's daughter Sam answers correctly with 100.

PRIOR KNOWLEDGE NEEDED:

Students should know how to convert time units and solve ratio problems.

CLASSROOM USE:

1. Show some or all of these clips.
2. Ask students to solve the problem given or check that the solution given is correct.

CONNECTION TO COMMON CORE:

Students model with mathematics since these problems all involve real-world situations.

The Music of Algebra

On *South Park* (season 15, episode 3), Mr. Garrison teaches the class algebra using music. In the first verse of the song "Bibbidi-Bobbidi-Boo," x = salagadoola mechicca boola and y = bibbidi-bobbidi-boo. Put them together and what have you got? Bibbidi-bobbidi-boo. So $x + y = y$ and $x = 0$. Mr. Garrison says the song was badly written. Later, he says that in the second verse x = bibbidi-bobbidi^3 + boo.

PRIOR KNOWLEDGE NEEDED:

Students should understand algebraic equations.

CLASSROOM USE:

1. Show this clip to students.
2. Have students in pairs, pick a different song and express it as an algebraic equation.
3. Have each pair share their song and equation.

Students have to attend to precision so that their classmates can understand their work.

What Is Algebra?

Some people are clueless when it comes to algebra. They don't understand that x is a variable that stands for a number. For example, in *That '70s Show* (season 3, episode 16), Eric tells his parents that he is tutoring Kelso in math. His parents try to quiz him to find out if he's telling the truth. His dad asks him what the squsare root of x is. Eric says that he can't answer that because x is a variable so he can't answer until someone defines its parameters.

Another clueless character is Nelson from *The Simpsons*. In an episode (season 22, episode 3), Nelson tries to impress a visitor with Lisa's math skills. He asks Lisa what x is. But not having been given a problem to solve, Lisa says it depends.

Yet another person not understanding algebra is Maeby from *Arrested Development*. In one episode (season 4, episode 13), George Michael is tutoring Maeby in algebra. He tries to seduce her by saying there is a man, a woman, and a bedroom; let's solve for x. Unfortunately, Maeby is very bad at algebra, and she doesn't understand what he is talking about. George Michael tries to explain that in algebra there is an unknown element called x that is a number that has to be solved for. She does not understand what George Michael means when he says x is a number, because it is a letter. This causes George Michael to take out his dry erase board and write the equation $3x + 1 = 10$ to show that they need to solve it for x.

Another character understands that x stands for a number but doesn't appreciate algebra. In an episode of *New Girl* (season 3, episode 11), the school that Jess works at is having space issues, so three different classes have to share the same room. Jess has to share her room with a biology class and a math class. The biology teacher says that they are getting stuck with the math kids who use letters instead of numbers. Jess asks if he means algebra.

Another character not impressed with algebra is Claire from *Six Feet Under*. In one episode (season 1, episode 7), Claire is in a math class reading while her teacher goes over multiplying y^4 by y^4 to get y^8 and then combining $x^3y^4 + x^3y^4$ to get $2x^3y^4$. When the teacher calls on Claire to explain a formula, Claire is unable to. The teacher says she might be able to if she paid attention in class rather than reading. Claire says she would pay attention if there was something useful being taught. The teacher says that algebra is very useful for physicists and for everyone else, because it forces your mind to solve problems logically and is one of the world's perfect sciences. Claire is not impressed and imagines her teacher's head exploding.

PRIOR KNOWLEDGE NEEDED:

For this activity students should be familiar with algebra already.

CLASSROOM USE:

1. Show these clips to students.
2. Have students write a letter to one of these characters explaining what algebra is and why it is useful.

CONNECTION TO COMMON CORE:

Students attend to precision as they explain what algebra is in a way that other people can understand.

Kayak Math

On the show *Shark Tank*, there are six business tycoons who are looking for companies to invest in. On each episode a series of entrepreneurs present their company to the sharks in hopes of gaining money and guidance in return for a percent of their company. In one episode (season 5, episode 28), the first company to present is Oro Kayak. They build foldable kayaks that sell for $1,100. Through the shark's questions it is revealed that the company has sold 1,228 kayaks so far, leading to $1.1 million in sales. Calculating the cost times the number of units sold yields $(1,100)(1,228) = 1,350,800$. This means that they actually had $1.3 million in sales. The kayaks cost $505 to build, but they hope to get the cost down to $350 in the next year. Since they have sold 1,228 units, the company has made $1,228(1,100–505) = \$730,660$. They project $4 million in revenue in the next year. According to the owners, at some point during the year the company will make the change from manufacturing the kayaks for $505 to manufacturing them for $350. We are interested in knowing how many kayaks need to be sold at each price point in order to get to the projected $4 million in revenue. Let's assume that there are a total of 5,850 kayaks sold in the next year. If x = the number of units sold for $505 and y = the number of units sold for $350, then we know $x + y = 5,850$. We also know that the profit will be the price the kayak sells for minus the cost of production times the number of kayaks sold at that production price. This gives us $(1100 - 505)x + (1100 - 350)y = \$4$ million. Reducing the second equation yields $595x + 750y = \$4$ million. Then substituting in $x = 5850 - y$ yields $3{,}480{,}750 + 155y = \$4$ million. Solving this gives us $y = 3{,}350$. Then $x = 5{,}850 – 3{,}350 = 2{,}500$. This means that 2,500 kayaks sold for $505 and 3,350 kayaks sold for $350.

The original offer the owners of Oro Kayak ask of the sharks is to get $500,000 in exchange for a 12 percent stake in the company. To figure out what the owners of Oro Kayak value their company at, we can solve $.12x = 500{,}000$ to get 4,166,666.67. One of the sharks, Robert, makes an offer for $500,000 in exchange for a 25 percent stake in the company. This means that Robert values the company at two million dollars. They take the offer.

PRIOR KNOWLEDGE NEEDED:

For this activity students need to know how to solve a system of linear equations.

CLASSROOM USE:

1. Show this clip to students.
2. Ask students to calculate the correct dollar amount of sales made so far. Also, have them calculate how much the owners value their company at and how much Robert values their company at.
3. Next, students can calculate how much revenue the company has earned so far.
4. Finally, have students calculate how many kayaks need to be sold at each price point in order to get to the projected $4 million in revenue.

CONNECTION TO COMMON CORE:

Students model with mathematics as they apply their knowledge of systems of linear equations to a real-world problem.

Simultaneous Equations

In an episode of *Grounded for Life* (season 2, episode 22), Jimmy is tutoring a girl in math. He says that when you have an equation with two variables you have to solve for y in terms of x or x in terms of y. This is a good preparation for solving simultaneous equations by substitution.

In *The Be All and End All*, Ziggy is shown in his math class while the teacher goes over solving simultaneous equations. She says it is easy to solve the equations using graphs. She asks the students to draw the equation lines, and that the point where they cross is the solution.

PRIOR KNOWLEDGE NEEDED:

Students should know how to solve algebraic equations and graph equations of lines.

CLASSROOM USE:

1. Show students the clip from *Grounded for Life*.
2. Give students examples of equations with two variables and have them solve for one variable in terms of the other.
3. Give students systems of two equations with two unknowns and ask them to solve for both variables. Start with problems where it is easy to solve for one of the variables in one equation so that students make the connection to use the substitution method. An example set of equations is $x + y = 10$ and $3x + 4y = 8$.
4. Show students the clip from *The Be All and End All*.
5. Take one of the previous examples and have students graph the two lines. They can see that the point where the two lines cross is the same solution that they get using substitution. Ask students if the two lines will always cross at a single point and, if not, what other possible cases are there. Students should answer that there will be no intersection (lines will be parallel) when there is no answer to the system of equations. Students should also be able to answer that there will be infinite intersections (the equations describe the same line) when there are infinite solutions to the system of equations.
6. To conclude this lesson, give students a word problem to solve using any of the above methods. An example word problem is this: There are children and dogs on a beach. There are a total of 41 heads and 110 feet. How many dogs and children are there?

CONNECTION TO COMMON CORE:

In this activity students make sense of problems and persevere in solving them when they solve systems of equations two different ways.

Polynomials

Polynomials are difficult to describe using a concise definition but easy to recognize by example. In an episode of *The O.C.* (season 3, episode 21), Summer and Seth are in a math class where the teacher reviews polynomials. He describes a polynomial as an expression in which variables and constants are combined using only addition, subtraction, and multiplication.

PRIOR KNOWLEDGE NEEDED:

Students should be familiar with polynomials.

CLASSROOM USE:

1. Show this clip to students.
2. Ask students if the teacher's definition is good and how they would define a polynomial in their own words. Students can also list properties of polynomials, such as that variables are always raised to positive integers or that each term has a constant and variable(s).

CONNECTION TO COMMON CORE:

In this activity students attend to precision when they have to be clear about defining and describing a polynomial.

Chapter Four

Functions

In this chapter students learn about Euler's number e and its relation to exponential growth and compound interest. They also learn how this number is featured in what some consider the most beautiful mathematical equation. Students will also use functions to study robots and pigeons. The topic of functions involves understanding and analyzing functions and being able to use them in real-world contexts. This chapter discusses different types of functions including trigonometric, linear, quadratic, and exponential functions.

Function of My Hand

In an episode of *The Simpsons* (season 10, episode 11), the children of Springfield are put on a curfew after being falsely accused of vandalizing Springfield Elementary School. To retaliate, they form a pirate radio station on which they reveal the adult population's secrets. The adults try to track down the station in order to stop the kids. Professor Frink invents a device to locate the radio station. As he is using the device, Professor Frink says that he is compressing the data in order to express it as a function of his hand. He then points in the direction of the radio station. This is a good example to use when students are first learning about functions. Professor Frink is inputting the x value as the compressed data, and his device outputs the y value as the direction his finger points. This is analogous to the function machine that is often used to introduce the concept of a function. Given an input (x value), the machine will perform some type of function and then produce an output (y value). In this example we don't know what the actual function is, so it is best used to go over the concept of a function in general.

PRIOR KNOWLEDGE NEEDED:

Students should know the definition of a function.

CLASSROOM USE:

1. Show this clip to students.
2. Have students explain why the example is a function.

CONNECTION TO COMMON CORE:

Students have to attend to precision as they explain why this is a function in a way that other people can understand.

The Origin

In an episode of *The Big Bang Theory* (season 2, episode 16), Penny sits in Sheldon's spot on the couch. When Sheldon sees Penny sitting there, he says she is in his spot and asks her to move. To explain how important the spot is to him Sheldon says that if his life were expressed as a four-dimensional function, then the coordinates of that spot would be (0, 0, 0, 0). Typically time is considered the fourth dimension, so that is probably the fourth dimension in his statement. One interpretation of why Sheldon used the couch cushion to represent the origin of the graph of his life is that it represents his home base, and all other locations are described in relation to this spot. The time position may be zero to represent his life beginning the moment he found that spot. If Sheldon were referring to his spot in the present tense then he should have called it $(0, 0, 0, t)$, where t is the elapsed time since he found his spot.

PRIOR KNOWLEDGE NEEDED:

Students need to know what the Cartesian Plane is.

CLASSROOM USE:

1. Show this clip to students.
2. Ask them to give a possible reason that Sheldon named his spot (0, 0, 0, 0).

CONNECTION TO COMMON CORE:

Students make sense of the problem as they explain Sheldon's reasoning.

The Mendoza Line

In an episode of *How I Met Your Mother* (season 3, episode 5), Ted meets a girl online, and he discusses with Barney how hot she is. Barney thinks that means she is also crazy. He goes on to explain the hot/crazy scale. Barney draws a set of axes with crazy on the x axis and hot on the y axis. A girl can be crazy as long as she is equally hot. He plots a few points showing the x and y value are approximately the same, saying that if she is x amount of crazy she is also x amount of hot. Barney then draws the $y = x$ diagonal line and says that girls should be above that line. He calls this line the Vickie Mendoza Diagonal, after an ex-girlfriend who kept wavering between doing crazy and non-crazy things. This is a baseball reference to the Mendoza line, named after the baseball player Mario Mendoza. Mendoza's batting average wavered around .2, and that is considered the minimum number to maintain in order to be thought of as a competent hitter. Any player whose batting average is below .2 is said to be below the Mendoza Line.

Barney draws points on the graph to represent his opinion of Vickie Mendoza's actions. First she shaved her head, giving her a point that is high on crazy and low on hot, putting her below the diagonal. Then she lost ten pounds, putting her above the diagonal with equal hotness but less craziness. Next she tries to stab Barney with a fork, moving her below the diagonal again with a high crazy and a higher hotness. Finally she gets a breast augmentation, which moves her above the diagonal again as her hotness stays the same but her craziness decreases. There seems to be some error with these placements. For example, losing ten pounds would presumably increase her hotness and not affect her craziness. Additionally, stabbing Barney with a fork should not increase her hotness and getting a breast augmentation should increase her hotness, especially considering Barney is the one plotting the points. The bottom right corner of the graph is called the Shelly Galezby Zone and is named after another ex-girlfriend who gained twenty pounds and then tried to kill Barney with a brick. Barney's silly conclusions can illustrate an application of functions in a fun, memorable way.

PRIOR KNOWLEDGE NEEDED:

For this activity students should know how to plot points in the Cartesian Plane.

CLASSROOM USE:

1. Show this clip to students.

2. Ask students to find the errors in the points Barney plotted when explaining Vickie Mendoza's actions and have them plot the dots correctly.
3. In pairs, have students think of ten characters from movies or television shows and rank each on a scale from one to ten based on how sane they are and how attractive they are. Even though the original premise for this graph was based on females, males can be included for this exercise to avoid any discrimination. Next, students can exchange their charts with another group and plot the values for the other group's characters.
4. Have some pairs share their graphs. Students can explain which points fall above, below, or on the Vickie Mendoza Diagonal. They can also explain why they think a point would fall in one of those spots.

CONNECTION TO COMMON CORE:

In this activity students make sense of the problem and reason abstractly and quantitatively. Students are thinking about the problem as they explain the errors in Barney's reasoning. When plotting the points from another pair's chart, students are solving the problem. Then, when they explain how they know a point would fall above, below, or on the Vickie Mendoza Diagonal, students are explaining what the solution means and reflecting on their thinking. Additionally, students model with mathematics when solving this problem.

Secondary Trigonometry Ratios

In the Disney version of *The Prince and the Pauper*, there is a scene where the prince is being tutored in math. His tutor is reviewing triangles and says that all triangles have three sides and that the relations between them are known as ratios. As the tutor discusses trigonometry, the prince looks out the window, longingly watching the other children playing outside in the snow. The tutor then asks for the three secondary trigonometry ratios. The prince says tangent and secant, and then can't think of a third ratio. The tutor says it is hypotenuse.

PRIOR KNOWLEDGE NEEDED:

Students should know all of the trigonometric functions.

CLASSROOM USE:

1. Show this clip to students.
2. Ask students which one of the prince's answers was correct and what the secondary trigonometry functions actually are (see Appendix B).

3. Ask students to explain how they can get the values of each secondary trigonometry function, given the value of the primary trigonometry functions (see Appendix B).
4. Ask students what other trigonometry values they can get, given only a sine value (see Appendix B).

Connection to Common Core:

Students makes sense of the problem by having to understand what the secondary trigonometry functions are when they explain how to get each one from a primary trigonometry function.

Inverse Tangent Function

In *The Big Bang Theory* (season 2, episode 13), Sheldon is trying to make new friends, so he goes indoor rock climbing. Everything is going well until he looks down. Looking down makes Sheldon feel like an inverse tangent function that is approaching an asymptote.

Prior knowledge needed:

Students should be familiar with the tangent function, including knowing how to evaluate different angles and graphing the function.

Classroom use:

1. Show this clip to students.
2. Ask students to find the values of the tangent function at the x values of $-\frac{\pi}{2}, -\frac{\pi}{4}, 0, \frac{\pi}{4}$, and $\frac{\pi}{2}$. Then have them draw one period of the tangent function from $-\frac{\pi}{2}$ to $\frac{\pi}{2}$ and describe the behavior of the function between these values.
3. To have the students graph the inverse tangent function, ask them to switch the x and y values they calculated earlier. They should see the vertical asymptotes turn into horizontal asymptotes and note that the graph is similar, just reflected over the line $y = x$. In figure 11 the tangent function is shown in black and the inverse tangent function is shown in gray.
4. While both the tangent and the inverse tangent functions have asymptotes, have students explain why the tangent function would fit this joke better. One possible answer is that since the asymptotes are vertical in the tangent function, this mimics the idea of falling better than a horizontal asymptote, which would mean traveling to the right or left forever.

In this activity students attend to precision, as they need to explain their work so that others are able to understand it.

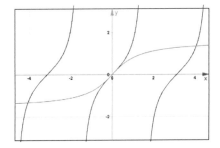

Fig. 11. The tangent (black) and inverse tangent (gray) functions.

Trigonometry Calculations

In an episode of *Jane by Design* (season 1, episode 3), Billy is helping Jane study for a math test. He asks, if $\sin\theta = \frac{3}{5}$, what is $\cos\theta$?

In *The Big Bang Theory* (season 1, episode 2), Sheldon and Leonard try to bring a large box up a flight of stairs. Leonard says that the stairs are an inclined plane, so the force needed to lift the box is reduced by the sine of the angle of the stairs, which he guesses to be 30 degrees. Leonard says this is about a half and Sheldon corrects him by saying it is exactly one half.

In an episode of *Freaks and Geeks* (season 1, episode 11), Lindsey crashes her parents' car and starts to think her new friends are a bad influence. She decides to re-join her old friends on the mathletes team. During a competition one of the questions they ask is this: If arcsin$x$ equals 2arccos$x$, then what does x equal? They give the answer of 0.9. This answer is incorrect because arcsin(.9) = 1.12 and 2arccos(.9) = .90. This problem is actually a lot harder than it appears. One way to solve it is to apply the sine to both sides to get x = sin(2arccos$x$). Looking at the right side, we can apply the double angle formula (thinking of arccos$x$ as the angle) to get 2sin(arccos$x$)cos(arccos$x$). Since cos(arccos$x$) is equal to x, we will focus on the sin(arccos$x$) term. We can think of setting up a right triangle where the cosine of some angle is equal to x. This means that the side adjacent to this angle is x and the hypotenuse is 1. Using the Pythagorean Theorem gives us the side opposite this angle as $\sqrt{1-x^2}$. This means that the sine of this angle will be $\frac{\sqrt{1-x^2}}{1} = \sqrt{1-x^2}$. Putting everything together, we get 2sin(arccos$x$)cos(arccos$x$) = $2\sqrt{1-x^2}(x)$. Going back to our earlier equation, x = sin(2arccos$x$) now becomes $x = 2\sqrt{1-x^2}(x)$. Solving this gives us $x = \frac{\sqrt{3}}{2}$. We can check this solution and see that it gives us 1.05 for both sides of the original equation. In decimal form, $\frac{\sqrt{3}}{2} = .866$, so it is possible the writers rounded the answer to the nearest tenth. Unfortunately, rounding like that throws off the solution substantially.

In an episode of *Boy Meets World* (season 4, episode 18), Corey, Topanga, and Sean are studying for the SAT. Topanga asks if angle A has a sine of 30 degrees, what is the cosine of angle B? Assuming she meant to say angle A, the answer is $\frac{1}{2}$.

In an episode of *Melissa and Joey* (season 3, episode 31), Ryder needs to get a B on his trigonometry test or else his aunt won't let him go on the senior trip. He asks Preston for help studying. Preston agrees to help him only if Ryder helps him get Layla interested in him. Layla also needs help studying for the trigonometry test. At their study session, Preston asks this question: In a scalene right triangle, if the tangent of 65 degrees is equal to 8 over 5, what is the slope of the hypotenuse? There are many things wrong with this question. First, there is no reason to say that the triangle is scalene. While this may be true because the angles will be 90, 65, and 35, this is extraneous information. Next, the tangent of 65 is not equal to 8 over 5. Finally, he probably wants to know the length of the hypotenuse rather than the slope of it.

PRIOR KNOWLEDGE NEEDED:

For this activity, students should know how to evaluate various trigonometric functions and inverse trigonometric functions.

CLASSROOM USE:

1. Show some or all of these clips to students.
2. After each clip, ask students to perform the calculation, explain the answer given in the clip, or explain why the question is incorrect.

CONNECTION TO COMMON CORE:

Students make sense of problems and persevere in solving them as they have to explain how the characters in the clips got their answers or how to solve the problem suggested by the characters.

SOHCAHTOA

A popular mnemonic used for remembering the three main trigonometric functions is SOHCAHTOA. This represents the ratios of each function using the sides of a right triangle: sine is opposite over hypotenuse, cosine is adjacent over hypotenuse, and tangent is opposite over adjacent. While it is unknown where this mnemonic came from, one tale is that a Native American was walking one day and stubbed his toe. He found a river to soak his foot in and his Native American name became SOHCAHTOA.

This mnemonic is found in an episode of *Switched at Birth* (season 1, episode 25). Bay is behind in schoolwork, so Daphne helps her study trigonometry. Bay learns that trigonometry is all about relationships between sides and ratios. They go over SOHCAHTOA and what each part stands for.

PRIOR KNOWLEDGE NEEDED:

Students should know the sine, cosine, and tangent functions and the value for each function at 30 degrees and 60 degrees.

CLASSROOM USE:

1. Give students pictures of three similar right triangles labeled A, B, and C that also have 30-degree angles. Have students measure the length of each side with a ruler.
2. Give students a chart similar to the one shown here to fill out (see Appendix B):

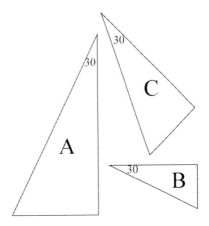

Fig. 12. **Three similar right triangles with thirty-degree angles.**

Triangle	Opposite	Adjacent	Hypotenuse	Opposite / Hypotenuse	Adjacent / Hypotenuse	Opposite / Adjacent
A						
B						
C						

3. Ask students what they might conclude from this chart. Ask them what they would expect to be in the last three columns if they did the same for a triangle with a sixty degree angle. (See Appendix B.)
4. Show this clip to students.

CONNECTION TO COMMON CORE:

In this activity students use appropriate tools when they use a ruler to measure the sides of the triangles. They also construct viable arguments when they figure out the table's pattern, seeing that the ratios lead to the sine, cosine, and tangent functions.

e

Pi is probably the most famous irrational number, but the next most popular one is Euler's number *e*. An easy way to remember the beginning digits is to think of it as 2.7 1828 1828.... This number shows up in many mathematical topics and has some interesting properties. The number *e* is the base for the natural logarithm. The derivative of the function e^x is e^x itself. A few other properties will be discussed in the next set of examples in this chapter.

The number *e* made an appearance in a billboard placed by Google in 2004.[1] The billboard read "{first 10-digit prime found in consecutive digits of *e*}.com." Anyone who figured out that the correct answer is 7427466391.com and visited the Web site was presented with another equation to solve. Anyone who was able to solve this equation was led to an invitation to apply for a job at Google.

Another mention of *e* occurs in an episode of *The Simpsons* (season 22, episode 8), which is a spoof of *Sesame Street*. Since episodes of *Sesame Street* are always sponsored by letters and numbers, this episode was sponsored by the umlaut symbol and the number *e*; not the letter "e," but the number whose exponential function is the derivative of itself.

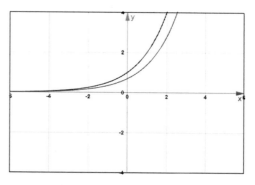

Fig. 13. Graph of 2^x (black) and its average rate of change (gray).

To see why the number *e* is a good base, we can look at various values plugged in for *a* in the expression a^x. In figure 13 the black line is 2^x and the gray line is its average rate of change. Notice that the graphs are similarly shaped but the average rate of change falls below the 2^x function. Next we will look at the graph (fig. 14) for 3^x (in black) and its average

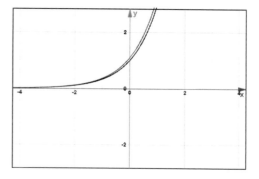

Fig. 14. Graph of 3^x (black) and its average rate of change (gray).

rate of change (in gray). Again, the graphs are similarly shaped, but this time the average rate of change is above the function. This tells us that there is a value between 2 and 3 where the graph of that number raised to the x power and its average rate of change will be the same. That special number is e. This is the same as saying that the derivative of $e^x = e^x$. Those familiar with calculus can easily see this, since we know $(a^x)' = a^x \ln a$. When the value of a is equal to e we get $(e^x)' = e^x \ln e = e^x(1) = e^x$.

PRIOR KNOWLEDGE NEEDED:

Students should have familiarity with various types of numbers such as square roots, fractions, and decimals.

CLASSROOM USE:

1. Give students a list of rational numbers and a list of irrational numbers. Make sure the numbers are written in different types of notations. On the list include some integers, fractions, terminating decimals, non-terminating repeating decimals, non-terminating non-repeating decimals, square roots of perfect squares, and square roots of non-perfect squares. Have them work in pairs to come up with a definition for a rational number and a definition for an irrational number.
2. Ask some students to share their definitions and come up with a consensus for each definition.
3. Show students the clip from *The Simpsons*.
4. Share some properties of the number e.

CONNECTION TO COMMON CORE:

In this activity students look for structure as they figure out a definition for rational and irrational numbers.

Exponential Growth

In *Pay It Forward*, Trevor's social studies teacher challenges his students to make a plan to change the world and put it into action. Trevor devises a plan to pay it forward. In one scene Trevor describes his plan to his class. He will help three people by doing something good that they can't do themselves. Then those three people are asked to each help three other people, and so on. Trevor draws a tree diagram on the blackboard illustrating his idea (fig. 15).

The top row is the original good-doer, but before he has done any good deeds the good-doer has not helped anyone yet, so call the top row 0, or $x =$

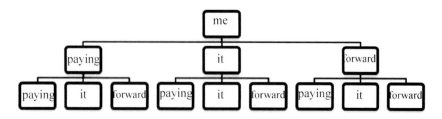

Fig. 15. "Paying it forward" tree diagram.

0. The next row, $x = 1$, has three people who have received a good deed, so its value is 3. Use this idea to think of modeling this situation with a function. Thus, $f(0) = 1$ and $f(1) = 3$.

Prior knowledge needed:

Students should be familiar with exponential functions, evaluating functions, and plotting graphs.

Classroom use:

1. Show the clip to students.
2. Have students in groups draw a tree diagram similar to the one in the movie. Then have them make a guess as to how many rows there need to be for there to be as many good deeds as there are students in their school (assuming that people receive at most one good deed). This will also require students to estimate how many students there are at their school.
3. Ask students to give different values for the function defined by the tree diagram. Students can find values such as $f(3)$, $f(4)$, or $f(15)$. Maybe students will draw the diagram for $f(3)$ or $f(4)$, but hopefully when trying to evaluate $f(15)$ they will realize that it will get big pretty fast and decide to find a pattern to get from one level to the next level.
4. Ask students to share their answers and how they derived them. The recursive formula is probably easier for the students to see, since each answer is just multiplied by three each time, but some students may also get the closed form, $f(x) = 3^x$. If students have trouble getting the closed form, ask them if they can figure out a way to quickly find $f(100)$.
5. Once students have the closed form, have them check the original guess about the number of rows needed to have the number of people in their school receive a good deed. Is it what they expected?
6. From the above work, students will have some x and y values for the good-deed function. Have them plot these points and sketch a graph.

7. Ask students to think about how the function would change if Trevor decided to help a different number of people.
8. To make this lesson more challenging, the idea of transformations of exponential functions can also be added. Change the original scenario to one in which two friends have the idea together, but one friend pays it forward to three people, as Trevor did, while the second friend only helps one person and asks his help-ee to also only help one person. Students can go through the same steps as above to get the function $f(x) = 3^x + 1$.

CONNECTION TO COMMON CORE:

In this activity students look for and make use of structure as they come up with a formula for the situation. Students also model with mathematics when they represent this real world situation as a mathematical model.

Euler's Identity

In *1600 Penn* (season 1, episode 8), President Gilchrist goes to the "Let's Multiply" awards ceremony to hand out trophies to the nation's brightest scientists and mathematicians. One of the young scholars makes this joke: "So," she said, "There's no *e* to the pi *i* in team," and I said, "Stop being negative."

This one joke can lead to some tough mathematics. Probably at this point students have not yet encountered Euler's Identity, what some consider to be the most beautiful mathematical equation. For this joke, the identity would be written as $e^{\pi i} = -1$, but to be even more beautiful it can be written as $e^{\pi i} + 1 = 0$. This equation contains all of the great numbers: 0, 1, π, and e. Devlin considers this equation "to be the most beautiful mathematical equation of all time, the mathematical equivalent of Da Vinci's Mona Lisa or Michelangelo's David."[2] Another popular joke involving this equation asks how many mathematicians it takes to change a light bulb. The answer is $-e^{\pi i}$.

To understand Euler's Identity it must first be noted that $e^{ix} = \cos x + i\sin x$. The reason this holds true is hard to prove without calculus knowledge. The simplest way to think of it is to look at the Taylor Series expansions for e^x, $\sin x$, and $\cos x$. If students do not know how to calculate derivatives, they can be given the expansions and do some explorations to observe that they hold true. For example, $e^x = 1 + x + \frac{x^2}{2!} + \frac{x^3}{3!} + \frac{x^4}{4!} + \frac{x^5}{5!} \ldots$, so students can evaluate this at $x = 1$ to see that it gets closer to the value of e (2.71828…) as more terms are added. Once students are comfortable with the Taylor expansions, they can get into the proof for why $e^{ix} = \cos x + i\sin x$. Starting with the expansion for e^x but plugging in ix for x yields: $e^{ix} = 1 + ix + \frac{(ix)^2}{2!} + \frac{(ix)^3}{3!} + \frac{(ix)^4}{4!} + \frac{(ix)^5}{5!} \ldots$. Since

$i^2 = -1$, this will become $e^{ix} = 1 + ix - \frac{x^2}{2!} - \frac{ix^3}{3!} + \frac{x^4}{4!} + \frac{ix^5}{5!} \ldots$. Then grouping to put the real parts together and the imaginary parts together yields: $(1 - \frac{x^2}{2!} + \frac{x^4}{4!} - \cdots) + i(x - \frac{x^3}{3!} + \frac{x^5}{5!} - \cdots)$. The first sum is the Taylor expansion for $\cos(x)$ and the second sum is the Taylor expansion for $\sin(x)$. Thus we get $e^{ix} = \cos x + i\sin x$. Now to see what $e^{i\pi}$ equals, the π can be plugged in for the x. This gives $e^{i\pi} = \cos x + i\sin \pi$.

Euler's Identity also shows up in a couple of episodes of *The Simpsons*. In one episode (season 22, episode 3), it is shown on the spine of a book that Lisa is studying. In another (season 7, episode 6), the equation is seen floating by when Homer enters a three-dimensional world. It can also be seen in an episode of *Veronica Mars* (season 2, episode 21), in the background on a poster in a math classroom. The equation is also mentioned in an episode of *Rizzoli and Isles* (season 1, episode 6), when Isles describes how she appreciates art and fashion. This clip can also be used to discuss the correct pronunciation of Euler's name since Isles makes the same mistake many students do by pronouncing it like "youler" rather than "oiler."

Prior knowledge needed:

Students should know how to evaluate the sine and cosine of an angle, what the number e is, how to evaluate factorials, and how to evaluate a function, and they should be familiar with imaginary numbers.

Classroom use:

1. Show the *1600 Penn* clip to students and some or all of the remaining clips.
2. Give students Euler's Identity and go through the proof for it as explained above.
3. Ask students to explain the joke shown in the *1600 Penn* clip.

Connection to Common Core:

Students construct viable arguments as they write the proof for the Euler Identity.

Compound Interest

In *The Bank*, a bank representative visits a classroom and explains why saving for retirement is very important. He says that if each student saves 50 cents a week at the bank, doubling the investment every 3 years, then in 25 years the student would have $727,000. One student claims that this is impossible because there are only 52 weeks in a year. The speaker agrees and writes out $52 \times 25 = 1{,}300$ weeks. He goes on to explain how compound interest gives interest on interest and writes the formula $FV = PV(1 + r)^n$. In this formula FV stands for the future value of the investment, PV stands for the present value of the investment, r stands for the interest rate per period, and n stands for the number of periods.

To figure out why this formula works, let's look at an example. Starting with an initial \$10 investment with a 10 percent interest rate that compounds every year yields the following table:

Year	Value at Start of Year	Interest	Value at End of Year
0	10	1	11
1	11	1.10	12.10
2	12.10	1.21	13.31
3	13.31	1.331	14.641
4	14.641	1.4641	16.1051

Rather than going through the two calculations of finding 10 percent of the start value and then adding it to the original, this can be shortened to one calculation by multiplying the start value by 1.1. But what if we want the end-of-the-year value in a given year without having to go through all of the earlier calculations? This is equivalent to multiplying by 1.1 for each year. So, to get the value at the start of year three, we can multiply the initial value by $(1.1)^3$. This gives us $10(1.1)^3 = 13.31$, which is the same value we got in the table. Now we can generalize this formula. Our initial value, \$10, is PV. The interest rate is 10 percent, which can be written as a decimal as .1. The 1.1 in our formula then represents $1 +$ interest rate $= 1 + r$. In this example the period is one year, so the $1 + r$ value gets raised to the number of periods. This gives us $(1 + r)^n$. Putting everything together gives us the original formula $FV = PV(1 + r)^n$.

This formula can be changed a little bit to reflect compounding more than once per year. Let m be the number of times we compound per year and t be the number of years. Then the interest rate per term becomes $\frac{r}{m}$. For example, if we take the same \$10 invested at a 10 percent yearly interest rate that is compounded quarterly, then each quarter the rate would be $\frac{10}{4} = 2.5$ percent. The other change in the formula occurs with the exponent. The interest is calculated mt times, the number of terms times the number of years. This gives us a formula of $FV = PV(1 + \frac{r}{m})^{mt}$.

Now think about increasing the number of times per year the interest is compounded. We'll look at the limit as m goes to infinity: $\lim_{m \to \infty} PV(1 + \frac{r}{m})^{mt} = PV \lim_{m \to \infty}(1 + \frac{r}{m})^{mt}$. If we do a change of variables letting $n = \frac{m}{r}$ this becomes $PV \lim_{n \to \infty}(1 + \frac{1}{n})^{nrt} = PV \lim_{n \to \infty}\left((1 + \frac{1}{n})^n\right)^{rt} = PV\left[\lim_{n \to \infty}\left((1 + \frac{1}{n})^n\right)\right]^{rt}$.

Those familiar with calculus will recognize that $\lim_{n \to \infty}\left((1 + \frac{1}{n})^n\right)$ is equal to e. Anyone who has not seen this before can plug in increasingly larger values of n and see that the value of $(1 + \frac{1}{n})^n$ gets closer and closer to the value of e. Thus our formula for interest compounded continuously becomes $FV = PVe^{rt}$.

In an episode of *Futurama* (season 1, episode 6), Fry needs some money. He sees his bank where he had 93 cents in an account in 1999. In this episode the current year is 2999. With an average of two and a quarter percent interest over one thousand years, he now has 4.3 billion dollars in his bank account. They don't give the interest rate, but since the final value is given, the interest rate can be calculated. We will assume the interest is compounded continuously. Then plugging known values into the formula gives: $4.3 \cdot 10^9 = .93e^{1000r}$. Dividing by .93 and taking the natural log of both sides gives us $1000r = 22.2545$. This gives us an interest rate of 2.225 percent.

PRIOR KNOWLEDGE NEEDED:

Students should know how to evaluate functions and exponents. Students should also know what the value of e is and understand what a limit is. The concept of limits can be used without the formal notation in lower level classes.

CLASSROOM USE:

1. Show students the clip from *The Bank*.
2. Explain the formula the banker gives and have students go through an example to derive the formula, giving guidance as needed.
3. Ask students to come up with a formula for compounding interest more than once per year and then compounding continuously. Students may need to see and work with the limit definition for e before finding the formula for continuous compounding.
4. Show students the clip from *Futurama*.
5. Ask students to find the interest rate Fry was given if the interest was compounded continuously.

CONNECTION TO COMMON CORE:

Students construct viable arguments when they come up with the formulas for compounding interest. Students also model with mathematics when they derive a formula for a real-world situation.

Angles in Clocks

In *Scorpion* (season 1, episode 2), Walter is one of the smartest people in the world, with an IQ of 197. As a point of reference he often points out that Albert Einstein's IQ was 160. Walter befriends a waitress named Paige who has a young boy. Paige doesn't realize that her son is a genius until Walter points it out. The boy doesn't like going to school so he hacks the thermometer to make his mom believe that he is sick. Walter figures this out and says that when he got bored in school he looked at the clock and created trigonometric functions out of the clock hands.

It is a little unclear how Walter would have made a trig function out of the clock hands, but a related problem would be to find the angle between the hour hand and the minute hand on a clock. It is possible to imagine rotating the clock so that one of the hands lies in the 3 position, and then the trig values of the angles between the two hands could be found similarly to how we find values using the unit circle.

To figure out the angle between the minute hand and the hour hand on a clock, we can first think about how fast they each move. The minute hand covers 360 degrees in 60 minutes, so it covers 360/60 = 6 degrees per minute. To get the hour hand speed we can first calculate the angle between any two numbers to be 30 degrees. This can be measured with a protractor, or this value can be given to students. Thus, the minute hand covers 30 degrees in 60 minutes. This equates to 30/60 = .5 degrees per minute. The angle between the hour hand and the 12 position will be 30 times the number of hours plus .5 times the number of minutes. Then the angle between the hour hand and the minute hand will be the absolute value of the angle between the hour hand and 12 minus the angle between the minute hand and 12. This equates to |30(number of hours) + .5(number of minutes)—6(number of minutes)|. This can be reduced to |30(number of hours)—5.5(number of minutes)|. For example, at 3:41 the angle between the hour hand and the minute hand will be |30(3)-5.5(41)|=|90–225.5|=135.5 degrees.

PRIOR KNOWLEDGE NEEDED:

For this activity students need to know how many degrees are in a circle. They also need to be familiar with the concept of absolute value.

CLASSROOM USE:

1. Show this clip to students.
2. Ask students to figure out how many degrees the minute and hour hand each move per minute. Then have them figure out the angle between the

hour hand and the 12. Finally, have them figure out the smaller angle between the minute and hour hands.

3. Give some example times for students to calculate the angle, using the formula they derived.

4. Have students explain their reasoning to the class.

CONNECTION TO COMMON CORE:

Students construct viable arguments when they derive the formula for the angle between the minute and hour hands.

Quadratic Formula

In *Nancy Drew*, Nancy goes to a new school in California. She is shown in a montage reciting the quadratic formula.

In an episode of *Freaks and Geeks* (season 1, episode 5), Lindsey helps Daniel study for a math test. While studying, Lindsey asks Daniel how he would solve a problem. Daniel says he would use the quadratic formula, so Lindsey asks him what the formula is. He gets the "*x* equals," and she has to fill in the rest.

In *Outside Providence*, Tim is sent to a boarding school. On the first day of school he is shown in a math class where the teacher has an example using the quadratic formula. Written on the board is: $x = \frac{-7 \pm \sqrt{7^2 - 4(2)(3)}}{2(2)}, x = \frac{-7 \pm 5}{4}$. The teacher asks Tim what *x* is equal to, but he doesn't know the answer. Later in the movie, Tim is influenced by his smart girlfriend, who makes him study. He is seen in math class again and the same problem is shown on the blackboard. This time Tim gets the correct answer.

In an episode of *Glee* (season 3, episode 7), the students are in a math class and the teacher asks what the quadratic equation is. Puck gives the correct answer.

In an episode of *The Secret World of Alex Mac* (season 1, episode 1), Alex is shown in a math class on her first day of junior high school. The teacher says she is reviewing things they should have learned in sixth grade. She says that if $ax^2 + bx + c$ equals zero, then *x* equals negative *b* plus or minus the square root of $b^2 - 4ac$; then she asks Alex what the denominator should be.

PRIOR KNOWLEDGE NEEDED:

For this activity students should have already learned the quadratic formula.

CLASSROOM USE:

1. Show some or all of these clips to students.
2. One popular way to teach students the quadratic formula is to teach them to sing it to the tune of "Pop Goes the Weasel." To put a spin on this, have students work in groups to create their own quadratic formula song. They can base it on a different melody or add in additional lyrics.
3. Have students share their songs either by recording them or singing them to the class.

CONNECTION TO COMMON CORE:

In this activity students attend to precision when they write lyrics that they share. The lyrics must be clear so that their classmates can understand the song.

Infinite Benders

In an episode of *Futurama* (season 6, episode 105), the Professor invents a scanning machine that will produce two copies of an object that are 60 percent of their original size. The purpose of his machine is to make sweaters because the Professor is shrinking as he gets older and gets twice as cold. Bender is instructed to fold the sweaters, but he doesn't want to. To avoid the work, Bender uses the machine to make two smaller copies of himself so that they can fold the sweaters. The Bender copies have the same idea and also duplicate themselves. This process keeps going until there are eleven generations. The Professor is worried that if they keep replicating, the Benders will eventually have so much collective mass that they will take over the whole earth. He shows everyone the following equation: $M = \sum_{n=0}^{\infty} 2^n \left[\frac{M_0}{2^n(n+1)}\right]$, where M is the mass of all Benders and M_0 is the mass of the original Bender. This formula doesn't prove what the Professor fears, because the 2^n's cancel out and it becomes: $\sum_{n=0}^{\infty} \frac{M_0}{(n+1)}$. The M_0 term is a constant, so it can be factored out to make the formula $M_0 \sum_{n=0}^{\infty} \frac{1}{(n+1)}$. Then $\sum_{n=0}^{\infty} \frac{1}{(n+1)}$ converges to 0, which means $M_0 \sum_{n=0}^{\infty} \frac{1}{(n+1)}$ converges to $M_0(0) = 0$. This means that the Benders would eventually get so tiny that their mass becomes nothing, and the Professor was incorrect about them overtaking earth.

A more accurate equation for this situation can be derived. Thinking about the first set of copies, they are 60 percent of the original Bender in terms of length, width, and height. Assuming Bender has a uniform density, each of bender's copies has a mass of $(.6)^3$. There are two of them, so that gives a total mass of $2(.6)^3M_0$ for the two copies. The total mass of all Benders now becomes $M_0 + 2(.6)^3M_0$. The same process can be used to think about the next set of copies. Each of the second-generation copy's mass will be 60 percent of a first-generation copy's mass, or $(.6)^3((.6)^3M_0) = (.6)^6M_0$. There were two copies, and each of those will be copied twice, for a total of four copies. This yields a total mass for these four copies of $4(.6)^6M_0$. Now the total mass of all Benders is $M_0 + 2(.6)^3M_0 + 4(.6)^6M_0$. Keep going with this pattern until it becomes obvious that the nth set of copies will have a total mass of $2^n(.6)3^nM_0$. This means that the total mass of all Benders from the original to an infinite set of copies becomes $\sum_{n=0}^{\infty} 2^n(.6)^{3n}M_0$. Rearranging and reducing this expression gives $M_0\sum_{n=0}^{\infty}2^n(.216)^n = M_0\sum_{n=0}^{\infty}(.432)^n$. Since this is the sum of an infinite geometric series, it is known to converge to $\frac{M_0}{1-.432} = \frac{M_0}{.568} = 1.76M_0$. This means that even with the correct equation, the mass of all of the Benders if they kept producing forever will be less than the mass of two of the original Benders. Again, it is seen that the Professor had nothing to worry about.

Besides just looking at the mass of the Benders, it may be interesting to think about the number of Benders. This is an example of exponential growth. One formula that can be used for exponential growth is $y(t) = ab^{t/r}$, where a is the initial value, b is the growth factor, t is the time in minutes, and r is the growth period. If we assume that it takes five minutes to make the copies, then we arrive at the formula $y(t) = 2^{t/5}$ because the initial number of Benders $= a = 1$, the growth factor b (how many copies are made each time) is 2, and the growth period r is the 5 minutes it takes for each copy to be made. This function can be used to calculate the number of Benders there will be in t minutes. For example, in one hour there will be $y(60) = 2^{60/5} = 2^{12} = 4096$ Benders. Another way the formula for exponential growth can be written is this: $y(t) = ae^{kt}$, where k is the growth rate. In our example a is 1, so this equation reduces to $y(t) = e^{kt}$. To figure out k we can use the example of 60 minutes and then solve for k. We get $2^{12} = e^{60k}$. Taking the natural log of both sides yields $\ln 2^{12} = 60k$. This gives us $k = \frac{12\ln2}{60} = \frac{\ln2}{5}$. The equation becomes $y(t) = e^{\frac{\ln2}{5}t}$.

In order to get these functions we had to make an assumption about how long it took for the machine to make a copy. Another way to look at this problem without making time a factor is to just think about the number of Bender generations we are at in relation to how many Benders there are. In this episode the Professor begins to worry in the eleventh generation. At this point there will be $2^{11} = 2,048$ Benders. This is assuming that the first two copies are considered the first generation.

PRIOR KNOWLEDGE NEEDED:

In this activity students should know how to evaluate exponents and natural logarithms.

CLASSROOM USE:

1. Show the clip from *Futurama*.
2. Tell students that the formula the Professor gives is incorrect and ask them to work together in groups to create a more accurate formula. This activity can be scaffolded to meet the needs of the students.
3. Have students go through some problems using various times to evaluate how many Benders there will be at the given time.
4. Ask students to change the $y(t) = ab^{t/r}$ formula for exponential growth to the $y(t) = ae^{kt}$ formula.
5. Ask students to figure out how many Benders there will be in a given generation and how many there will be in the nth generation.

CONNECTION TO COMMON CORE:

Students have to make sense of this problem and persevere in solving it when they figure out the correct formula for the mass of infinite Benders. Students are also modeling with mathematics since this involves a real-world (in the world of *Futurama*) problem.

The Pigeonhole Principle

In an episode of the reality television show *Top Chef* (season 7, episode 2), there was a competition among the chefs that required them to work in pairs. In order to make the pairs, contestants had to pick a knife from a knife block that had 16 knives numbered 1 through 8. The two chefs with the same number became a pair. A pair wasn't formed until the sixth draw because the numbers on the knives drawn were 2, 1, 3, 6, 7, and 7. This can be thought of as a function with the set of knives 1 through 16 as the domain and the set with the numbers 1 through 8 as the co-domain. It may seem somewhat surprising that the first pair was not formed until the sixth draw, but after further analysis it really is not that surprising. One way to analyze this situation is by thinking of the two extreme possibilities. The quickest scenario occurs when a pair is made on the second draw. The most number of draws needed would be nine, because the first eight could all be different numbers but the ninth draw would have to match one of the previous eight. This is an illustration of the Pigeonhole Principle: if there are n pigeons and m holes with $n > m$ then at least one hole has two or more pigeons. In terms of functions, the Pigeonhole Principle says that if f is a function mapping from the finite set A to the finite set B with the cardinality of A greater than the cardinality of B, then f can't be one-to-one. While the principle seems pretty obvious and straightforward, it can lead to somewhat surprising results. For instance, if Yankee Stadium is at least half full, then there will be at least two people who share the same first, middle, and last initial. This is because Yankee Stadium holds 50,287 people,[3] while there are 17,576 possible combinations of a first, middle, and last initial. This comes from the fact that there are 26 letters in the alphabet, giving each initial 26 possibilities. Using the multiplication rule yields $26 \cdot 26 \cdot 26 = 17{,}576$ sets of initials. Since Yankee Stadium at half capacity holds 25,143 people, there are more elements in this set than there are in the set of possible initials, and the Pigeonhole Principle applies. The worst possible case is that the first 17,576 people all have different initials, but once the 17,577th person is looked at he must have the same initials as one of the previous 17,576 people, because there are not any other possible choices.

PRIOR KNOWLEDGE NEEDED:

Students should know the definition of a function and how to draw arrow diagrams to represent functions. Students should also know the definitions of "one-to-one" and "onto" functions.

CLASSROOM USE:

1. Show this clip to students.
2. Explain the Pigeonhole Principle and give examples or have students make up their own examples of sets and functions to see if the principle will apply.
3. Below is a sample set of exercises to give on this topic for students to get practice with the definitions for function, one-to-one function, and onto function (see Appendix B):

John has m keys and n locks, but he has forgotten which keys open which locks.

a) Assume that each key can open one and only one lock.
   i) Think about this problem in terms of functions. Let the function "open" go from the set of keys to the set of locks. Draw an arrow diagram for this situation.
   ii) Let $m = 6$ and $n = 8$. Can all of the locks be opened?

iii) Again letting $m = 6$ and $n = 8$, is this function one-to-one? Onto? Why or why not?

iv) What needs to be true about m and n to ensure that every lock gets opened?

b) Now assume that there are two keys that open the same lock, while the rest of the keys open one and only one lock.

i) Draw an arrow diagram for this situation.

ii) Let $m = 6$ and $n = 5$. Can John open all of the locks?

iii) Again letting $m = 6$ and $n = 5$, is this function one-to-one? Onto? Why or why not?

iv) What is the minimum number of keys needed to open n locks?

c) Now assume that there is one key that opens exactly two locks while the other keys open one and only one lock.

i) Draw an arrow diagram for this situation.

ii) In this case is "open" a function? Why or why not?

CONNECTION TO COMMON CORE:

In this activity students model with mathematics as they use the concepts and properties of functions in the real-world situation of keys opening locks.

Infinity

In *Revenge*, Emily's father was framed as a terrorist. He was put in jail and is believed to have been stabbed to death (although we later learn that he did not actually die). As a result, Emily grows up parentless. She decides to seek revenge on everybody who played a part in framing her father. Her father left her a wooden box filled with journals he kept and various photographs. The symbol on top of this box is two infinity symbols intertwined. There are many references to this symbol throughout the show. Often (for example, in season 3, episode 20), there are flashbacks to Emily's childhood in which her father is shown asking Emily if she knows how much he loves her. Emily replies that he loves her infinity times infinity. The symbol is also seen etched into the porch railing at the house she grew up in. Additionally, Emily has a tattoo of the infinity symbol on her arm.

The idea of infinity is difficult for students to understand, because it is not an actual number. This is especially confusing because we assign a symbol for it. One way to help students realize that infinity is not an actual number is to look at some properties of infinity. For example, $\infty + 1 = \infty$. Infinity is endless so adding one to something that is endless will still be endless. Similarly, $\infty \cdot 2 = \infty$. If we think of multiplication as repeated additions then this is equivalent to adding $\infty + \infty$. Something endless plus something endless will still be endless. In the same way, $\infty \cdot \infty$ can be thought of as adding infinite infinities. Again, something endless plus something endless plus something endless, etc., will still be endless. This means that $\infty \cdot \infty$ is actually equal to infinity. Thus, there is no need for Emily's father to love her infinity times infinity because that is the same as loving her infinity. It may also be interesting for students to see that infinity divided by infinity does not equal one. Again, if they think of infinity as a number, then this would be the expected result, but keeping in mind infinity is not really a number will help show why this is not true. The proof technique used here is proof by contradiction. First, let's assume that it is true. Then we can re-write the numerator to get $\frac{\infty+\infty}{\infty}$ because, as we said earlier, adding two infinities still results in infinity. Then we have $1 = \frac{\infty}{\infty} = \frac{\infty+\infty}{\infty} = \frac{\infty}{\infty} + \frac{\infty}{\infty} = 1 + 1 = 2$. Thus, assuming infinity divided by infinity is equal to 1 led to the result of 1 equal to 2, which we know is not true. This means that infinity divided by infinity does not equal one.

Another way to look at these properties of infinity is in terms of sets and functions. One way to tell if two sets have the same number of elements is to define a one-to-one and onto function mapping from one set to the other. This definition is pointless for finite sets because it is much easier to just count the number of elements in each set and see that they are the same. However, finite sets are a lot easier to understand than infinite sets, so an example with finite sets is provided first. Let the set $A = \{1, 2, 3\}$ and the set $B = \{a, b, c\}$. Then we can define a function that maps 1 to a, 2 to b, and 3 to c. This function is one-to-one because no two elements of the first set map to the same element in the second set, and it is onto because every element of B has an element mapped to it. Then we can conclude that A and B have the same number of elements. This concurs with what we get by counting that each set has three elements.

It may also be helpful to give a non-example. If we keep the set $A = \{1, 2, 3\}$ and let set $B = \{a, b\}$ we know that they do not have the same number of elements because A has three while B has two. To see where the definition fails, we can try to find a one-to-one and onto function between these two sets. We can let 1 map to a and 2 map to b. But now 3 has to be mapped somewhere (or else this will not be a function). Once 3 gets mapped to either a or b then the function is no longer one-to-one.

Now that students understand the definition a little better they can move on to infinite sets. We know that the set of counting numbers = $\{1, 2, 3,...\}$ is infinite. Let's imagine adding one element, say an a, to the set of counting numbers. This set would look like $\{a, 1, 2, 3,...\}$. Now we want to know if these two sets have the same number of elements in them. We will try to define a one-to-one and onto function between the two sets. The 1 can be mapped to *a*, 2 can be mapped to 1, 3 can be mapped to 2, and so on. Since the number of counting numbers is infinite, given an element in the first set we can always find an element in the set to map to. This is similar to what we said earlier that $\infty + 1 = \infty$.

A similar idea can be used to show that $\infty \cdot \infty = \infty$. However, this proof is probably too difficult for many high school students. The idea is to think of infinity times infinity as the addition of infinite infinities. This can be done using the positive rational numbers. The first infinite list will be fractions that have one as the numerator, {1/1, 1/2, 1/3,...}. The next list will have two as the numerator, {2/1, 2/2, 2/3,...}. This will continue with each new list having a numerator one bigger than the last. The result is an infinite amount of lists where each list has an infinite number of elements, or $\infty + \infty + \infty + \cdots$, which we know is equal to $\infty \cdot \infty$. These lists will also give all possible positive fractions, which is the set of positive rational numbers. A German mathematician named Georg Cantor was the first to come up with a way to define a one-to-one and onto function between the set of rational numbers and the set of integers. The way to define one such function is to put 0 in the center then above it and to the right put the lists as described above starting with the largest value and moving up. The negative numbers will be placed similarly but below and to the left of the zero. Then to pick the number from this picture to match with a positive integer we will go around in a spiral. Start with 0 mapped to the first positive integer, 1. Then 1/1 is mapped to the next positive integer, 2. Keep going like this to have ½ mapped to 3, -1/1 is mapped to 4, -1/2 is mapped to 5, and so on. In this way, all of the rational numbers will be matched with a counting number.

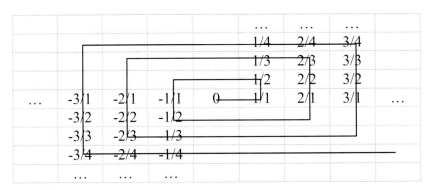

Advanced students may be interested to see a proof that the set of real numbers does not have the same number of elements as the set of counting numbers. The argument shows that no matter how one tries to write out all of the real numbers in decimal form, there will always be a real number that is not on one of these lists. The full argument is detailed by Robert Milson.[4]

In *The Fault in Our Stars*, Hazel gives a eulogy to Gus while he is still alive. One of their favorite authors told them about the existence of more than one kind of infinity. In the eulogy Hazel says that there are an infinite amount of numbers between zero and one and that there is an even bigger infinite set of numbers between zero and two. She uses this idea of infinity as a metaphor for their lives. Hazel says that Gus gave her forever within her numbered days, and she is grateful for their little infinity. Hazel got it partly right. The author she referred to did correctly tell them about the different types of infinities, saying one infinity can be smaller than another infinity. For example, as we discussed earlier, the set of real numbers has more elements than the set of natural numbers. This means that the infinite set of real numbers is larger than the infinite set of natural numbers. Unfortunately, Hazel did not fully understand this concept, because there are the same amount of real numbers between zero and one as there are between zero and two. In fact, the number of elements between any two real numbers is the same. This movie is based on a book of the same name written by John Green. Green has been asked about this mistake; he said that he intentionally made Hazel take a correct piece of information from her favorite author and make an incorrect assumption from it that, to non-math people, seems obvious.[5] If one infinity can be larger than another, it would make sense to a sixteen-year-old that there would be more values between zero and two than there would be between zero and one. It is only after careful study of the idea of infinity that she would realize that this is incorrect. Although Hazel's infinity concept is wrong, she was correct in saying that Gus gave her forever within her numbered days. Between meeting Gus (zero) and his dying (the number of days they knew each other) there are an infinite amount of real numbers.

PRIOR KNOWLEDGE NEEDED:

For this activity students should know the definitions for function, one-to-one, and onto.

CLASSROOM USE:

1. Show students a clip from *Revenge* that shows Emily and her father talking about infinity times infinity.
2. Ask students to define what infinity is and what they think infinity times infinity is.

3. Go through some of the properties of infinity addition and multiplication as shown earlier.
4. Next, give students the definition for two sets having the same number of elements, and go through an example with finite sets.
5. Have students try another example with finite sets on their own.
6. Go over the example, shown earlier, that a set with infinite elements and a set with infinity plus one elements actually have the same number of elements.
7. Have students try a similar example, such as that the set of all positive even integers has the same number of elements as the set of counting numbers $(2 \cdot \infty = \infty)$.

CONNECTION TO COMMON CORE:

In this activity students look for and make use of structure when they represent multiplication as repeated additions.

Logarithms

In an episode of *NCIS: Naval Criminal Investigative Service* (season 6, episode 1), McGee works in a cyber-crimes unit. One of his co-workers says that the logarithm of the quotient is the excess of the logarithm of the dividend over the logarithm of the divisor. McGee says that's high school math. This is a fancy way of saying that $\log_a(x/y) = \log_a(x)\text{-}\log_a(y)$.

This logarithm rule can be proven by changing it into exponential form and using the properties of exponents. To start we will let $\log_a(x) = m$ and $\log_a(y) = n$. By definition this means that $a^m = x$ and $a^n = y$. If we divide x over y this becomes $x/y = a^m/a^n$. By the exponent rule for dividing $a^m/a^n = a^{m-n}$. So we end up with $x/y = a^{m-n}$. Taking the logarithm of both sides yields $\log_a(x/y) = \log_a(a^{m-n})$. The right side becomes $(m - n)\log_a(a)$, and we know that $\log_a(a) = 1$. This leaves us with $\log_a(x/y) = m - n$. Finally, we can substitute back in for m and n to get $\log_a(x/y) = \log_a(x)\text{-} \log_a(y)$.

One game to give students practice with logarithms is speed dating.[6] In this activity students arrange their desks in two rows facing each other or stand up in two lines facing each other. Each student is given a card with a logarithm problem written on it, such as $2\log_9\left(\sqrt{x}\right) - \log_9(6x - 1) = 0$ or $\log_5(2x + 4) = 2$. Each student solves their problem and becomes the expert on it. Then, each student solves the problem of the person across from them. If they have any questions or problems they ask the expert, not the teacher.

The expert should coach his or her partner until they get the correct answer. After a few minutes, one row shifts over and each student now has a new partner. The same process is repeated until all partners are exhausted.

Prior knowledge needed:

For this activity students should know properties of exponents, such as that when multiplying two numbers with the same base, the exponents get added. They should also know what logarithms are.

Classroom use:

1. Show this clip to students.
2. Review the exponent properties such as $(2^x)(2^y) = 2^{x+y}$. Then go over the logarithm rules for multiplying and dividing and the proofs for these rules.
3. Have students play the speed dating game.

Connection to Common Core:

In this activity students attend to precision when they share their expertise on their logarithm problem.

CHAPTER FIVE

Modeling

In mathematical modeling, students constantly make decisions regarding how to solve everyday problems. These decisions include deciding the correct branch of mathematics to use, choosing appropriate technologies, and determining how to best represent the solution. This topic leaves a lot of room for creativity, depending on how open-ended the problems are. Activities in this chapter include swinging from vines, launching rockets, measuring mountains, graphing laughs, and calculating baseball statistics. They draw from various branches of mathematics including trigonometry, graph theory, and algebra. Since all of the activities in this chapter involve modeling, the "Connection to Common Core" section will only be included if there are additional Standards for Mathematical Practice utilized in them beyond "model with mathematics."

Modeling with Vines

In *George of the Jungle*, George grew up in the jungle swinging from vines like an ape. George is transported to San Francisco after he meets some travelers. While exploring the city, George finds the Bay Bridge and walks to the very top of it. There is a parasailor entangled in the cables of the bridge five hundred feet above the water. George sees a rope and decides to rescue him. The narrator says that George calculates the angle and velocity of his swing in order to do so.

A similar problem that has some of the numbers included as givens can be provided to students. Here is one example problem. George swings on a 30-meter-long vine initially inclined at an angle of 37° from the vertical. What is his speed at the bottom of the swing if he starts from rest?

103

Students need to start with the formula saying that the initial sum of the kinetic energy and the potential energy is equal to the final sum of the kinetic energy and the potential energy. Plugging in the potential energy and kinetic energy formulas will give the equation $\frac{1}{2}mv_i^2 + mgh_i = \frac{1}{2}mv_f^2 + mgh_f$, where m = mass, g is the gravitational acceleration constant, v is the velocity, and h is the height. Since his initial velocity and final height are both zero, this formula can be simplified to $mgh_i = \frac{1}{2}mv_f^2$. Solving this equation for the final velocity yields $v_f = \sqrt{2gh_i}$. Trigonometry can be used to find the initial height. The length of the rope is given as 30 meters and the angle is given as 37°. Forming a right triangle from the end of the initial vine allows for the use of the cosine formula, giving $\cos37 = \frac{adjacent\ side}{30}$. This tells us that the adjacent side is equal to 30cos37. Since the length of the whole vine is 30, we get the initial height is 30–30cos37, or 6.04 meters when rounded to two decimal places. Going back to the formula $v_f = \sqrt{2gh_i}$, we now get that the final velocity = $\sqrt{2(9.8)(6.04)}$ = 10.9 m/s.

PRIOR KNOWLEDGE NEEDED:

Students need to know algebra and trigonometry for this activity. It may be helpful for some students to have a physics background as well.

CLASSROOM USE:

1. Show students the clip to introduce the topic.
2. Have students solve a problem similar to the one above. If any students have a physics background, they can help explain the formulas needed to solve this problem.
3. Replay the movie clip. Then, have students calculate the swing angle and velocity needed to save the man. Not enough

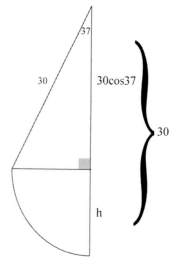

Fig. 16. George's swing.

information is given in the movie to solve the problem, so students will have to figure out the length of the rope George uses. It will be helpful for them to be given or search for the height of the bridge, which is 526 feet.[1]

CONNECTION TO COMMON CORE:

Students make sense of problems and persevere in solving them when they solve the problem from *George of the Jungle*.

Rocket Motion

Another example of a physics modeling problem is given in the movie *October Sky*. Homer and his friends build rockets and launch them. They get arrested when one of their missing rockets supposedly starts a fire. Homer figures out the equation to calculate where the missing rocket landed in order to prove it didn't start the fire. They know the time it took to fall was 14 seconds, because that was how long the previous rocket that was made with the same material took. After accounting for wind, they find their missing rocket to prove that theirs was not the one that caused the fire. Later Homer defends himself to the school principal by showing that the fire was started 3 miles from their launch pad, but at that time the greatest distance their rockets could travel was 1.2 miles. He uses the equation displacement = ½ acceleration times time squared ($s = \frac{1}{2}at^2$) to get a distance of 3,000 feet. Plugging in the 14 seconds for time and the gravity constant of 32 feet per second squared for acceleration gives 3,136 feet, or .6 miles. The book that this movie was based on, *Rocket Boys,* also has a large amount of math in it.

PRIOR KNOWLEDGE NEEDED:

Students should have a familiarity with parametric equations and how to change them to rectangular equations. Students should also know the equation of a parabola.

CLASSROOM USE:

1. Show this clip and have students think about the shape of the rocket's trajectory.
2. The formulas for vertical and horizontal displacement can be given as parametric equations with $x = (v_0cos\theta)t$ and $y = (v_0sin\theta)t - \frac{1}{2}at^2$. Have students prove that the path given by these equations is parabolic by eliminating the t parameter and showing that the resulting equation is a parabola. (See Appendix B.)

CONNECTION TO COMMON CORE:

Students reason abstractly and quantitatively as they think about what the solution will look like, solve the problem, and then check that their result matches what they expected.

Drip Rate

In an episode of *Grey's Anatomy* (season 9, episode 14), the emergency room of the hospital has been shut down. The doctors don't agree with this and they sneak in a patient. They don't have all of their usual equipment. At one point they need to calculate the patient's IV drip rate. Usually one of the nurses does this calculation, but because the ER is closed they don't have any nurses with them. One of the doctors quickly runs through some calculations and comes up with 5.625 ccs per minute. When all of the other doctors look at her, amazed, she admits to being really good at math. The patient needs 5 micrograms per kilogram per minute of dopamine. They know the standard concentration of dopamine is 1,600 micrograms per cubic centimeter and that the patient weighs 30 kilograms. The doctor multiplies the patient's weight (30 kilograms) by the desired dosage (5 micrograms per kilogram per minute) to get 150 micrograms per minute. She then multiplies the 150 micrograms per minute by 60 minutes to get 9,000 micrograms. Finally, she divides the 9,000 micrograms by the standard concentration of 1,600 micrograms per cubic centimeter to get 5.625 cubic centimeters.

PRIOR KNOWLEDGE NEEDED:

For this activity students need to know algebra.

CLASSROOM USE:

1. Show students this clip.
2. In this clip, the doctor runs through her calculations very quickly and doesn't fully explain things. Ask students to use the numbers she gives and show how the units work out correctly, similarly to what was described above.
3. Additional problems can be given to students with different values and other types of drugs.

Logic Riddle

In *Die Hard: With a Vengeance*, John and Zeus are in contact with a criminal who has them solve riddles in order to avoid detonating a bomb. In one scene, they use a five-gallon jug and a three-gallon jug to measure exactly four gallons of water. This problem is actually an example of a linear Diophantine equation. These are equations of the form $ax + by = c$ where a, b, and c are given integers with a and b not both equal to zero. We are looking for integer solutions x and y. This equation will have a solution as long as c is divisible by the greatest common divisor of a and b. In the movie, a and b are the size of the water jugs (5 and 3), and c is the amount we want to measure (4). Positive x or y values indicate the jug being filled and negative x or y values indicate the jug being emptied. The goal is to solve for integer values of x and y to see how many times each jug is filled or emptied to arrive at four gallons. The first step in the standard procedure for solving a linear Diophantine equation is to check if a solution exists. In this case we are solving $5x + 3y = 4$. Since the greatest common divisor of 5 and 3 is 1, and 4 is divisible by 1, we know there is a solution. Next, use the Euclidean algorithm (see appendix A) to get the greatest common divisor of the water jug sizes. When the numbers are this small it is easy to calculate the greatest common divisor without using the Euclidean algorithm; however, doing it this way will help with calculations later on. In this case we get:

$$5 = 3(1) + 2$$
$$3 = 2(1) + 1$$

The next step is to use these equations to write the greatest common divisor as a linear combination of 3 and 5. Start with the bottom equation to get $1 = 3 - 2(1)$. Then use the top equation written as $2 = 5 - 3(1)$ to plug in for the 2: $1 = 3 - 2(1) = 3 - [5 - 3(1)](1) = 3 - 2(1) = 3 - 5 + 3(1) = 3(2) + 5(-1)$. This leads us to the equation $1 = 3(2) + 5(-1)$. Finally, multiply both sides by 4, because that leads to the right side of the original equation. This yields $4 = 3(8) + 5(-4)$ and gives us the solution $x = -4$ and $y = 8$ This means that one solution is to empty the five-gallon jug 4 times and to fill the three-gallon jug 8 times. This is not the most efficient solution, though.

Once one solution is found, it is easy to find other solutions. To find more x values, take the existing solution and add multiples of the coefficient in front of the y divided by the greatest common divisor $\left(\frac{b}{\gcd(a,b)}\right)$. In this case x was -4, so all additional solutions will look like $-4 + \left(\frac{3}{1}\right)m = -4 + 3m$, where m is any integer. To find more y values, take the existing solution and subtract multiples of the coefficient in front of the x divided by the greatest common divisor $\left(\frac{a}{\gcd(a,b)}\right)$. In this case y was 8, so other solutions look like $8 - \left(\frac{5}{1}\right)m = 8 - 5m$. Letting $m = 1$ yields the solution $x = -4 + 3(1) = -4 + 3 = -1$ and $y = 8 - 5(1) = 8 - 5 = 3$. This tells us that the five-gallon jug can be emptied once and the three-gallon jug can be filled 3 times.

Our solution here corresponds to the movie's solution. The three-gallon jug is filled once and poured into the five-gallon jug. The three-gallon jug is filled a second time and poured into the five-gallon jug until it is full, leaving 1 gallon left in the three-gallon jug. The five-gallon jug is emptied once. The 1 gallon left is poured into the five-gallon jug. The three-gallon jug is filled a third time and poured into the five-gallon jug. This leaves 4 gallons in the five gallon jug and, as suggested by our solution, the three-gallon jug was filled 3 times while the five-gallon jug was emptied once.

In *Idiocracy* there is a similar question involving buckets. The premise of this movie is that Joe was part of a hibernation program, but he was forgotten. He wakes up five hundred years in the future in a dumbed-down society. In one scene Joe is taking a test that asks, If you have one bucket that holds two gallons and another bucket that holds five gallons then how many buckets do you have?

PRIOR KNOWLEDGE NEEDED:

No background knowledge is needed to do this activity unless students are asked to work with linear Diophantine equations. In that case they will need to know how to use the Euclidean algorithm to find the greatest common divisor of two numbers, and they will need to be strong in algebra.

CLASSROOM USE:

1. Show the *Die Hard* clip where the criminal explains the riddle and sets forth the rules.
2. Have students work out the solution in groups.
3. Show the remainder of the clip where the characters solve the riddle, and see if students come up with the same solution.
4. Give students another solution, such as the one found above of emptying the five-gallon jug 4 times and filling the three-gallon jug 8 times. Have students translate the solution to the equation into the sequence of pours that results in the desired four gallons.
5. If further analysis is desired, students can be taught linear Diophantine equations.

Zeno's Paradox

Zeno of Elea was a Greek philosopher who wrote a book of paradoxes. According to Aristotle, Zeno invented a style of debate in which one person presents an idea and the other reduces that idea to absurdity. This is the earliest form of proof by contradiction (*reductio ad absurdum*).[2] One of Zeno's most famous paradoxes is called the Dichotomy paradox. It says that motion can't exist because "whatever moves must reach the middle of its course before it reaches the end; but before it has reached the middle it must have reached the quarter-mark, and so on, indefinitely."[3]

This means that for a given distance, half of it must be traveled first. Then travel half of a half. Follow with half of that distance and keep going. Looking at motion this way, it can never start.

The scenario described in this paradox leads to the geometric series $\frac{1}{2} + \frac{1}{4} + \frac{1}{8} + \cdots$. We can show that this converges to 1 by letting $\frac{1}{2} + \frac{1}{4} + \frac{1}{8} + \cdots = x$. Multiplying both sides by 2 yields $1 + \left(\frac{1}{2} + \frac{1}{4} + \cdots\right) = 2x$. This can be written as $1 + (x) = 2x$, and solving for x yields $x = 1$. This example is often given as an introduction to limits, since it is fairly easy to understand and it converges.

In the movie *I.Q.*, Edward asks Catherine to dance, and she says that he can't ever get to her because of Zeno's paradox. She then explains that he would have to keep coming halfway and there are infinite halves left so he would never reach her.

PRIOR KNOWLEDGE NEEDED:

Students should know how to do algebra for this activity.

CLASSROOM USE:

1. Describe the paradox in as much detail as deemed necessary and then show students the movie clip.
2. Have students consider if what Catherine said makes sense or if she would eventually reach Edward if she had an infinite amount of time.
3. The method shown above, proving that this sum converges to 1, doesn't involve knowledge of calculus, so students can either be shown it or can try to come up with it themselves. It may be perplexing at first for students to see that an infinite sum is equal to a finite number.

Triangulation

Triangulation uses triangles and trigonometry to find unknown distances. Applications include measuring the heights of large objects such as mountains, finding earthquakes[4] or meteorites,[5] and locating places with a GPS.[6] This method has been around since ancient Greek times when men such as Eratosthenes measured the heights of mountains.[7]

In *The Englishman Who Went Up a Hill and Came Down a Mountain*, locals of a small Welsh village named Ffynnon Garw are very proud to have the first mountain in Wales. A pair of English cartographers come to measure it and find that it is actually 16 feet short of being called a mountain. The mountain is currently measured at 984 feet, but it has to be 1,000 feet tall in order to be called a mountain. The villagers decide to add dirt to the top to make it to mountain status. To measure the hill the cartographers used the heights of two known hills (Newton Beacon and Whitchurch Hill) and the known distance between them. The villagers ask how the other two hills were measured, and the cartographers say they were measured the same way—by looking at two other known hills. One villager asks how the first hill was measured. The reverend says it was measured by God.

There are two steps to finding the height of the mountain in Ffynnon Garw. First, the distance between this mountain and one of the known mountains is needed. Think of an aerial view with each mountain being at one of the vertices of the triangle connecting them (fig. 17). Given the known distance between the two known mountains is 1,840 feet and the

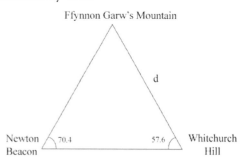

Fig. 17. Aerial view of the three mountains.

angles as shown in the diagram, the unknown distance d can be computed to the nearest foot. Using the fact that the sum of the angles in a triangle is 180 degrees and the law of sines, d is calculated to be 2,200 feet. Next, think of a side view showing Ffynnon Garw's mountain and Whitchurch Hill. The height of Ffynnon Garw's hill can be found, given that the height of Whitchurch Hill is 772 feet and the angle of depression of the top of Whitchurch Hill is 5.5 degrees. This scenario is shown in figure 18.

To calculate the unknown height, first realize that the angle of depression's complementary angle will be 84.5 degrees. Then the tangent function can be used to find the x value to be 211.8. When this is added to the known height of Whitchurch hill, the height becomes 983.8, or 984 rounded to the nearest foot. This is the same height that was found in the movie.

Another example of triangulation occurs in *Touch* (season 1, episode 8). The kids at the Child and Family Services institution are talking via satellite to an astronaut in space who says that their ship is currently the same distance from

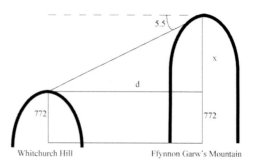

Fig. 18. Side view of the two mountains.

Houston (where the space station is) as it is from New York (where the children are), 5,191 miles. She says this is called triangulation, and that in this case it forms an isosceles triangle. The astronaut then shows a picture of the triangle and asks who can find the distance of the missing side if the top angle is 18 degrees. Jake does the work on his tablet and correctly gets 1,624 miles.

PRIOR KNOWLEDGE NEEDED:

Students need to know that the angles of a triangle sum to 180 degrees, the law of sines, what complementary angles are, and how to calculate the tangent function in a right triangle.

CLASSROOM USE:

1. Show students the clip from *Touch* and ask them to show how Jake arrives at his answer.
2. Show the clip from *The Englishman Who Went Up a Hill and Came Down a Mountain*.
3. Have students calculate the height of the mountain as described above.

Graphical Representation of Poems

In *Dead Poets Society*, Mr. Keating is the new English teacher at a private school. He has a student read aloud the introduction to poetry in their textbook. One part discusses how to find a poem's greatness by plotting the poem's perfection on the horizontal axis and its importance on the vertical axis. Calculating the area of the poem yields the measure of its greatness. Mr. Keating draws the axes on the board, and one student is shown using a ruler to also draw it. Examples are given such as a sonnet by Byron, which scores high on the vertical and average on the horizontal. A Shakespearean sonnet scores high on both. Mr. Keating draws bar graphs to represent them. He then continues to say that this is rubbish and asks everyone to rip out that page of the book.

PRIOR KNOWLEDGE NEEDED:

For this activity students just need some familiarity with drawing graphs.

CLASSROOM USE:

1. Show this clip to students.
2. Ask students to draw graphs for other poems. There can be a list of poems provided or students can come up with the poems on their own. This

works well when taught in conjunction with a poetry unit in the student's English class.

Shrinking and Growing

In *Alice in Wonderland* (2010 version), Alice wants to go through a tiny door, but she won't fit through. There is a bottle on a nearby table labeled "drink me." Once she drinks the potion, Alice shrinks and is able to fit through the door. But then she is too small to get the potion from the table where she left it. She then finds a small piece of cake that is labeled "eat me." Alice takes a bite and grows so tall that she has to bend her head to fit in the room. She drinks more of the potion and shrinks back down to fit through the door.

Students can come up with a model in which Alice drinks the potion and eats the cake at least twice each until she returns to her normal height. For example, if the cake makes Alice grow to three times her height and the potion makes Alice shrink to 1/9 of her height, then Alice can eat the cake four times and drink the potion twice to get back to her original height.

Given any growth rate and any shrinking rate, will there always be a solution? One way to answer this is to write out the equation $h \cdot g^x \cdot \left(\frac{1}{s}\right)^y = h$, with g = the growth factor, x = the number of times the cake is eaten, s = the shrink factor, y = the number of times the potion is drunk, and h is Alice's height. This equation can be reduced to $g^x \cdot \left(\frac{1}{s}\right)^y = 1$, which becomes $g^x = s^y$. If s can be written as a power of g or g can be written as a power of s, then this equation can be solved to find the relationship between x and y. Using the example with g is 3 and s is 9, $3^x = 9^y$ can be solved because 9 can be written as 3^2. Then $3^x = (3^2)^y$ becomes $3^x = 3^{2y}$, and $x = 2y$. To show that there isn't always a solution, students can find a counterexample such as $g = 3$ and $s = 4$. This leads to $3^x = 4^y$, which becomes $x\ln3 = y\ln4$. Then $\frac{x}{y}$ is equal to $\frac{\ln4}{\ln3}$. If students plug this into their calculator and try to convert it to a fraction, they will see that it is impossible. Since there are no integral solutions, there is no acceptable solution. This is because x and y need to be integers, since they represent the amount of times Alice is growing and shrinking.

PRIOR KNOWLEDGE NEEDED:

For this activity students need to know algebra and be familiar with exponents and logarithms.

CLASSROOM USE:

1. Show this clip to students.

2. In groups, ask students to pick a shrinking factor that is assigned to the bottle and a growing factor assigned to the cake. Then have them come up with a model in which Alice drinks the potion and eats the cake at least twice each until she returns to her normal height.

3. Next, ask students if they will always be able to solve this problem for any growth and shrinking factors.

CONNECTION TO COMMON CORE:

Students construct viable arguments as they try to figure out if there will be a solution for any growth and shrinking factors.

Spherical Geometry

In *G.I. Joe: The Rise of Cobra*, Breaker uses spherical trigonometry to find the location of a base from information in a photograph. Knowing the height of the object, the length of the shadow, and the time and date the image was taken, he can figure out the base's location. Breaker has an image of McCullen, who is 180 cm tall; his shadow is 46 cm long, and the image is 51 hours and 17 minutes old. This leads him to finding the location as the polar ice cap. Solving this problem with only the given measurements will be too difficult, if not impossible, for students. However, this can lead to a lesson on spherical geometry.

A great circle is defined as any circle that cuts a sphere in half. Great circles in spherical geometry are equivalent to lines in plane geometry. Given any two distinct points on a sphere, there is a great circle passing through them. This is something that students can explore through the use of a software program called Spherical Easel.[8] This is the spherical geometry equivalent of Geometer's Sketchpad.

PRIOR KNOWLEDGE NEEDED:

For this activity students need to have a solid background in geometry, including circles and spheres.

CLASSROOM USE:

1. Show the clip to students.

2. Explain in as much detail as desired the basic ideas of spherical geometry. Strike the right balance between teacher-given information and student-discovered information.

3. Have students in groups use a computer lab with Spherical Easel to dis-

cover properties of spherical geometry. Students can be asked leading questions, such as whether parallel great circles exist.

Connection to Common Core:

Students use appropriate tools strategically when they make use of Spherical Easel.

Time Needed to Complete a Task

In *Extremely Loud and Incredibly Close*, Oskar's father, who died in the September 11 attacks, used to make up puzzles for Oskar. To solve these puzzles Oskar would go on expeditions around New York City. When Oskar finds a key in a vase with the word "Black" written on it, he thinks it is one last expedition left by his father. He decides to visit every person with the last name Black in New York City. In one scene he calculates how long it would take to visit them all. Some of the calculations shown include the total number of miles he would have to travel (2,880) divided by the number of miles he could travel each day (24) to get 120 days. Looking through his calendar Oskar sees that he is busy on 36 days. This gives him a total of 156 days. Oskar is only able to go out looking on Saturdays, so he then divided the 156 days by 52 for the number of weeks in a year and gets a total time of 3 years.

Prior knowledge needed:

Students just need basic arithmetic skills for this activity.

Classroom use:

1. Show students this clip.
2. In groups ask them to come up with a scenario like Oskar's in which they have to figure out how long it will take them to complete a task.
3. Have each group switch problems with another group and then find a solution.

Connection to Common Core:

Students attend to precision as they make up a problem. They have to make it clear so that another group is able to understand and solve it.

P Versus *NP*

In an episode of *Elementary* (season 2, episode 2), two mathematicians are murdered because they are close to solving *P* versus *NP*. *P* problems are easy for computers to solve, and *NP* problems are easy for computers to check if a possible solution is given, but they are not easy to solve. It is unknown whether *P* = *NP*, meaning we are not sure if there exists a fast method for solving *NP* problems. Holmes discovers mathematical formulas written in invisible ink on the walls of the first victim's house. He brings in a mathematician friend to analyze the formulas. The friend explains to Holmes what *P* versus *NP* is by saying it is like asking if every problem that can be quickly verified by a computer can also be quickly solved by a computer. Holmes figures out that somebody was video-taping one of the victims, and they trace the tapes to a security company. When they confront the owner of this company it is revealed that solving *P* versus *NP* would have many real-world applications, such as making the encryption used for computer security obsolete. The reason for this is that encryption deals with keys that are so complicated that computers cannot solve them. Knowing the solution to *P* versus *NP* would allow the computer to go through all possible solutions fast enough to crack the code. This episode also mentions the Millennium Problems, of which *P* versus *NP* is one. These are seven famous unsolved problems chosen by the Clay Mathematics Institute of Cambridge at the turn of the century in 2000. There is a one-million-dollar reward for anyone who can solve one of these problems. The purpose of these problems was to have a record of some of the problems mathematicians were working on during this time and to show the public that mathematics is still an open field with unsolved problems.[9]

One application that illustrates the *P*-versus-*NP* question is the Traveling Salesman Problem. This problem is accessible to high school students. First, students need to be familiar with graphs. These are sets

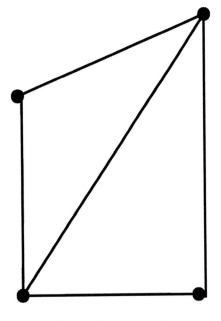

Fig. 19. Graph example.

of vertices (points) and edges (lines) where each edge ends in a vertex on each side. An example of a graph is in figure 19.

A fun way to introduce graphs is to use the "Six Degrees of Kevin Bacon," also known as the Kevin Bacon game. This game uses the "six degrees of separation" theory[10] applied to actors with Kevin Bacon as the connector. Actors that are in a movie with Kevin Bacon have a Bacon number of 1. Actors that are in a movie with an actor who was in a movie with Kevin Bacon have a Bacon number of 2, and so on. Hopkins[11] suggests using actors as vertices with an edge connecting them if they were in a movie together. The Oracle of Bacon[12] provides a search engine for finding how actors are linked together through movies. For example, Seth Rogen has a Bacon number of 2 because he was in *Neighbors* with Rose Byrne, and Rose Byrne was in *X Men: First Class* with Kevin Bacon. The corresponding graph looks like figure 20.

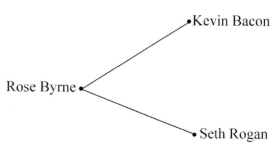

Fig. 20. Kevin Bacon graph example.

On a historical side note, the same concept as the Kevin Bacon game is used in the field of article publication in mathematics with Paul Erdős. Erdős is one of the most prolific writers of mathematical papers, and he liked to collaborate with other mathematicians. A mathematician who wrote a paper with Erdős is said to have an Erdős number of 1. A person who wrote a paper with somebody who wrote a paper with Erdős has an Erdős number of 2, and so on.

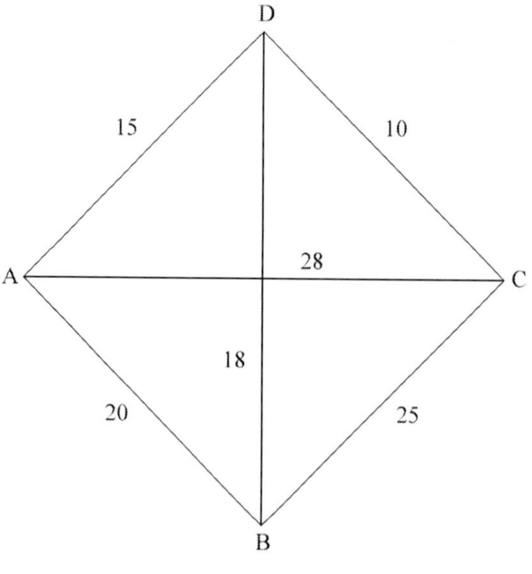

An example of a graph is shown in *Good*

Fig. 21. Traveling Salesman example.

Will Hunting. In one scene Professor Lambeau wrote what was meant to be an incredibly difficult problem on a hallway blackboard. Will solved it while working as a janitor.

In the Traveling Salesman Problem, a salesman must visit a certain number of cities. He can visit each city only once and must start and end at the same city. We want to know what route he should take in order to minimize his travel distance. The salesman's route is an example of a Hamiltonian circuit because he starts and ends at the same point, hits each vertex exactly once (other than the starting point), and cannot repeat an edge.

For example, suppose a salesman starts at city A and has to travel to cities B, C, and D, and then return back to city A. The distance between each city is labeled in figure 21.

One way to solve this problem is to list every possible route and calculate the distance for each. This is shown in the following table:

Route	Distance
ABCDA	20 + 25 + 10 + 15 = 70
ABDCA	20 + 18 + 10 + 28 = 76
ACBDA	28 + 25 + 18 + 15 = 86
ACDBA	=ABDCA backwards = 76
ADBCA	=ACBDA backwards = 86
ADCBA	=ABCDA backwards = 70

Routes ABCDA or ADCBA are shown to be the shortest distance at 70, so the salesman should use one of these two routes. This method is an exhaustive method because every possible outcome needed to be computed before we can arrive at an answer. For a problem like this with only 4 cities it wasn't too much work, but imagine using this method for a problem with 10 cities. The starting city is fixed. For the next city there are 9 choices, then 8, then 7, etc. This means there are $9 \cdot 8 \cdot 7 \cdot 6 \cdot 5 \cdot 4 \cdot 3 \cdot 2 \cdot 1 = 9! = 362,880$ possible paths. Even accounting for symmetry, that leaves 181,440 paths that would need to be calculated. In general, a problem with n cities will have $(n - 1)!$ different paths. As the problem gets larger it becomes infeasible to do by hand, and even using a computer would take too long. A problem with 30 cities would take $2.8 \cdot 10^{14}$ years to calculate if it took the computer one nanosecond to compute each path.[13] There is no known algorithm that will solve the traveling salesman problem. There are some methods that can find a pretty good answer, but it is not guaranteed to be the minimal distance. This type of problem is an example of an *NP* problem. It is similar to the encryption example given in *Elementary*, in that it isn't possible for a computer to compute every single possible solution in an efficient manner.

PRIOR KNOWLEDGE NEEDED:

No background knowledge is needed for this activity beyond being able to sum numbers.

CLASSROOM USE:

1. Show clips from this episode of *Elementary* to students.
2. Introduce graphs and explain the Traveling Salesman Problem.
3. Give examples or have students come up with their own examples of the Traveling Salesman Problem. Students can be given a list of cities, and they can find the distances between each and then find the shortest path.
4. Ask students whether this is an example of a *P* problem or an *NP* problem and have some students share their reasoning.

Ratios

In an episode of *The Wonder Years* (season 3, episode 2), Kevin imagines that his bad math grades will be found out by his parents. He imagines that his mom asks him to solve a math problem: if a pitcher of lemonade makes 8 servings of 1 cup each, then how many servings will it make when the cups are only filled 2/3 of the way?

PRIOR KNOWLEDGE NEEDED:

Students need to know how to calculate with fractions and make ratios.

CLASSROOM USE:

1. Show this clip to students.
2. Students can solve this problem and can also be given similar problems with the fractional amount changed. Tactile learners can be given a pitcher of water and a set of cups so that they can act out the problems.

Graphing with Laughs

In the movie *Dumbo*, Dumbo is a disgrace to the other elephants because of his big ears and, as a result, he gets sent to perform in the clown's circus act. He jumps from a burning building as part of his act. The clowns think they should raise the platform that Dumbo jumps off of because if the audience laughed when he jumps 20 feet then they will laugh twice as hard if he jumps 40 feet. Then they want to make it 80 feet, 180 feet, 300 feet, and 1,000 feet. Is the height of Dumbo's platform and the amount the audience laughs positively correlated? There's no way to know for sure, but students can make a guess. Try drawing a graph showing Dumbo's platform height on the *x*-axis and the amount the audience laughs (in laughs per minute) on the *y*-axis. At some point the platform will probably be too high, and Dumbo won't be able to jump or the audience will be too scared. A possible graph can look like figure 22.

In this example the first part of the graph began at *x* = 40 because that is Dumbo's current platform height. It is assumed that at this height there are 10 laughs per minute. Up until a platform height of 80 feet there will be a positive slope because as the height increases the amount of laughter will also increase. However, 80 feet is pretty high up, so after that if the platform height were to increase, not as many people would laugh because they would be nervous for Dumbo. At this point the slope changes to negative, because the higher the platform height the more people will be nervous and won't laugh. Finally, at 150 feet everybody is too nervous and nobody will laugh. The equation for the first part

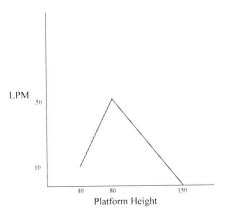

Fig. 22. Dumbo's height versus audience laughs per minute.

of this piecewise function can be found using the two endpoints (40, 10) and (80, 50). The slope is $\frac{50-10}{80-40} = \frac{40}{40} = 1$. Using point-slope form, the equation becomes $y - 10 = x - 40$, or $y = x - 30$. The second equation can be found similarly to be $y = \frac{-5}{7}x + \frac{750}{7}$. Thus, the piecewise equation is

$$y = \begin{cases} x - 30 & 40 \leq x \leq 80 \\ \frac{-5}{7}x + \frac{750}{7} & 80 < x \leq 150 \end{cases}.$$

PRIOR KNOWLEDGE NEEDED:

For this activity students need to know how to draw graphs and calculate slopes. They will also need to know how to find equations of lines and/or parabolas.

CLASSROOM USE:

1. Show this clip to students.

2. Have students make up a graph similar to the example given here. Also ask them to give the equation of their graph.
3. Have students explain their reasoning for why they chose to make the graph the way they did. Ask about concepts such as slope and the shape of the graph. Students will most likely pick a linear graph or a parabolic graph, because they are most familiar with these types.

CONNECTION TO COMMON CORE:

Students reason abstractly and quantitatively as they think about what the graph will look like, draw it, and then explain why they drew it as they did.

Sabermetrics

In *Moneyball*, Peter is hired by the Oakland A's general manager to use mathematical formulas to figure out the value of a baseball player. He uses statistics called sabermetrics that differ from the typical baseball statistics of batting average, runs batted in, etc. Sabermetrics measure activity within the baseball game and try to give values to players beyond the traditional statistics. Peter finds an equation that tells wins percentage by taking runs scored squared over runs scored squared plus runs allowed squared. He predicts that they have to win at least 99 games to make it to the pro season, they need to score at least 814 runs to win those games, and they can allow no more than 645 runs. Using mathematical formulas, Peter shows that players that have been overlooked for various reasons, such as age, appearance, and personality, can be bought at a price that the Oakland A's can afford to help form a championship team.

Sabermetrics are also used in an episode of *The Simpsons* (season 22, episode 3). Lisa uses sabermetrics to coach Bart's Little League team. Additionally, in an episode of *Numb3rs* (season 3, episode 8), a mathematician uses sabermetrics to determine when baseball players began using performance enhancing drugs.

There are many sabermatric statistics that students can study. One example is cumulative home-run ratio (CHR). This is calculated by taking a player's cumulative home runs divided by his cumulative at-bats. It was found that Babe Ruth's CHR started to level off in his mid to late twenties.[14] The authors of this study were interested to see if the same was true for other players who hit at least 500 home runs, so they calculated the CHR for each player and made corresponding graphs. This article was written in 2005, so there are some players that have joined the 500-home-run club since then, including

Alex Rodriguez, Jim Thome, Manny Ramirez, Frank Thomas, Albert Pujols, and Gary Sheffield.

Another sabermetrics statistic worth studying is the Pythagorean Expectation. This tells us how many games a baseball team should have won. It is calculated as the number of runs scored squared over number of runs scored squared plus the number of runs allowed squared. For example, in 2009 the Florida Marlins scored 772 runs and allowed 766 runs. This means that their Pythagorean Expectation was $\frac{772^2}{772^2+766^2} = .504$. This means that they should have won 50.4 percent of their 162 games. With rounding, this leads to 82 games. They actually won 87 games. Since their actual wins were more than their Pythagorean Expectation, the Marlins are said to have been lucky in 2009.

PRIOR KNOWLEDGE NEEDED:

Students should know how to calculate and understand percentages and draw scatterplots either by hand or using computer software.

CLASSROOM USE:

1. Show any of the clips to students.
2. Explain what sabermetrics is and how it is conventionally applied.
3. Explain what CHR is and have students go through some examples calculating it. Baseball statistics can be found online.[15]
4. Have students read the article mentioned above[16] or give students a summary of the results.
5. Have students calculate the CHR and plot graphs for the players that have hit 500 home runs since the publication of this article. They can see whether the article's conclusions still hold true or try to find their own patterns in the CHR graphs.
6. Next, explain what the Pythagorean Expectation is.
7. Give students data for different teams and seasons. Include number of runs scored, number of runs allowed, number of games played, and number of games won. Have students figure out when teams were lucky or unlucky.
8. Ask students to analyze the Pythagorean Expectation formula by thinking about the maximum and minimum values and what has to happen in order to attain those values.

CONNECTION TO COMMON CORE:

Students look for structure as they analyze the CHR graphs and come up with patterns.

D = *RT*

Here's proof that James Bond is not good at math. In *The World Is Not Enough*, there is a planned bomb attack that Bond wants to stop. He asks the computer technician how far away the bomb is and how fast it is travelling. The tech says it is 106 miles from its destination and travelling at 70 miles per hour. Bond says that it will take 78 minutes. The formula distance = rate times time would be used to calculate the time. Solving this leaves 1.514 hours. Converted to minutes, this becomes around 91 minutes.

Prior knowledge needed:

In this activity students should know the distance = rate × time formula.

Classroom use:

1. Mark off a distance such as 100 meters in a hallway or outside. In groups of four have one student run this distance, one student speed-walk it, one student walk it, and the final student time the other three.
2. Have each group calculate the rate for the runner, speed walker, and walker, making sure to include units.
3. Ask additional questions such as these:
   - If each student kept the same pace for double the distance, how long would it take each of them?
   - If each student kept the same pace but ran for twice as long, how far would they each go?
4. Show this clip to students and have them find the correct time.

Using Logic

In the book version of *Harry Potter and the Sorcerer's Stone*, Harry and Hermione are in a room whose exits are blocked by fire. Seven bottles are on table in the room, along with a piece of paper with the following poem:

> Danger lies before you, while safety lies behind,
> Two of us will help you, whichever you would find,
> One among us seven will let you move ahead,
> Another will transport the drinker back instead,
> Two among our number hold only nettle wine,
> Three of us are killers, waiting hidden in line.
> Choose, unless you wish to stay here forevermore,
> To help you in your choice, we give you these clues four:

First, however slyly the poison tries to hide
You will always find some on nettle wine's left side;
Second, different are those who stand at either end,
But if you would move onward, neither is your friend;
Third, as you see clearly, all are different size,
Neither dwarf nor giant holds death in their insides;
Fourth, the second left and second on the right
Are twins once you taste them, though different at first sight.[17]

Hermione realizes that she can use logic to find the right bottle rather than relying on magic. She figures out the correct bottle and they move forward. The book does not give a picture of the bottles, so it is not possible to fully solve this riddle. Let's try to solve it and see what happens. From the riddle we know there are seven bottles with one that moves ahead (A), one that moves backward (B), two that are wine (W), and three that are poison (P). The second clue tells us that the two ends are different and neither of them are A. We know from the first clue that P is always to the left of W, so the left end cannot be W. This leaves us with the possibilities: $P????PW$, $P?????B$, $B????PW$, or $B?????P$. The fourth clue says that the second bottle to the left and the second bottle to the right are the same. This rules out A and B for those positions because there is only one of each. Of the four cases we had, let's start with $P????PW$. In this case, the fourth clue tells us that P must go in the second from the left position. From the first clue we know that wherever W is, there is a P to the left. But since we know where three P's are, the W must go to the right of this P, yielding $PPW??PW$. The remaining two spots cannot be solved. They would most likely come from the third clue about bottle size. This leaves two possibilities for case one. Let's move on to the second case: $P?????B$. Here we still know that the second from the right and the second from the left are both P or both W. Assume they are both P. Then we wouldn't be able to place the two W's since they both need a P to their left. This means those two spots are both W. That means the third from the right has to be P, giving $PW??PWB$. Again there are two remaining spots that are unknown, giving us two possibilities for case two. For the third case, $B????PW$, we know the second from the left has to be P. At this point we are stuck, leaving $BP???PW$. Of the six possible ways to arrange the remaining three bottles (calculated by $3! = 6$), two of them won't work because W needs to have P to the left of it. This leaves us with four possibilities for case three. In the fourth case, W cannot be in the second from the left position since it needs a P to the left of it. This means that the second from the left and the second from the right are both P, leaving $BP???PP$. But this means that there would be a W that did not have a P to the left of it. Since that can't happen, we can get rid of this case. Altogether, that leaves eight possible bottle positions. That is as far as we can take the solution without knowing the bottle sizes. However, in the book we are told that Hermione drank from the bottle at the right end and she moved backwards. This helps reduce our number of possible solutions to only two, since the second case is the only one that had B on the right end. We are still unsure whether the move-ahead bottle is in the third or fourth from the left position. Unfortunately, the movie version does not contain this scene at all.

Prior knowledge needed:

Students should have some familiarity with reading and understanding word problems.

Classroom use:

1. While the discussed scene is not shown in the movie, students can be shown the introduction to what Harry, Ron, and Hermione are doing as they go through each obstacle that is meant to guard the Philosopher's Stone. The first obstacle is to get past a three-headed dog named Fluffy. The second is to avoid strangulation by a Devil's Snare plant. Next, they need to find the right flying key. Finally, they have to win a game of chess. At this point it can be mentioned that the logic game was originally included here as another obstacle.
2. Depending on the level of difficulty desired, there are two options at this point. For a greater challenge students can just be given the poem with the clues, and they have to get possible solutions in the same method described earlier. For an easier option, students can also be given a picture of the bottles showing the different sizes of them. A possible arrangement for the bottles can be found here.[18]

Connection to Common Core:

Students have to make sense of this problem as they try to use the given clues to figure out the possible bottle arrangements.

CHAPTER SIX

Geometry

Geometric objects are everywhere around us. Architects use geometry to design buildings. Artists use geometry in their paintings. Computer scientists use geometry when designing video games. Students can use geometry to solve a crime, study art, and play basketball. This chapter includes topics from Euclidian geometry such as geometric objects, angles, the calculation of area, and logic.

The Perfect Student

In *Better Off Dead* there is a scene in a mathematics classroom where all of the students are excited to learn about geometry. The teacher talks about trapezoids and triangles. We do not see the diagram, and the teacher says a lot of nonsensical mathspeak, but this is still a great clip to show students because the entire class acts really excited about math. When the teacher asks for volunteers to put up the homework, everyone wants to get picked because they are so enthusiastic about learning math.

PRIOR KNOWLEDGE NEEDED:
No prior knowledge is needed for this activity.

CLASSROOM USE:
1. Show this clip before starting the geometry unit and use it as a way to get students interested in learning more about geometry. As an opening activity, have students go to the board and draw different shapes they know.
2. Hold a class discussion to see if students know the names of the different shapes and what properties each shape has.

In this activity students tend to precision as they explain the properties of geometric shapes to the class and ensure that their explanations are clear so that other students can understand them.

Triangles in Motion

One of the more basic shapes is the triangle. It is featured in various movies and television shows. In an episode of *Buffy the Vampire Slayer* (season 5, episode 19), Willow talks about acting out a geometry problem because she read an article that said that kids learn better if you stimulate their visual learning. Willow said that she and Xander made a triangle with their bodies, and then she called Xander obtuse, and he got really grumpy. Then Dawn said they were a cute triangle.

Prior knowledge needed:

Students need to have already learned about different types of triangles, such as acute, obtuse, right, scalene, equilateral, and isosceles triangles.

Classroom use:

1. Show this clip.
2. Have students act out the activity that Willow is talking about. In groups of four, students can form various types of triangles and the fourth person can take a picture. Have students alternate so that everyone gets a chance to participate in the formation of the triangles. This type of activity is great for kinesthetic learners because it utilizes movement.
3. After the groups have finished, have a class discussion. If a computer is available in the room, upload the pictures and display each group's pictures. Have students name the type of each triangle. If a computer is not available then this follow-up can be done the following class after the teacher has a chance to print the pictures.

Connection to Common Core:

Students will make sense of this problem before solving it since they have to first think about what type of triangle they want to make before they can figure out how to arrange themselves in the correct positions. Students also use appropriate tools strategically as they take pictures and upload them to a computer.

Name That Triangle

In an episode of *Seinfeld* (season 4, episode 20), Jerry draws a doodle of a triangle on a napkin, and Kramer says that it is nice. Jerry says that it is isosceles, and Kramer loves the name isosceles. The viewers are not shown the picture of the triangle.

In an episode of *Family Ties* (season 4, episode 7), Alex is getting tutored in non-Euclidean geometry by a thirteen-year-old math genius named Eugene. At an office party the professor asks how they are getting along, and Alex says they are like two sides of an isosceles triangle.

Other types of triangles are mentioned in *Like Mike*. Calvin is a fourteen-year-old orphan who joins the NBA. He is having difficulty understanding geometry. Tracy, one of the players on his team, shows him that the key to understanding triangles is to super-size them. Tracy paints giant triangles on his house using basketball players as the vertices and asks Calvin to think about different basketball plays to figure out the names of the triangles. The Bulls use an isosceles triangle, giving room for Michael Jordan to isolate. The Lakers use an equilateral triangle to give equal sides for Kobe and Shaq. Their team uses an acute triangle.

PRIOR KNOWLEDGE NEEDED:

This activity should be done after the students have already learned about the various types of triangles.

CLASSROOM USE:

1. Show the *Seinfeld* and *Family Ties* clips during review. Then, have students draw an isosceles triangle.
2. Show the *Like Mike* clip, but pause it after each triangle is shown to have students name the triangle before Calvin does.

CONNECTION TO COMMON CORE:

In this activity, technology is used to help students review. Students must interpret the types of triangles based on what they see in the video.

Similar Triangles

In *A Walk to Remember*, one student tutors another student in geometry using basketball. The tutor has himself standing on the basketball court in one corner, the student in another corner, with the basket forming the third point of a triangle. He then has them both take a step towards the basket and asks if they are each at the same angle to the basket as before. When the student answers yes, the tutor then asks what they just made. The student answers, a similar triangle.

Students can make a reasonable guess as to how far each of the two people are from the basket originally and how far apart they are from each other. In an NBA court the distance from the basket to the three-point line is 23.9 feet. If one person is a little to the left of center and the other person is the same distance to the right, then a fair guess is to say that they are each 24.5 feet from the basket. The distance each person is from the center can be calculated using the Pythagorean Theorem. This will be calculated from the equation $(23.9)^2 + x^2 = (24.5)^2$. Each person is 5.39 feet from the center, making them 10.78 feet apart. Then ask students how far they are from each other after moving. Let's say they each move to a distance of 14.5 feet. Have students figure out how far each person is from the basket after they moved, using the properties of similar triangles. This can be calculated from the equation $\frac{24.5}{14.5} = \frac{10.78}{x}$. The solution is 6.38 feet.

Prior knowledge needed:

Students should know what similar triangles are. They should also be able to use the idea of proportionality to find the lengths of missing sides in similar triangles.

Classroom use:

1. Show this clip to students.
2. Have students explain why the two triangles are similar.
3. Ask students in groups to find the distances each person is from the basket and from each other as described above.

Connection to Common Core:

Students make sense of the problem when they have to think about why the two triangles formed are similar. Students are modeling with mathematics when they estimate distances and calculate missing distances.

Angle Bisectors

In an episode of *Buffy the Vampire Slayer* (season 1, episode 6), Willow tutors Xander in geometry. She tells him that the bisector of an angle divides the angle into two equal parts. This clip can be used to give the definition of an angle bisector. The clip can be followed by an activity in which students bisect different angles. Starting with triangle *ABC*, students can draw an angle bisector of one of these angles and see that it splits the triangle into two smaller triangles. The angle bisector theorem says that the ratio of the other two sides of each triangle (not the bisector side) are in proportion. If we bisect angle *B* and name the point where the bisector hits the triangle *D*, then the theorem tells us that $\frac{AB}{AD} = \frac{BC}{CD}$. To prove this we can extend the bisector line and draw a line through *C* that is parallel to *AB*. Then, because of alternate interior angles, we know angle *ABD* is the same measure as *DFC*. We also know that angle *ABD* and angle *DBC* are the same because we drew in the angle bisector. This means that *DBC* and *DFC* are the same. Looking at the triangle *BCF*, we now know that this is an isosceles triangle because two of its angles are the same. That means the sides *BC* and *FC* are the same. We also know that angle *ADB* and angle *FDC* have the same measure because they are vertical angles. This tells us that the triangle *BDA* and the triangle *FDC* have two angles that are the same, which means their third angles must also be the same, since all three must sum to 180. By Angle-Angle-Angle (AAA) we find that the two triangles are similar. Since they are similar we can say $\frac{AB}{AD} = \frac{CF}{CD}$. But we said earlier that *BC* = *FC*, so that gives us $\frac{AB}{AD} = \frac{BC}{CD}$.

PRIOR KNOWLEDGE NEEDED:

In this activity, students should know how to use a protractor to measure angles, and should be familiar with parallel lines, isosceles triangles, and similar triangles.

CLASSROOM USE:

1. Show this clip to students.
2. Ask students in groups to draw a triangle using a ruler. Then have them draw the bisector of one of the angles using a protractor and measure the sides of the two triangles formed.
3. Have each group calculate the ratio of the non-bisector sides of each of the two triangles and then share their results with the class. By this point students should be fairly convinced that the angle bisector theorem is true.
4. Next, ask students to prove the angle

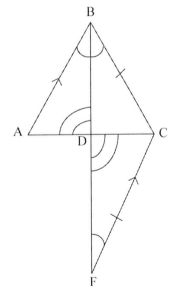

Fig. 23. Picture to prove the angle bisector theorem.

bisector theorem. Depending on their ability level, students can try to prove it themselves, or the proof can be teacher-directed.

Connection to Common Core:

In this activity students construct viable arguments when they prove the angle bisector theorem.

The Center of a Triangle

In an episode of *The Cosby Show* (season 2, episode 21), Theo and his friend are studying for a math test together. Theo asks what an acute triangle is, and his friend says it is a triangle with three acute angles. Next, Theo asks for the theorem for the centroid of a triangle. His friend says the centroid is the point of concurrency of the medians. Theo then asks what a median is. His friend is a little unsure, so Theo gives him the book to read the definition.

This clip is useful because it gives the definitions of median and centroid. After students have seen it, they can begin to explore different triangles and find their medians and centroids. There are actually many different types of triangle centers. Another is called the incenter. This is located at the intersection of the three angle bisectors. The circumcenter is located at the intersection of the perpendicular bisectors of the sides of the triangle.

Prior knowledge needed:

For this activity, students should know how to bisect angles and draw perpendicular bisectors.

Classroom use:

1. Show this clip to students.
2. Ask students to restate the definitions of median and centroid in their own words.
3. Give students cardboard cutouts of various triangles. Be sure to include an equilateral triangle and at least one non-equilateral triangle. Have students use a ruler to locate the midpoint for each side of each triangle and then draw the medians in red. They can then label the centroid of the triangle.
4. Next, have students use a protractor to bisect each angle and label the incenter in green.
5. Finally, have students find the circumcenter and label it in blue.

6. Ask students for any observations they have about the various centers they found. One thing they should notice is that for the equilateral triangle, all three points will be the same. They also may notice that the centroid and the circumcenter are always collinear. The line that they lie on is called the Euler line (another center not previously mentioned is called the ortho-center, and it also lies on this line). Another thing to note is that some of the centers may lie outside the triangle, although the centroid never will.
7. Have students take a sharpened pencil and try to balance each of the triangles on the pencil at the centroid. They will see why the centroid is referred to as the center of gravity of the triangle.

CONNECTION TO COMMON CORE:

In this activity, students use appropriate tools strategically when they measure with a ruler and protractor. Students also look for structure when they look for patterns in the center values of the triangles.

Pythagorean Theorem

In *The Wizard of Oz*, the scarecrow gets an honorary degree in "thinkol-ogy" from the wizard. Then he says, "The sum of the square roots of any two sides of an isosceles triangle is equal to the square root of the remaining side." An episode of *The Simpsons* (season 5, episode 10) pokes fun at this scene. While in the bathroom Homer finds a pair of glasses and thinks that they make him smart. He says the same thing that the scarecrow said.

It is interesting to think about whether the scarecrow's statement is true or not. It should be easy to come up with an example to show that this state-ment is false. For example, if the sides of the triangle are 16 and the base is 25, then $\sqrt{16} + \sqrt{16} = 4 + 4 = 8 \neq \sqrt{25} = 5$ and $\sqrt{16} + \sqrt{25} = 4 + 5 = 9 \neq \sqrt{16} = 4$. This counterexample shows the statement is false, but are there any cases that it does work for? If we name the sides of the isosceles triangle x, x, and y, then this means we want to know if either of these can ever be true: $\sqrt{x} + \sqrt{y} = \sqrt{x}$ or $\sqrt{x} + \sqrt{x} = \sqrt{y}$. The first case is easy since the equation reduces to $\sqrt{y} = 0$, which is equivalent to saying $y = 0$. A triangle can't have a side with length zero, so this will never happen. The second case becomes $2\sqrt{x} = \sqrt{y}$. Squaring both sides yields $4x = y$, or $x = y/4$. This, also, can never be true. To see why let's add in the height of the triangle and call it h. This splits it into two right tri-angles. Using the Pythagorean Theorem gives us $h^2 + \left(\frac{y}{2}\right)^2 = x^2$. If we let $x = y/4$, then this becomes $h^2 + \left(\frac{y}{2}\right)^2 = \left(\frac{y}{4}\right)^2$. This becomes $h^2 = -\frac{3y^2}{16}$. This can never happen, since $-\frac{3y^2}{16}$ is a negative number and h^2 must be a positive number.

In fact, for this to work, x has to be greater than $y/2$. If $x = y/2$ then $h^2 + \left(\frac{y}{2}\right)^2 = \left(\frac{y}{2}\right)^2$. This implies that h is zero. Recall that h is the height of the triangle, so in order for the triangle to exist the height h has to be greater than 0. If $x < y/2$ then h is imaginary, as seen with $x = y/4$.

While the scarecrow didn't quite get it right, the Pythagorean Theorem is a popular reference. In *Family Guy* (season 2, episode 10), Lois is running for school board president, and she bad-mouths her opponent for not supporting background checks for new teachers. The scene flashes to a teacher going over the Pythagorean Theorem while he flirts with one of the students. The hypotenuse is labeled c, making the sides opposite the acute angles a and b. He says that the square of the hypotenuse will always equal the sum of the squares of the other sides and writes $a^2 + b^2 = c^2$ on the board.

In *Saved by the Bell* (season 2, episode 9), Jesse needs straight A's to get into Stanford. When she gets a C on a geometry quiz, Jesse begins to worry about the midterm. She drinks lots of coffee and starts taking pills to stay awake to study. One day in the locker room Jesse asks if anyone knows how to bisect the vertex angle of an isosceles triangle. Then on the day of the midterm Jesse has a lot of energy from taking the pills, so she is talking fast. She declares herself ready for the test and says the square of the hypotenuse in a right triangle equals the sum of the squares of the other two sides.

In *The Man Without a Face*, Chuck spends the summer studying for the entrance exam to a boarding school that his late father attended. In one scene he states Euclid's 47th proposition: in any right-angled triangle, the square on the side opposite the right angle is equal to the sum of the squares of each two sides.

In *Super Fun Night* (season 1, episode 10), Kimmie is making her video diary and talking about how she used to rap. She gives one example of rapping to study for math tests. The scene flashes to high school Kimmie rapping, "Ok let's get this Pythagorean theorem right, $a^2 + b^2 = c^2$ that's tight."

In *My Name Is Earl* (season 3, episode 18), Earl is in a coma, but Randy takes him home from the hospital and takes care of him. In Earl's coma dream sequence, he recalls Randy getting hit in the head by a wooden board. The usually dim-witted Randy spews smart-sounding lines, including that in a right triangle the sum of the squared sides equal the hypotenuse squared. After getting hit again, Randy is back to normal.

In *The New Normal* (season 1, episode 13), Brian and David are looking for a nanny for their unborn child; but they are unhappy with all of the applicants, so they decide that one of them will be a stay-at-home dad. They babysit nine-year-old Shania for a week to see what it would be like to be a dad. One morning on the way to school, David is quizzing Shania on her math and asks, in a right triangle the sum of the squares of the legs is equal to what? Shania answers, the square of the hypotenuse.

Prior knowledge needed:

Students should know what an isosceles triangle is and the rules for verifying what numbers form the lengths of the sides of a triangle.

Classroom use:

1. Show *The Wizard of Oz* clip and ask students if what the scarecrow said is true. Have students work in groups, trying different examples to see if it looks true. If they believe it is not true, have them provide a counter-example.
2. Ask students to prove or disprove if there is ever a case where the scarecrow's statement is true.
3. Once students figure out that it is false, show the *Simpsons* clip. Then ask them to state the correct theorem, if they have already learned the Pythagorean Theorem, or use this as an introduction to it. Follow with the remaining clips showing the theorem used in other shows.

Connection to Common Core:

Students will reason abstractly and quantitatively, make sense of a problem, and persevere in solving it as they try to decide if what the scarecrow said was true and, once they realize it is not true, come up with the correct statement.

Quadrilaterals

Squares, rectangles, rhombuses, and trapezoids are also mentioned in movies and television shows. In an episode of *Suburgatory* (season 2, episode 17), it is George's birthday and his daughter Tessa gives him a wrapped present. Dalia says, "Wow, you got him a square." To which Tessa replies, "That's the shape of what I got him, except it's a rectangle."

In an episode of *Curb Your Enthusiasm* (season 1, episode 7), Larry is having a dinner party. During dinner, one guest tells him about a piece of property he just bought and describes the lot as trapezoidal.

In an episode of *Monk* (season 3, episode 6), Monk describes four dead bugs on a windshield as being in the shape of a trapezoid.

In the movie *Death and the Compass*, based on the short story by Jorge Luis Borges, there are three murders occurring at locations that form an equilateral triangle. The first murder occurs on December 3. The inspector assigned to the case receives a message saying that the first letter of the name has been uttered. The inspector figures out that this clue refers to the four-letter name for the Judeo-Christian God, YHWH. The next month on January 3, the second murder takes place, and a second clue reveals that the second letter has been uttered. Then on February 3 the third murder takes place, and this time the clue says that the last letter of the name has been uttered. With this clue most people believe that the murders are over. However, the inspector realizes that the murders actually took place on the fourth of each month because Jewish people consider the new day to begin at sundown. Additionally, the name of God the murderer is referring to has four letters, with two of them being the same. This means that even though the last letter has been uttered, there could still be a repeat of one of the letters. The inspector predicts a fourth murder will occur, forming a rhombus.

PRIOR KNOWLEDGE NEEDED:

Students need familiarity with quadrilaterals.

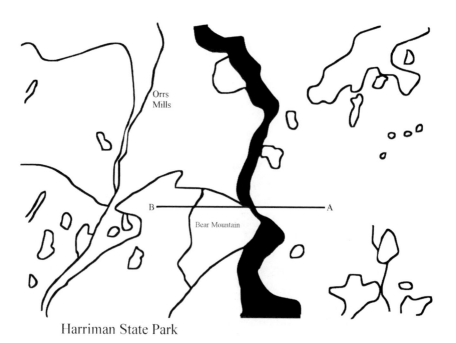

Fig. 24. Map of upstate New York.

CLASSROOM USE:

1. Show the first three clips and then have students describe the differences between a rectangle and a square. Also ask about the differences between a rhombus and a trapezoid.
2. Show the fourth clip and then have students work in groups to solve a similar crime. This example is based in upstate New York, but a map from any region can be used with appropriate clues.
3. Meet as a class and have groups share their results.

Can You Stop the Crime?

The police in upstate New York are stumped, so you are called in as a math special agent. So far there have been two murders (shown in the map, figure 24, as point A and point B), and the killer left notes at each location implying there will be a third and final murder. Your job is to figure out where the final crime will occur so the police can get to the scene beforehand and prevent it.

At the first crime the following clue was found:

> Unlike its salmon
> When I cross and climb Bear Mountain
> My bridges will be burned
> For I will not return.
> There will be three dead by the third night.
> Say what you will, I am always RIGHT.

And on the second night this clue was found:

> The north better be armed
> For the third time won't be a charm.
> My crime spree will be terminated
> Thirty degrees northwest of where I originated.

Can you help the police figure out where the third crime will be?*

CONNECTION TO COMMON CORE:

In this activity, students model with mathematics when they use their knowledge of triangles to solve the crime.

Area of a Rhombus

In the episode of *Freaks and Geeks* mentioned in Chapter Four (season 1, episode 11) Lindsey participated in a math competition. One of the questions asked is this: If the longer diagonal of a rhombus is 10 and the large angle is 100 degrees, then what is the area of the rhombus? Lindsey says the answer is 42.

One way to calculate this area is to use the fact that the diagonals of a rhombus are perpendicular and they bisect each other. Take one of the right triangles formed by the diagonals' intersection. The length of one side is 5, since we were given the diagonal length of 10 and it has been cut in half. If we call the length of the side of the rhombus s, then the remaining side will have length $s\cos50$ by using cosine of an angle is equal to the length of the adjacent side over the hypotenuse. Thus, the length of the other diagonal is $2s\cos50$. There are two different formulas for the area of a rhombus that can be combined to solve for s. One area formula calls for multiplying the diagonals and dividing by 2. This leaves us with $10s\cos50$. Another formula for area is to take a side squared multiplied by the sine of an interior angle. This tells us that the area can also be expressed as $s^2\sin100$. Putting these together gives $10s\cos50 = s^2\sin100$. This reduces to $10\cos50 = s\sin100$. Solving for s gives the approximate value of 6.53. Then plugging back into the area formula yields an area of approximately 41.95. Depending on the rounding rules of this competition, 42 may have been an acceptable answer.

PRIOR KNOWLEDGE NEEDED:

Students should know properties of a rhombus such as the diagonals of a rhombus are perpendicular and they bisect each other and how to calculate the area of a rhombus.

CLASSROOM USE:

1. Show this clip to students.
2. Ask students to solve the problem given in the clip.
3. Have some students share how they solved it. Try to include students who used different approaches.

CONNECTION TO COMMON CORE:

In this activity students reason abstractly and quantitatively when they understand what the problem is asking, figure out how to solve the problem, and then share their solution.

Other Shapes

In *Touch* (season 1, episode 10), Clea asks Abram what a set of large dice are; Abram says they are the five Platonic Solids. Plato thought they were the building blocks of life itself, with each shape corresponding to an element: fire, earth, air, water, and ether (what constellations and the heavens are made of). Clea picks up a dodecahedron, and Abram says it has twelve sides for the twelve zodiacal signs the sun passes through in a year, said to represent the universe itself. The five Platonic Solids are the only five three-dimensional solids with regular (all sides being of equal length) and convex (all interior angles being less than 180 degrees) polygonal faces. This fact was proved by Euclid in his book *The Elements.* The solids include the tetrahedron, with four triangular faces, which is said to represent fire; the cube, with six square faces, said to represent earth; the octahedron, with eight triangular faces, said to represent air; the dodecahedron, with twelve pentagonal faces, said to represent ether; and the icosahedrons, with twenty triangular faces, said to represent water. A demonstration of Euclid's construction of a dodecahedron is available on this Web site.[1]

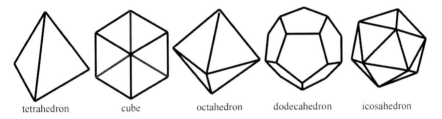

tetrahedron   cube   octahedron   dodecahedron   icosahedron

Fig. 25. The five Platonic Solids.

PRIOR KNOWLEDGE NEEDED:

Students will need to know various facts about pentagons and possibly other polygons.

CLASSROOM USE:

1. Show the clip.
2. Show the demonstration of how Euclid described constructing the dodecahedron. Students may also be interested in seeing the wording from the original text, but it is probably difficult for them to follow.
3. There is a dodecahedron template at this Web site.[2] In groups of three, have students decorate four faces of the dodecahedron with mathematical facts pertaining to the pentagon. Facts they could include are the measure of each interior angle (108), the measure of the central angle (72), why the pentagon is regular, why it is convex, and how many diagonals a pentagon has. Students can also include formulas for the area of a pentagon, the circumference of a pentagon, and so on. If students can't think of twelve facts about

pentagons, then they can include facts about other polygons. After the pentagons are decorated, the dodecahedrons can be glued together to make nice classroom decorations.

4. Have each group explain the sides of their dodecahedron.

Connection to Common Core:

In this activity, students must attend to precision as they write the facts on their pentagons and as they explain these facts to the class.

Hexagons

In an episode of *Sonny with a Chance* (season 1, episode 5), Sonny has been doing poorly in math, and she has a big geometry test coming up. In one scene Zora helps her study by explaining that a hexagon is two trapezoids, one on top of the other. She then starts talking about finding the area, but Sonny begins to daydream. Next, Zora tries to explain geometry with a model. She says that a hexagon is made up of six triangles. The model has six triangles, each a different color, that are stuck together to form a hexagon. She pulls one triangle off and explains that if you find the area of one triangle you can find the area of the hexagon. Sonny begins to daydream again and asks Zora to explain it one more time. Zora draws a circle on the blackboard and says this is a circle.

We can take this idea of a hexagon being made up of six triangles and take it a step further. If the hexagon is regular, then the six triangles formed will be equilateral. In a regular hexagon the sum of the interior angles will be $(6-2)180 = 720$ degrees. Since each angle is equivalent, the measure of each interior angle will be $720/6 = 120$ degrees. Drawing a diagonal from each vertex to its opposite vertex will bisect the angle into two 60-degree angles. Now each triangle has two 60-degree angles, so the remaining angle must be $180 - (60 + 60) = 60$ degrees. This gives us six equilateral triangles. As Zora started to explain, to get the area of the hexagon it is only necessary to know the area of one of these equilateral triangles. Each triangle is the same since the hexagon is regular and we know all sides have the same length. That means the area of the hexagon will be six times the area of one of the triangles.

In another scene, Sonny and Tawni are arguing because Sonny almost cheated on her test based on Tawni's suggestion. When Tawni complains that they both were banned from working on their television show, Sonny says that the whole world doesn't revolve around Tawni. The world is a sphere, and we are all points on its perimeter, which means we are all equidistant to the center. Then they both get excited that Sonny gave an insult with geometry. Tawni tells her to do it again, and Sonny says she is a rhombus, a parallelogram with four equal sides.

PRIOR KNOWLEDGE NEEDED:

For this activity, students should know what a hexagon is and how to calculate the measure of an interior angle of a regular polygon. Students should also know what an equilateral triangle is and what its properties are.

CLASSROOM USE:

1. Show students this clip.
2. Give students a paper with a regular hexagon drawn on it or ask students to construct their own.
3. Ask students to calculate the degree of an interior angle. Also have them draw the three main diagonals.
4. Have students prove that each triangle is equilateral.
5. Give examples where the side of the hexagon is known and have students calculate the area of it. For example, if each side has length 2 cm, then we can take one of the equilateral triangles and know that each side of it has a length of 2 cm. To find the area of the triangle we can draw a perpendicular to form two right triangles. The hypotenuse is still 2 cm, and the base will be 1 cm because it was bisected. Thus, the height can be found by solving $h^2 + 1^2 = 2^2$. The height is found to be $\sqrt{3}$ cm. This means that the area of the equilateral triangle is $2\left(\frac{1}{2}(1)\sqrt{3}\right) = \sqrt{3}$ cm^2. Thus, the area of the hexagon is $6\sqrt{3}$ cm^2.

CONNECTION TO COMMON CORE:

Students construct viable arguments when they prove the hexagon can be split into six equilateral triangles.

Parallel Lines

In an episode of *House M.D.* (season 5, episode 19), Lee has just had brain surgery and can only move his eyes. The doctors want to check a few things, so they ask him various yes-or-no questions. For one question, the doctor holds up a card with parallel lines and asks if the lines shown are parallel. Lee blinks once for yes and the doctor says that his spatial relationships are intact.

Students should already be familiar with parallel lines by the time they get to high school, but this clip can be used as a motivator to prove that two parallel lines have the same slope. One way to prove this is to draw two non-vertical and non-horizontal lines that are parallel. Then make each line into a triangle by drawing a line parallel to the *y*-axis as the second side and a line parallel to the *x*-axis as the third side of the triangle (fig. 26). These two triangles are congruent because their corresponding sides are par-allel. This means that their sides are in proportion, and we can say

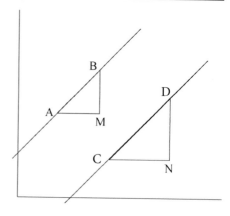

Fig. 26. Picture to prove the slope of two parallel lines are the same.

$\frac{BM}{DN} = \frac{MA}{NC}$. Manipulating this equation leads to $\frac{BM}{MA} = \frac{DN}{NC}$. The distance BM is the change in *y* from point *A* to point *B* and *MA* is the change in *x*. This means that $\frac{BM}{MA}$ is the slope of line *AB*. Similarly, $\frac{DN}{NC}$ is the slope of line *CD*. Since they are equal, we can say the slope of two parallel lines is equal. Vertical parallel lines can be thought of as having the same slope because they have no slope, since there is no change in their *x* values. Horizontal parallel lines will also have the same slope because they have no change in their *y* values (i.e., a slope of 0).

Prior knowledge needed:

Students should know what parallel lines are as well as how to prove tri-angles are similar, properties of similar triangles, and the definition of slope of a line.

Classroom use:

1. Show this clip to students.
2. Ask students to think of real-world examples of parallel lines. A few exam-ples include double yellow lines on a road, railroad tracks, and telephone wires.
3. Have students prove that all horizontal lines have the same slope.
4. Ask students why all vertical lines have no slope.
5. Have students draw two non-horizontal and non-vertical lines on a set of axes. Explain how to construct two similar triangles from the lines as described above. Then have students explain why the two triangles are similar and prove that the lines have the same slope.

In this activity students construct viable arguments when they prove that two parallel lines have the same slope.

The Fourth Dimension

In *Flatland,* Arthur Square lives in a two-dimensional world where everything happens along a flat surface. In the opening scene Arthur quizzes his granddaughter Hex on the rules of Flatland. She explains how every generation has children with one additional side until they have so many sides they become circles. The rule in Flatland is the more sides a shape has, the higher class it is. Thus, the circles are the priests and make all the rules. Later, Arthur explains that forming a line segment of length three then extending it three units up will yield a square of area 3^2, or nine units. Hex hypothesizes that taking three squares and somehow extending them would form a new object of 3^3, or 27 units, that could be called a super-square.

Arthur has a dream where he sees other dimensions. First, he sees a zero-dimensional point who is the only occupant of Pointland. In a one-dimensional world, there is a line segment king and two queens, one on either side of him. Arthur says he is above the king, but the king is confused and says there is no such thing as above and below, only left and right. Arthur enters the line segment and the king is surprised. Finally, Arthur is approached by

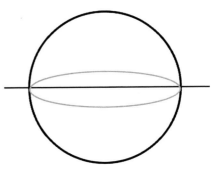

Fig. 27. Sphere appearing as a circle in two dimensions.

Sphereus, a sphere that appears in Arthur's two-dimensional world as a circle.

The movie *Flatland* is based on a book entitled *Flatland: A Romance of Many Dimensions,* written by Edwin Abbott in 1884. Because the book was written so long ago it is available in the public domain for free.[3] The book is actually denser than the movie, because it was written as a satire of the Victorian era in Great Britain. Women are represented by line segments while men are represented by polygons, with the same class distinctions as described in the movie. The movie does not make this distinction between men and women and mainly focuses on the geometric aspects of the book.

In an episode of *The Simpsons* (season 7, episode 6), Homer finds a portal behind a bookcase that transforms him from two-dimensional to three-dimensional. Much like the characters in *Flatland*, Homer is confused by his new appearance, specifically his bulgy stomach. Professor Frink offers an explanation of the third dimension to Chief Wiggum by starting with a square and then extending it onto the hypothetical z-axis, forming a cube.

In an episode of *The Twilight Zone* (season 3, episode 26), a young girl named Tina has fallen into a fourth dimension. Her parents can't see her but they can hear her.

The concept of going from two to three dimensions as discussed in *Flatland* is a good way to have students understand (rather than just memorize) the volume formulas for rectangular prism, cylinder, cone, and sphere.

PRIOR KNOWLEDGE NEEDED:

Students should have already studied two-dimensional objects, such as squares, rectangles, and circles. They need to know the area formulas for these two-dimensional objects, as well as the surface area of a sphere.

CLASSROOM USE:

Part 1:

1. Ask students to pick a two-dimensional shape and draw it by hand or on the computer using interactive geometry software such as Geometer's Sketchpad.[4]
2. Next, have them think of stacking many copies of the same shape on top of it to add a third dimension of height, and have them draw that object. Then have them calculate the volume of this new three-dimensional object. Most likely at least one student will each start with a rectangle, square, and circle. With these objects students will get the formulas for the volume of a rectangular prism, cube, and cylinder.
3. Have each student share their shape and its volume formula with the rest of the class.

Part 2:

1. After completing part 1, students should know the formula for calculating the volume of a solid cube. Have them split the cube into three equal shapes so that each shape has a full side of the cube. This can be done with manipulatives or using software. Something like Play-Doh works as a manipulative if the student makes a solid cube and then uses a plastic knife to split up the cube.

2. Once students get the three equal objects ask what the volume of each one is. They should use the fact that the volume of a cube is the side cubed to calculate the volume of each object as the side cubed divided by 3. At this point, the objects can be referred to as pyramids.

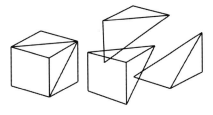

Fig. 28. Cube split into three pyramids.

3. Next, ask students to think about how the volume formula would change if instead of having a square base, the pyramid had a rectangular base. From there they can brainstorm in groups to try to come up with a general formula for the volume of a pyramid with any base shape. Once they calculate the formula as $\left(\frac{1}{3} \cdot \text{area of base} \cdot \text{height}\right)$, they can determine the formula for the volume of a cone, which has a circular base, as $\frac{1}{3}\pi r^2 h$.

Part 3:

1. The formula for the volume of a sphere is nicely explained in this video.[5] The video uses the idea of splitting the sphere into several pyramids with square bases and summing the area of each of these pyramids. Students will already know the volume of each pyramid from part 2, and the video shows that the height of each pyramid is the same as the radius of the sphere, r. The sum of all of the bases of the pyramids will be the same as the surface area of the sphere, $4\pi r^2$. Putting this all together gives the volume of the sphere as $\left(\frac{1}{3} \cdot \text{area of base} \cdot \text{height}\right) = \frac{1}{3}(4\pi r^2)(r) = \frac{4}{3}\pi r^3$. Students can be shown this video and then asked to explain the process that was shown.

CONNECTION TO COMMON CORE:

Students use appropriate tools when they use geometry software for this activity. Students look for and make use of structure as they come up with the formula for volumes of pyramids and cones.

How to Make a Basket

In an episode of *How I Met Your Mother* (season 8, episode 6), Ted uses geometry to make a basket. He bounces the basketball 77 degrees under his opponent's legs, 93 degrees against the wall, 91 off another wall, 170 off another wall, and $17 \cdot \frac{5}{6}\pi$ off another wall and into the basket. Unfortunately, Ted's basket does not count because the ball went out of bounds, which is one reason why people don't play basketball this way. Ted's idea of bouncing the basketball off walls at certain angles is related to playing billiards. Using this clip in the classroom can lead to a discussion of geometry and angles in billiards.

A similar situation is shown in an episode of *The Simpsons* (season 2, episode 6). Bart is preparing to compete in a miniature golf tournament. He asks Lisa for advice on his putting technique. While on the putting course, Lisa takes out a tape measure and figures out where Bart has to hit the ball to make it bounce several times before going in the hole. Bart can't believe that Lisa found a practical use for geometry.

Prior knowledge needed:

Students should have some familiarity with angles.

Classroom use:

1. Show the two clips and make the billiards connection.
2. Have handouts or project on the board a picture of a billiards table and a path that a ball would need to take to

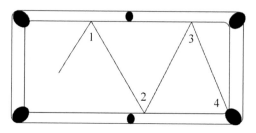

Fig. 29. Billiard table example.

get into a hole. Have students estimate the angles that the ball bounces off each wall. Figure 29 shows an example handout.

Connection to Common Core:

Students model with mathematics when they use their knowledge of angles and apply it to a real-world billiard table.

Circles

In *The Man Without a Face*, Chuck's tutor shows him how to find the center of a circle. The tutor's method is as follows: First, draw a circle *ABC* with *AB* as a chord. Bisect *AB* at *D* and draw a straight line to *C*, making a right angle. Then draw the line *AC* and bisect that to get the center where the two bisectors meet (fig. 30).

Prior knowledge needed:

Student should have already studied circles. They will need to know definitions for chord, bisect, and right angle.

CLASSROOM USE:

1. Show this clip.
2. Put up circles of various sizes on a SMART Board or have handouts with pictures of circles; have students find their centers using this technique.
3. Have students explain their solutions to the class.

CONNECTION TO
COMMON CORE:

Students have to attend to precision as they explain their solutions to the class.

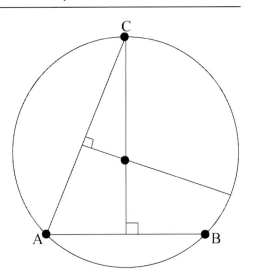

Fig. 30. Finding the center of a circle.

Chords of a Circle

In an episode of *My So-Called Life* (season 1, episode 12), Angela is in geometry class and the teacher asks the class to draw a circle with two intersecting chords. Then the teacher asks the students what the product of the segments of one chord is equal to. Angela is too busy daydreaming about kissing Jordan Catalano to draw the circle.

If she had been paying attention, Angela would have known that the product of the segments of one chord is equal to the product of the segments of the second chord. This can be proven by drawing a circle with two chords and then adding two lines connecting the points where the chords hit the circle. This will form two triangles. It can be proven that the two triangles are similar by showing that they both have three angles with the same measure. Since the triangles are similar, their sides will be in proportion. This proportionality leads to the previously mentioned property.

PRIOR KNOWLEDGE NEEDED:

Students should have seen the given property before. They will also need to know how to prove that triangles are similar and that the sides of similar triangles are in proportion.

Classroom use:

1. Show this clip to students.
2. Ask students what the correct answer is.
3. Have students prove this property, giving guidance as needed.
4. Have students come up with a few examples using the property.

Connection to Common Core:

In this activity, students construct viable arguments when they construct the proof.

Area of Circles

In *Castaway*, Chuck figures out how many miles rescuers would have to search to rescue him after his plane crashes—first by estimating the distance from where the plane was supposed to be and where it ended up, then by multiplying this radius squared by pi. He ends up with the area of the circle that needs to be searched.

In *Raising Hope* (season 2, episode 11), Jimmy and his parents return to high school. In one scene they are studying, and Jimmy's mom asks her mom, Maw Maw, to give them a math question. Maw Maw asks, if the radius of a circle is six, what is the circle's area? When they are stumped she adds that the area formula is πr^2. Everyone then goes off topic talking about pies.

In an episode of *Army Wives* (season 2, episode 11), Roxy is studying for her GED. Her friend asks her what the area of a circle with radius 3.5 inches is. They get sidetracked by a different discussion, but eventually Roxy answers 38.48 inches squared.

Prior knowledge needed:

Students should have some background on circles, such as what a radius is and what pi is.

Classroom use:

1. Show the *Castaway* clip. The area formula is not given, so students can use the calculations Chuck gives to figure out what the formula is as an introduction to the topic. This can also be shown during review to make sure students remember the formula.
2. Show the *Raising Hope* clip and have students calculate the area of the circle with radius 6 as a practice problem.

3. Show the first part of the *Army Wives* clip. After students figure out the correct answer, show the remaining clip.

CONNECTION TO COMMON CORE:

Students see Chuck modeling with mathematics because he uses his ability to calculate a circle's area to figure out his rescue area.

Pi

In *Life of Pi*, Piscine is tired of being mocked for his name, so on the first day of classes he declares his new nickname to be Pi. He goes on to describe some of the properties of pi. He says that pi is the ratio of a circle's circumference to its diameter and that it is an irrational number usually rounded to 3.14. In his math class Pi writes some of the digits of pi, taking up three blackboards.

In an episode of *Sliders* (season 1, episode 7), the sliders enter an alternate universe in which intelligence is highly prized and smart people are worshipped the way athletes are in ours. In this universe Quinn is a star player of a game called Mindgame. In this game players have to answer trivia questions while throwing a ball and trying to capture squares. The rules are too confusing to fully understand how the game works, but it is likened to Othello. In the final championships one of the questions is to give pi to thirteen places. Quinn is shown answering this question.

In an episode of *Person of Interest* (season 2, episode 11), a substitute teacher named Mr. Swift teaches a math class. One day Mr. Swift draws a picture of a circle, writes pi as 3.1415926535, and asks if anyone knows what it is. The only response he gets is from a student asking when she will ever need to use this. Mr. Swift says that pi is the ratio of the circumference of a circle to its diameter. He points to the number written on the board and says this is just the beginning, and that it keeps on going forever without ever repeating. He goes on to say that this means that within this string of numbers is every single other number such as your birth date, the combination to your locker, and your social security number. Converting these numbers into letters gives every word that ever existed. This finally gets the class interested.

In an episode of *Angel* (season 3, episode 5), Fred is planning to run away, so she goes to a bus station. She is shown talking to herself, saying things to try to convince herself that she will start over in a new town. She says that it will be as easy as pie and then starts reciting pi. A homeless guy sitting next to her is scared off by this. She says that she is just reciting pi to relax and that she has memorized 452 digits of pi.

In an episode of *Fringe* (season 3, episode 3), Milo is mentally challenged, having an IQ less than 65, but his sister signs him up for an experimental drug trial that raises his IQ. After one treatment Milo is shown reciting the digits of pi. The doctor says that he could go through one thousand digits while solving differential equations in his head.

In *Night at the Museum II*, Larry and Amelia are trying to find the number at the heart of the pyramid. They speak to a bunch of bobblehead Albert Einsteins and figure out that the number is pi. The Einsteins say it is 3.14159 265, to be exact.

In *Never Been Kissed*, the math team has a sign at their bake-sale table that says pi = 3.14578699869 and pie = 75 cents. Pi's value is only correct up to the first two decimal places.

In one scene in *The Virgin Suicides*, written above the blackboard in the math classroom is a decimal expansion of pi, written as 3.1415926535942987 64285691219800823164329155 2314. Only the first ten decimal places are correct.

In *Northern Exposure* (season 4, episode 3), Chris meets Amy when he accidentally runs over her dog. She is a mathematician studying pi. They discuss what pi is and that it goes on forever. Amy mentions that she also studies other transcendental numbers. Amy says that these numbers seems to be a random sequence of digits, but that if she can find enough digits of them there will be a mathematical sign.

PRIOR KNOWLEDGE NEEDED:

Students should know what the circumference and diameter of a circle are. Students should know what an irrational number is, or it can be discussed during the activity.

CLASSROOM USE:

1. Students should work in groups, with each group receiving a different-size circle. They should calculate the circle's circumference and diameter with string and a ruler and then divide them.
2. Have each group put their answers on the board and then discuss why all of them are similar.
3. The clip from *Life of Pi* can be shown to introduce or review some of pi's properties. Go over the definition for an irrational number if students are unfamiliar with it.
4. Show the *Night at the Museum II* clip and ask students what is wrong with what the bobbleheads said.

In this activity, students will be constructing viable arguments when they conjecture that the ratio of a circle's circumference to its diameter is the same value for any size circle. Students critique the reasoning of others when they explain why the mistakes occur in these movies.

Area

The movie *Rushmore* begins with a dream sequence in which Max is the class hero because he solves the hardest geometry problem in the world, finding the area of an ellipse. The teacher is in the middle of a different problem when another student named Isaac asks about the area problem that is shown on a different blackboard as an extra credit problem. The teacher says that he just put it up as a joke because it is probably the hardest geometry problem in the world. When Isaac asks how much extra credit it is worth, the teacher says that if anyone in the class solves it, he will make sure that none of them have to open a math book ever again. Max goes to the board to try it, and he gets the correct answer. The method that Max uses involves calculus, but high school students can make a conjecture about what the area of an ellipse is and form an argument to support it, even if they can't prove it yet.

Something similar actually happened to a mathematician named George Dantzig, best known for his work in linear programming. As a graduate student at Berkeley, Dantzig arrived late one day to class and saw some problems written on the board. Assuming these were homework problems, he copied them down and handed the correct solutions in a few days later. Dantzig later found out that they were actually two famous unsolved problems in the field of statistics.[6]

Prior knowledge needed:

Students should have knowledge of circles and ellipses, such as the definition of an ellipse's major and minor axis, the standard forms for the equations of the circle and the ellipse, and the formula for the area of a circle.

Classroom use:

1. Show the clip.
2. Have students draw an ellipse centered at the origin with major axis length $2a$ and minor axis length $2b$. Ask them to write the equation of the ellipse in standard form $\left(\frac{x^2}{a^2} + \frac{y^2}{b^2} = 1\right)$.

3. Next ask them to think about how the circle and ellipse are related. In pairs, they can discuss how to make an ellipse turn into a circle and what happens to the *a* and *b* values. Once they realize that *a* has to equal *b*, have them substitute *a* in for the *b* in the equation and make it look like the equation of a circle ($x^2 + y^2 = a^2$).

4. Then have them write the formula for the area of this circle (πa^2) and ask them to make a guess as to what the formula for the area of an ellipse would be if *a* and *b* were different values (πab).

CONNECTION TO COMMON CORE:

Students construct viable arguments as they make a conjecture as to what the area of an ellipse is and back up their conjecture with the argument given in this activity.

Geometry and Art

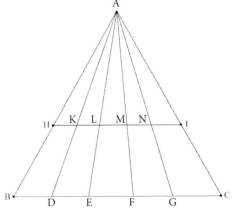

Fig. 31. Triangle showing perspective.

In *Touch*, Jake usually communicates through numbers, but in this episode (season 1, episode 5) he arranges sugar packets and leaves a maple syrup hand print in the shape of concentric circles. Dr. Teller shows Jake's dad that mathematicians use art to study geometry and that Jake's pattern is actually based on the centered heptagonal numbers. The first centered heptagonal number is 1. The next is found by drawing a heptagon (a seven-sided polygon) where a dot is placed at each vertex and in the center. This gives it a value of 8. The pattern continues like this, with a larger heptagon added surrounding the previous one. The centered heptagonal numbers are 1, 8, 22, 43, ... The formula to calculate the *n*th centered heptagonal number is $\frac{7n^2-7n+2}{2}$. Dr. Teller looks at the painting *The Brera Altarpiece* by Piero della Francesca and shows that the ceiling in this painting has the same pattern. The third centered heptagonal number is 22, and Dr. Teller shows that there are 22 dots within the circles Jake drew.

Piero della Francesca was a mathematician in addition to being an artist. He wrote three mathematical books, including one on perspective painting called *De prospectiva pingendi*. In the first book of this treatise he proves an original proposition on perspective (proposition 8). The given straight line *BC* is divided into equal parts. The line *HI* is drawn parallel to *BC*. If the lines from each point that divides the line *BC* meet up at a point *A*, then *HI* is divided into the same proportions as *BC*. (See figure 31.)

PRIOR KNOWLEDGE NEEDED:

For the first activity, students just need knowledge of various geometric shapes. For the second activity, students need familiarity with triangles and should know how to prove that two triangles are similar.

CLASSROOM USE:

Activity #1:

1. Show the clip to introduce the idea of geometry in art.
2. Have students search for famous paintings online, or bring in art books. Have students in pairs choose a painting and then find any geometric shapes they can within the painting.
3. Ask students to share the shapes they found. This works best if the class is equipped with a SMART Board. The painting can be displayed on the board and students can draw on the painting with the shapes that they found.

Activity #2:

This activity isn't related to the math shown in this clip but is based on the idea of math being an important part of art. The clip can be used to introduce *The Brera Altarpiece* painting. Students can see perspective used in this painting.

Show students the proposition that Piero della Francesca proved in his book and ask them to prove it themselves in groups. If they need help getting started, have them prove that triangle *AKH* is similar to triangle *ADB*. Similarly, they can prove triangle *ALK* is similar to triangle *AED*, and so on. From here they should be able to use the fact that the sides of similar triangles are in proportion, such as $AK/AD = HK/BD$ and $HK/BD = KL/DE$. Then they can use the fact that each segment in *BC* has the same length, so $BD = DE$. This means that $HK/DE = KL/DE$ and thus $HK = KL$. Similarly the remaining segments of *HI* can be shown to also be the same length as *HK*.

There are many additional activities that can be drawn from J.V. Field's book on the mathematics in Piero della Francesca's works of art.[7] These include calculating the optimal viewing distance and other types of perspective.

CONNECTION TO COMMON CORE:

In the first activity, students model with mathematics when they use their knowledge of geometry to describe the geometric shapes found in a work of art. In the second activity, students construct viable arguments when they complete the proof.

Russell's Paradox

Being able to think logically is an important skill for students studying geometry to have. Having students solve logic riddles is good practice for the type of logical thinking they will need in order to write geometry proofs.

In an episode of *The Office* (season 9, episode 22), Dwight is named the regional manager and chooses Jim to be the assistant to the regional manager. As Jim is constantly playing pranks on Dwight, he convinces Dwight that there needs to be an assistant to the assistant to the regional manager (A.A.R.M.). Jim devises a set of obstacles so that Dwight ends up choosing himself to be the A.A.R.M. As Dwight is getting crowned for the position, Jim says that he should kneel for this, but that the manager for Dunder Mifflin kneels for no man. This is an example of a famous logical riddle known as Russell's Paradox. The paradox is named after Bertrand Russell, who discovered it in 1901. Russell had been studying Cantor's proof that there is no greatest number and began thinking of a set, call it S, which contains all the sets that are not members of themselves.[8] But this led to a contradiction, because if S is not in S, then the definition says S is in S. If S is in S then it does not follow its own definition. The most famous example of Russell's paradox is given by the following riddle: A small town has a barber who shaves all the men in this town who do not shave themselves, and he does not shave anyone who shaves himself. Who shaves the barber? The barber cannot shave himself because then the statement is false. If the barber doesn't shave himself then the barber must shave himself, according to the statement. Both ways lead to a contradiction.

Another example of Russell's paradox occurs in *Proof*. Catherine is talking to her father and wondering if she will become crazy like he did. Her dad says that the fact that she is asking that question means that she is not crazy, because crazy people have better things to do than to ask if they are crazy. Catherine seems to accept that until she remembers that her father is crazy and wonders why he can admit to being crazy. We then find out that she is imagining talking to her father, because he actually died of an aneurism a week prior.

No prior knowledge is needed for this activity.

CLASSROOM USE:

1. Explain what Russell's Paradox is.
2. Show the clips and have students explain why the situations lead to a contradiction. Another popular example that can be shown to students is this: Consider a library that compiles a bibliographic catalog of all (and only those) catalogs that do not list themselves. Then does the library's catalog list itself?[9]

CONNECTION TO COMMON CORE:

Students construct viable arguments when they explain why Russell's Paradox occurs in these situations.

A Fox, a Goose and a Bag of Beans

In an episode of *The Simpsons* (season 20, episode 13), Homer goes to the store to get rat poison to deal with a rat infestation. He is driving Maggie and their dog, Santa's Little Helper, home. Homer gets distracted, which causes the car to go off a bridge. Homer needs to cross a river. There is a boat, but it can only carry two items at a time. Maggie can't be left alone with the poison because she may swallow it. Santa's Little Helper can't be left alone with Maggie because he may bite her. Homer has to figure out how to get everyone safely across.

This is a play on a famous riddle about a fox, a goose, and a bag of beans. The riddle says that a farmer goes to market and buys a fox, a goose, and a bag of beans. To get home the farmer has to cross a river in a boat that can only hold himself plus one other item. Left alone the fox would eat the goose and the goose would eat the bag of beans. The goal is to figure out how the farmer can get everything across safely. One solution is for the farmer to first take the goose to the other side. Next, he returns and brings the fox over. On the next return he brings the goose with him. Then he takes the bag of beans to the other side and returns. Finally he brings the goose back over.

To solve his riddle, Homer first takes Maggie over to the other side. Then he returns and brings the poison over. He brings Maggie back to the first side and brings Santa's Little Helper across. Finally, he returns and brings Maggie back over. In this version Maggie is equivalent to the goose, the poison is equivalent to the fox, and Santa's Little Helper is equivalent to the bag of beans.

PRIOR KNOWLEDGE NEEDED:

No prior knowledge is needed for this activity.

CLASSROOM USE:

1. Explain the riddle about the farmer who buys a fox, goose, and bag of beans. Ask students in groups to solve this riddle. Students can be given visuals to help solve the problem. Pictures of each object can be printed, laminated, and mounted on a popsicle stick. This way, students can act out the situation as they try to solve the riddle. Once a group has a solution, ask them if there are other solutions. One variation is to switch the roles of the fox and the bag of beans.
2. Have groups share their solutions. Ask them why it is necessary for the goose to be brought over first. Essentially, it works out this way because the goose can't be left alone with either the fox or the beans.
3. Show students this clip.
4. Have students figure out how this is equivalent to the previous riddle.

CONNECTION TO COMMON CORE:

In this activity, students have to make sense of the problem and persevere in solving it as they try to figure out this logic riddle.

Indirect Reasoning

In *Proof*, Hal compliments Catherine's dress, but she says that it doesn't fit. Hal says it does, but Catherine says that he can't prove it. Hal says he can prove the opposite—that it doesn't not fit. Later the same idea comes up: Catherine says she wrote a proof, but Hal is not sure if it was written by Catherine or her father. Catherine says there is no way to prove that she wrote it; Hal says, no, but we can talk it through and determine if you couldn't have written it.

These examples of indirect reasoning can serve as a way for students to begin thinking about proof by contradiction. It is a strange thing for students to think about proving a statement is true by proving that the negation of the statement is false.

PRIOR KNOWLEDGE NEEDED:

Prior knowledge for this activity will vary depending on what geometry proofs are chosen for number 4, below.

CLASSROOM USE:

1. Show the clips from *Proof* and ask students to explain why Hal's method is valid.
2. In groups, ask students to explain why the following statement must be true: If Beth buys two items and spends more than $50 at a toy store, then at least one of the items is more than $25.
3. Have each group share their arguments. Since they will have just discussed indirect reasoning, they will most likely come up with an explanation similar to the following: Assume both items are under $25 or exactly $25. Then their total would come to less than or equal to $50. This can't happen, because Beth spent more than $50. Therefore, at least one of the items had to have been more than $25.
4. Give each group a geometry proof that uses proof by contradiction to complete and then explain to the class.

CONNECTION TO COMMON CORE:

Students are constructing viable arguments when they come up with an argument for the toy store situation and when they solve the geometry proof.

Logic Riddle

In an episode of *Law and Order: Criminal Intent* (season 10, episode 2), Detective Goren is forced to see a therapist in order to keep his job. This episode features his first session with the therapist. He asks her to solve the following riddle: There are two doors and two guards. One of the doors leads to heaven, the other to hell. One of the guards always tells the truth and one always lies. You get to ask one guard one question without knowing whether that is the honest guard, and then you must pick a door. What question should you ask? It isn't until episode 8 that the therapist is able to provide a solution to the riddle. The solution is to ask one guard, what will the other guard say if you ask him if his is the door to heaven? If the guard says yes, then you know that the other door leads to heaven.

PRIOR KNOWLEDGE NEEDED:

No prior knowledge is needed for this activity.

CLASSROOM USE:

1. Show the clip from episode 2 where the riddle is posed.
2. Putting the students in groups of three, assign one student to be the guard that always tells the truth, one to be the guard that always lies, and the last to be the person questioning the guards, making sure that the student asking the guards questions does not know which guard lies. Have them role play to try to figure out the solution to the riddle.
3. Ask groups to share what solution they got and how they came to that solution.
4. Show the clip from episode 8 where the therapist gives her solution to the riddle.

CONNECTION TO COMMON CORE:

Students construct viable arguments when they come up with a solution to this riddle.

Transitivity

The transitive property is used in geometry proofs, so it is helpful for students to understand it. The property has been featured in several media examples.

In the movie *Lincoln*, Lincoln is talking to two young men and trying to decide whether to end slavery or extend his emancipation proclamation. He brings up Euclid and the idea that things that are equal to the same thing are equal to each other, speaking about the transitive property in Euclid's book *The Elements*.

In an episode of *30 Rock* (season 1, episode 15), Kenneth joins Tracy's entourage but doesn't quite understand that part of being an entourage requires him to kiss up to Tracy. Kenneth beats Tracy at a game of Halo, and Tracy is surprised because usually the other members of his entourage, Grizz and Dot Com, let Tracy win. Later Tracy sees Grizz beat Kenneth at Halo, and Tracy is confused because he says that if Grizz can beat Kenneth and Kenneth can beat him, then by the transitive property Grizz should beat him.

In another episode of *30 Rock* (season 5, episode 19), Pete discovers that he has a hidden talent and beats everyone at arm wrestling. After losing to

Pete, Jack says that by the transitive property, Pete just defeated Muammar Gaddafi.

PRIOR KNOWLEDGE NEEDED:

Prior knowledge for this activity will vary depending on what geometry proofs are chosen for number 3, below.

CLASSROOM USE:

1. Since the clip from *Lincoln* defines the transitive property and the clips from *30 Rock* give examples, together they can be used to introduce the concept. After showing the clips, have students write down in their own words what transitive means and provide their own example.
2. Students can meet with a partner and share their definition and example. Have them check each other's work and make sure that the definition and example make sense.
3. Have each pair of students prove a different geometry proof that uses the transitive property. For example, have students prove that all right angles are equal to each other.
4. Have each pair share their proofs with another pair. Have students check each other's work to make sure that the proofs were done correctly.

CONNECTION TO COMMON CORE:

In this activity students reason abstractly and quantitatively as they think about what transitive means, use that idea to write a geometry proof, and explain the proof to classmates.

CHAPTER SEVEN

Statistics and Probability

Let's begin our exploration of statistics and probability by considering a curious student with a quarter. The student starts flipping the quarter. First, the heads side comes up. Then the student flips again and the heads side of the coin reappears. A third flip yields heads yet again. All together, the student flips the coin ten times and sees heads all ten times. The student then makes what seems like an obvious conclusion: surely the next flip is more likely to be tails than heads.

The student's obvious conclusion turns out to be incorrect. The student has fallen for the Gambler's Fallacy, which treats independent events as if they were dependent. In the student's case, coin flips are independent events and are unrelated to the previous flips. The eleventh flip is just as likely to be heads again as it is to be tails (50 percent in each case). The coin has no memory and doesn't care if its eleventh flip brings another heads. In fact, that string of ten heads that the student got wasn't that amazing either. There was a 1-in-1,024 chance that the first ten flips were all heads, which is just as likely as getting alternating heads and tails, a sequence that people perceive as being more random.

The misunderstanding and mystery surrounding statistics and probability, combined with the number of everyday problems generated by them, makes these topics popular in television shows and motion pictures. There are many examples of randomness and other statistics and probability topics included in popular culture.

Statistics involves categorizing data with various charts and graphs and being able to make inferences from statistical experiments. Probability includes understanding the rules of probability and being able to use them to make decisions. Probability and statistics are probably the mathematical subjects that have the most accessible real-world examples.

The Monty Hall Problem

The Monty Hall Problem is one of the most famous problems in probability theory. This problem is named after Monty Hall, the host of the television game show *Let's Make a Deal*. The reason the Monty Hall Problem became so famous is that it appeared in an issue of *Parade* magazine as a problem posed to Marilyn vos Savant, a *Guinness Book of World Records* holder for highest IQ at 228.[1] A reader wrote in describing a situation in which a game-show contestant has a chance to pick one of three doors. Goats are behind two of the doors and a brand new car is behind the third door. After the contestant chooses, the host, who knows what is behind each door, opens one of the doors the contestant didn't pick to reveal a goat. The problem focuses on this question: should the contestant stick with the original door or switch to the other remaining one? Vos Savant argued with a clear and precise explanation that the contestant should switch. Her answer confused many readers and compelled a lot of them to write in to claim that she was wrong. They believed that there was no incentive to switch because at this point you are down to two doors so there's a 50/50 chance of getting the car.

This seems like the obvious answer. It is, in fact, what most students say when presented with this problem. In this case students are not alone in their assumptions. People with PhDs in mathematics also wrote in saying Vos Savant had answered incorrectly. Vos Savant knew she was right, took the criticism well, and gave another explanation of why the contestant should switch. But apparently this was still not good enough, because even more mathematicians wrote, saying she was mistaken. Not one to back down, Vos Savant tried a third explanation and asked math classes to try the experiment out and send in their results.

Clearly this is what she should have done from the start, because once people simulated the situation they saw that it worked out in their favor to switch. Readers can now find many java applets online that allow people to go through repeated trials of the choosing game and see that they win about two-thirds of the time if they switch and one-third of the time if they stay with the original choice.[2] This story shows that probability can be counterintuitive, even for mathematicians.

What Vos Savant kept stressing was the fact that the host knew what was behind each door, and so he would never open the door with the car. This fact is what completely changes the problem. Here is one way the solution to this problem can be explained: Originally there are three doors, so each door has a one-third chance of having the car. This also means that together, the two doors that the contestant did not pick have a two-thirds chance of having the car. Since the host knows what is behind each door, he opens a door that has a goat behind it. The original door still has that same one-third chance of having the car but that other two-thirds probability is now transferred to the remaining door, giving it a greater probability of having the car.

This problem is actually a simplified version of what happened on *Let's Make a Deal*, because Monty Hall usually would offer contestants money for their door. There is an article in the *New York Times*[3] that discusses this story and includes commentary from Monty Hall.

The Monty Hall Problem is so famous that it has been featured in movies and television shows. Consider the movie *21*. This is a movie based on a book (*Bringing Down the House*) that is based on a real-life story. The main character, Ben, is a math major at MIT. One of his professors uses the Monty Hall Problem as a test to find students who are good at probability to recruit them for a blackjack team. The scene takes place in a mathematics classroom. The professor poses the problem and asks Ben if he would stick or switch. Without hesitation Ben says he would switch and gives an explanation similar to the one given above.

The Monty Hall Problem was also featured on the television show *Numb3rs* (season 1, episode 13). In this episode, Charlie is giving a lecture on math for non-mathematicians. He has three posters set up to model the problem. After describing it, Charlie calls on a student to pick a door. He then turns over one card to reveal a goat and asks the student if it would be advantageous to switch. She says, no, because with two cards there is a 50/50 chance of getting the car. Charlie asks the class how many people agree and mostly everyone raises their hand. Charlie acknowledges that this is the intuitive answer but says it is incorrect. He then explains the solution.

Prior knowledge needed:

There is nothing sophisticated about the math in the Monty Hall Problem. All students need is a basic understanding of probability.

Classroom use:

These two clips can be used similarly in the classroom. While both clips do a good job of setting up the problem, the one from *Numb3rs* has a nice visual. In *21* the professor has three blackboards that he points at as representing doors, but in *Numb3rs* Charlie actually has the two goats and the car on posters. This saves a teacher the trouble and expense of making his or her own posters.

1. Show either clip, and pause it before the solution is given.
2. Ask the class to think about what they would do in this situation. Give them a few minutes to think about it or discuss it with a partner.
3. Take a class poll to see who would stick and who would switch.
4. Ask one sticker and one switcher to explain why they chose that answer.
5. Show the remainder of the clip.
6. Even after hearing the explanation, there will probably be some people who still don't believe it's true. For those people it will be helpful to run through some trials. This can be done using a java applet found online or by having students use paper as doors and labeling one side with the numbers one through three and writing or drawing two goats and one car on the other side. They can work in groups or pairs and run through the problem. They should keep track of how many times they won from switching and how many times they won by sticking. It is more beneficial to have them actually do the experiment, but it will be quicker to use an applet if there is not much class time.
7. Compile everyone's results and see that around two-thirds of the time, when students switched they won the car, and one-third of the time, when they didn't switch they won the car.

Going through this example is also beneficial for reinforcing or explaining the idea of repeated trials and the difference between theoretical probability and experimental probability. The explanations in these clips show that the theoretical probability of winning when switching is two-thirds. Your students should see that as they do more trials, the actual outcomes come closer to this theoretical probability.

CONNECTION TO COMMON CORE:

Students construct viable arguments when they explain why they chose to stick or switch. They may also critique the reasoning of others if teachers encourage them to explain why another student's argument is correct or incorrect. Students can use modeling if teachers have them set up an experimental version of the Monty Hall Problem to run through the trials. If teachers allow the students to choose how they want to set up their model, they can choose the appropriate tools, be it pen and paper or a computer.

Galton Board

In an episode of *The Simpsons* (season 24, episode 21), Marge wants the family to do something educational, so she takes them to the Springfield science museum. There they enter the Hall of Probability and see a Galton Board. This is a tool that was named after the scientist Sir Francis Galton. The board has evenly spaced pegs with a funnel on top and slots at the bottom for the balls to fall into. A ball is dropped from the top, and it bounces off the pegs to land in one of the slots. The pegs are placed to form a triangular shape. To think about what type of distribution the balls will drop in, it is easiest to start with a board with a small number of rows, such as the one in figure 32.

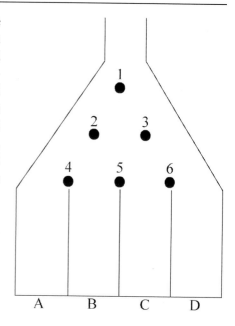

Fig. 32. Galton Board example.

A tree diagram (fig. 33) can be used to think about all of the possible situations. A ball that is dropped from the top at peg 1 can either go left (L1) or right (R1). If it goes left, the ball then goes to peg 2. Again the ball can either go left (L2) or right (R2). If it goes left again, then the ball goes to peg 4. At this point if the ball goes left (L4), then it fall into slot A, and if it goes right (R4), then it falls into slot B. The remaining possibilities are shown in the tree diagram. Assuming that the ball has an equal probability of going left or right at each peg results in the theoretical distribution shown in figure 34.

If a fourth row is added to the board then the distribution is as shown in figure 35.

This turns out to be the binomial distribution. In fact, this is what the Simpsons see when the balls are released on the board.

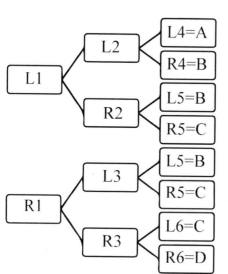

Fig. 33. All the possible choices for a ball to fall in the Galton Board example.

There is a Galton Board on display at the National Museum of Mathematics in New York City (as of August 2014). This board has an added feature that allows visitors to change the probability that balls will fall to either the left or right by moving a lever.

PRIOR KNOWLEDGE NEEDED:

Students should know how to draw tree diagrams and what the binomial distribution is.

CLASSROOM USE:

1. Explain to students what a Galton Board is.
2. Ask students to use a board with three rows to draw the tree diagram showing all possible outcomes, along with what the distribution would look like.
3. Show students this Web site,[4] which shows a demonstration of the Galton Board. Ask students what the probability distribution for this board is.
4. Show students this clip from *The Simpsons*.

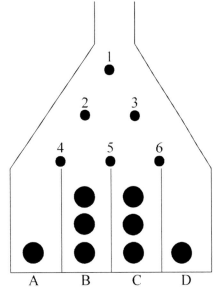

Fig. 34. Theoretical distribution of a Galton Board with three rows.

CONNECTION TO COMMON CORE:

In this activity, students construct viable arguments as they run through experiments and recognize the binomial distribution from the patterns they see.

Winning the Lottery

In the same episode of *The Simpsons* (season 24, episode 21) as

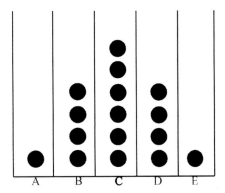

Fig. 35. Theoretical distribution of a Galton Board with four rows.

the previous example, the family watches a video featuring Blaise Pacal, an early pioneer of probability theory. He says that someone is more likely to be run over by a car, hit by lightening, or murdered by an acquaintance than to win the lottery, and that anyone who understands probability would never play the lottery. Of course, the next scene shows Homer having bought a lottery ticket. He echoes the lottery's catchphrase, saying, "You can't win if you don't play."

With such low odds it is a wonder that people play the lottery at all. One possible reason for this is that people in general do not understand really small probabilities, because they can't differentiate between numbers with many zeroes.[5] Additionally, people love the idea of a rescue fantasy, thinking that they will magically get saved from their debt.[6]

Calculating the odds of winning the lottery can be a fun activity for students. In New York the lottery balls have numbers 1 through 59 on them, and each player selects six numbers. Combinations can be used to determine how many possible number choices exist for the New York lottery. There are 59 total numbers to choose from, and the player selects six, meaning there are $\binom{59}{6} = 45,057,474$ possible lottery tickets. In order to win the first prize, all six numbers have to match. This gives a probability of $\frac{\binom{6}{6}\binom{53}{0}}{\binom{59}{6}} = 2.22 \cdot 10^{-8}$. In order to win the second prize, a player must match five of the numbers plus the bonus number. The bonus number is the seventh ball chosen and it is used only to determine a second-place winner. This gives a probability of $\frac{\binom{6}{5}\binom{53}{1}}{\binom{59}{6}} \cdot \frac{1}{53} = 1.33 \cdot 10^{-7}$. In order to win the third prize, a player must match five of the numbers. This gives a probability of $\frac{\binom{6}{5}\binom{53}{1}}{\binom{59}{6}} = 7.06 \cdot 10^{-6}$. In order to win the fourth prize, a player must match four of the numbers. This gives a probability of $\frac{\binom{6}{4}\binom{53}{2}}{\binom{59}{6}} = 4.59 \cdot 10^{-4}$. In order to win the fifth prize, a player must match three of the numbers. This gives a probability of $\frac{\binom{6}{3}\binom{53}{3}}{\binom{59}{6}} = .0104$.

Now that students know the odds of winning the jackpot in the New York State lottery are roughly 1 in 45 million, they can compare this to the odds of other unlikely events. The odds of being hit by lightening is 1 in a million.[7] Other events that are unlikely, but more likely than winning the jackpot, include becoming president of the United States (1 in 10 million) and being attacked by a shark (1 in 11.5 million).[8]

Prior knowledge needed:

For this activity students should know how to calculate combinations and probability.

Classroom use:

1. Show this clip to students.
2. Ask students to pick an event that they think is unlikely and look up its

odds. This can be assigned as homework the night before, or students can be given a list of events and their probabilities to choose from.

3. Have students calculate the odds of winning the lottery. The New York lottery can be used as shown above, or students can calculate the odds in the state or country they live in.

4. Hold a class discussion for students to share how they got their solutions and how the odds of winning the lottery compare to the odds of the other events.

CONNECTION TO COMMON CORE:

Students model with mathematics when they apply their probability knowledge to a real-world problem.

Bernoulli and Binomial

In an episode of *Community* (season 1, episode 7), Jeff is shown in his math class. The professor talks about the Bernoulli distribution. The typical example used to represent a Bernoulli trial is flipping a coin. When flipping a coin there are two possible outcomes, heads or tails. If we want to count the number of heads, then landing on heads will be considered a success. The probability of success for each coin flip is always $p = .5$ for a fair coin. For a weighted coin the probability will be different from .5, but it will still be a fixed number each flip. The probability of a failure (in this case a tails) will be $1 - p = 1 - .5 = .5$, since there are only two possible outcomes and we know the total sum of all possible probabilities is always 1. We also know that each coin toss is independent, because the outcome of one toss will not affect the outcome of other tosses. The probability of independent events is just the product of the probabilities of each event.

A sequence of independent Bernoulli trials is a binomial experiment. To figure out the number of arrangements of the possible outcomes of the trials, we can use combinations. For example, to find the probability of an event such as getting two heads and three tails on five tosses of a coin, there are five total trials, and two of those should be successes. This corresponds to $_5C_2 = 10$ possible arrangements. Thus, the probability of getting two heads and three tails on five tosses of a coin will be the product of the number of arrangements, the number of successes, and the number of failures, or $10(.5)^2(.5)^3$.

PRIOR KNOWLEDGE NEEDED:

Students should know probability rules, such as that the total sum of all possible probabilities is 1 and the probability of independent events occurring is the product of the probability of each event. Students also need to know how to do combinations.

CLASSROOM USE:

1. Show students this clip.
2. Go over the definition and an example for a Bernoulli trial.
3. Put students in groups and have each group pick a human trait that has two possible measures. They can pick a trait such as male or female, but they can also choose something, such as hair color, that appears to have more than two choices; they just need to pick one color to focus on. For example, they can choose blonde or non-blonde. Also ask that they assign a probability to each choice. It does not have to be accurate, but they will need a value to work with.
4. Next, have students collect data from the class to see how many students fall into each category.
5. Now have each group calculate the probability of the results they saw. For example, suppose they chose to measure gender and assigned a 50-percent chance of being male. If there are 25 students in the class and 11 of them are male, then the probability of this happening is $_{25}C_{11}(.5)^{11}(.5)^{14} = .13$.
6. Next, have students calculate the full distribution by figuring all of the possible outcomes. Since they are working in groups, students can split up the problems and each work on some. In this example they would have to figure out the probability of zero males, one male, two males, and so on.
7. Finally, ask students to put together their results and have each group share their results with the class. They can discuss properties such as what the shape of the distribution will be and what event is the most likely to occur.

CONNECTION TO COMMON CORE:

In this activity, students model with mathematics when they apply probability to a real-world problem. Students also attend to precision when they share their results with the class.

Dice Probability

In an episode of *The Wire* (season 4, episode 7), Prez talks to some of his students on their lunch break as they are playing poker. He talks about probability, and one student asks about the odds of winning with dice. Later Prez uses dice in class to teach his students probability. His students say there are more ways to roll a 7 than a 4. The following activity will also show students a comparison between experimental and theoretical probability.

Prior knowledge needed:

This activity requires students to know what probability is and how to calculate it. To find the theoretical probability, students should also know the multiplication rule.

Classroom use:

1. Ask students what the possible outcomes are when rolling two dice and summing the values. Keep discussing until they come up with the values 2 through 12. Also ask if they think any of these outcomes are more likely to occur.
2. Have students work in pairs and give each pair two dice. Have the students roll the dice ten times and record how many of each sum they get.
3. Make a big chart on the board and ask each group to aggregate their results together into this one chart.
4. Ask students to calculate the observed probability for each sum. Also have students calculate the theoretical probability of getting each sum and see how closely their results matched the theoretical probability.
5. Show the clip to reinforce the idea of some sums coming up more often than others.

Connection to Common Core:

In this activity, students model with mathematics as they perform the experiment.

Randomness

Human beings generally have a poor sense of what the word "random" means. Here is an experiment to try with students. For homework ask that they flip a coin 100 times and write down whether they get heads or tails on each toss. The teacher should be able to tell who actually did the experiment and who made up answers. Those who made up answers will mostly alternate between heads and tails, with some patterns of three in a row. Maybe there will be four or five in a row. Those who actually did the coin tosses will have much longer patterns of heads or tails in a row. Most people think of ran-

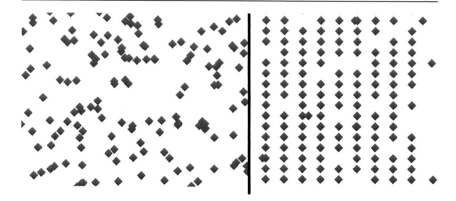

Fig. 36. Random dots versus dots perceived as random.

domness as being spread out evenly, when in fact, randomness has no pattern. We look for patterns in everything, even randomness. In figure 36, the dots on the left are random while the dots on the right are not. The dots on the right are fairly evenly spread out, but the dots on the left have clusters with uneven gaps.

A fallacy called the "Texas Sharpshooter Fallacy" shows one way people are bad at perceiving randomness. To demonstrate this fallacy, imagine a sharpshooter shoots at the side of a barn. Afterwards, he finds a spot on the barn where there is a cluster of bullets and draws a bull's-eye to make it look like he is a good shooter. People who fall for this fallacy gather evidence after the fact and use it to create a hypothesis that the data might suggest. This is opposed to the more accurate scientific method which is to make a hypothesis and then collect data to support or oppose it. One of the most famous examples is the list of coincidences there are between the murders of Abraham Lincoln and John F. Kennedy. Both were presidents, both were shot in the head on a Friday, both of their assassins had three names, and on it goes. The problem is that nobody looks at what elements these murders did not have in common. For example, pick any two people or events, and there are sure to be a list of commonalities. But there is also going to be a longer list of things they do not have in common. See Chapter Two for an example of this fallacy using numerology.

In an episode of *Numb3rs* (season 3, episode 5), Charlie explains this concept of randomness. He has two pictures similar to the dots shown earlier and asks his students which picture represents raindrops falling on a sidewalk. The majority of the class thinks it is the evenly spaced picture but Charlie says this is not the case; our brains misperceive evenness as random.

Another example occurs in an episode of *Psych* (season 8, episode 4). Sean and Gus are investigating a murder case, and they find lottery tickets in the victims' room. When they go to investigate at the store where the tickets were purchased, Gus asks the clerk to check if the tickets are winners. Gus comments that since the purchaser was murdered, math says he is due some good luck. This is a confusing point about probability that a lot of people have trouble with; when events are independent, the outcome of one does not affect the outcome of another. This means that the victim's having had one instance of (very) bad luck by being murdered doesn't mean that his lottery ticket will win to balance that out. This type of misconception is exploited in gambling. A simple example is the Big Six Wheel found in casinos; in this game the dealer spins a giant wheel, and people can bet on various numbers or symbols. If one spin lands on a 5, most people will avoid that 5 for the next game, even though the wheel is just as likely to stop at the 5 as it was in the first spin. A more popular example is slot machines. Many gamblers believe in myths about slot machines, such as the idea that a machine is having a hot streak if the player is winning and the machine will keep on winning. Another myth is that a machine that hasn't been winning is due some good luck and will win soon. These ideas are debunked by the fact that current slot machines use random-number generators that do not keep track of past performance.[9]

PRIOR KNOWLEDGE NEEDED:

No prior knowledge is needed.

CLASSROOM USE:

1. Give students a list of songs and ask them to pretend these songs are the playlist for an mp3 player. Make sure to include songs by the same artist.
2. Have students list an order for a randomly shuffled song list. What will probably happen is that most people will order the songs so that there aren't two songs by the same artist back to back.
3. Ask one or more students to explain why they ordered their list the way they did.
4. Show the *Numb3rs* clip for students to see why most of their song orders probably would not have been produced by a random system. This can also be demonstrated with an actual mp3 player or using the random-number generator in Excel.
5. The *Psych* clip can also be used as an extension when discussing random-number generators and casino games.

CONNECTION TO COMMON CORE:

In this activity, students are constructing viable arguments when they explain why they put the songs in the order they did.

The Birthday Problem

The Birthday Problem is a famous probability problem because its result is so unexpected. The Birthday Problem asks: What is the probability that there are at least two people in a group who share the same birthday, not including leap day? Basic probability can be used to calculate the odds of any group containing two people with the same birthday. It turns out that in a group of 23 people there is a roughly 50-percent chance of two people having the same birthday. One reason this number seems so low to most people is that they think of the question as this: What is the probability that somebody in the group shares *my* birthday? That is an entirely different question, since the date to match is fixed in that case. To match a given birthday, a group of 253 is needed to have a 50-percent chance of a match.

A similar problem can be seen in the movie *Identity*. In *Identity* there are ten strangers who get stranded at a motel during a storm. At one point it is discovered that they all share the same birthday of May 10. One of the characters guesses that the odds of this happening are 10 trillion to one. Actually, the odds are 1 in almost 115 sextillion. To calculate this, we know the probability of the first person having any birthday is 1. The probability that the second person matches that birthday is 1 in 365. Next find the probability that the third person matches that birthday, which is also 1 in 365, and keep going like this for each person in the group. Finally, multiply each probability to calculate the final probability of $\frac{1}{(365)^9}$.

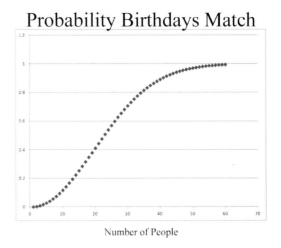

Probability Birthdays Match

Number of People

Fig. 37. Number of people versus the probability that birthdays match.

PRIOR KNOWLEDGE NEEDED:

Students should know certain probability facts including the multiplication rule and the fact that the probability of an event's not occurring is one minus the probability that it will occur.

CLASSROOM USE:

1. Show the movie clip to introduce the idea of finding the probability that people share the same birthday.
2. Ask students how likely they think it is that two people in the class will have the same birthday.
3. Have students go around the room to record everyone's name and birthday. Depending on class size, students might also give a relative's birthday to have a larger sample. If this activity is used on the first day of class, it can also serve as a way for students to get to know their classmates.
4. See if there are any matches.
5. Depending on when this activity is done and how much probability background students have, the answer can be given at this point or students can try to derive the formula. In either case it is nice to show them the graph so they have a visual of the probability. The graph shows the probability of a birthday match steadily rising with group size. It hits the 50-percent mark at about 23 and hits the 90-percent mark at about 41.

If a teacher chooses to have students calculate the formula, here are sample questions to give them:

1. What is the probability, in a group of two, that the two people have the same birthday?

    Start with just two people, call them Ann and Bob. Ann could have any one of 365 birthdays (ignoring leap day) and Bob could have any of 365 birthdays as well. Therefore, using the multiplication rule, there are 365 * 365 = 133,225 different possible birthdays the pair could have. There are 365 cases where Ann and Bob share a birthday because they could share a birthday, one for each day of the year. This gives a probability of $\frac{365}{133225}$ = .0027.

2. What is the probability in a group of three that at least two of them will have the same birthday?

    Once Cal joins the group, we have 365 * 365 * 365 = 365^3 = 48,627,125 possible birthday outcomes. Out of the over 48 million possibilities, there are 365 * 364 * 363 = 48,228,180 cases where all three people have different birthdays. This is because Ann can have any day of the year as her birthday;

Bob can have a birthday on any of the remaining 364 days; and Cal will have his birthday on one of the remaining 363 days. To get the probability that the birthdays are not all different, meaning at least two of them share a birthday, we can do 1 minus the probability that the birthdays are all different, which becomes $1 - \frac{48,228,180}{48,627,125} = .0082$.

3. Try to find the probability for a group of four people and then get a general formula for n people (see Appendix B).
4. (Extra Credit) Come up with a formula that includes the leap day (see Appendix B).

CONNECTION TO COMMON CORE:

Students who come up with the formula on their own make use of repeated reasoning when they start with the solution for two, three, and four people and use that to find a general formula for *n* people.

The Multiplication Rule

In *The Da Vinci Code*, one of the main characters has to open a cryptex. The term *cryptex* was invented by Dan Brown when he wrote *The Da Vinci Code*. It describes a locked vessel. It is so named because the science of cryptology is used to open the vessel, which contains a codex, or ancient book.[10] To unlock it there are five wheels, each with the letters of the alphabet. This is similar to a bike lock but with letters instead of numbers. The letters must be in the right position in order to open the cryptex. If someone attempts to open it with the letters in the wrong position, ink is released that will ruin the paper contained inside the cryptex. In the movie they calculate how many letter arrangements are possible using the multiplication rule.

PRIOR KNOWLEDGE NEEDED:

Students should already know the multiplication rule. This exercise can serve as an example of using the rule or as a review of it.

CLASSROOM USE:

1. Show *The Da Vinci Code* clip in which they calculate how many cryptex arrangements exist.
2. Ask students to explain how they got the answer in the movie. When they do the calculation, students will notice that the answer given in the movie was rounded.

CONNECTION TO COMMON CORE:

This activity helps students model with mathematics. They see how the multiplication rule can be applied in a real-life situation.

What Are the Odds? Part 1

In an episode of *Monk* (season 6, episode 13), there are two crime victims with the same first and last name. While at the crime scene for one victim named Julie Teeger, the police get a call saying there is another victim named Julie Teeger. This obviously worries Monk's assistant, because her daughter's name is Julie Teeger. Luckily neither of the victims turns out to be her daughter. As they are at the second crime scene, everyone marvels at how unlikely this is, but another detective says that these coincidences happen all the time. He mentions taking a course in statistics and tries to explain but then admits to dropping the class because he didn't understand it.

The Social Security Administration lists the top ten names for the 20,285,168 female babies born in the United States from 2000 to 2009 as: Emily (223,448 occurrences), Madison (192,976 occurrences), Emma (181,055 occurrences), Olivia (155,848 occurrences), Hannah (155,525 occurrences), Abigail (150,746 occurrences), Isabella (149,310 occurrences), Samantha (134,148 occurrences), Elizabeth (133,166 occurrences), and Ashley (132,934 occurrences).[11] Julie wasn't one of the top 200 names in this decade, but in the previous decade (1990–1999) Julie was the 125th most popular name, with 25,422 occurrences. There is also a Web site that uses the United States Census Bureau database to show how many people have a certain first and last name.[12] When "Julie Teeger" is entered, the results show 547,098 people named Julie, 117 people with the last name Teeger, and 1 or fewer with both names. Using these sites, the likelihood of an American in a certain age range having a specific name can be determined.

PRIOR KNOWLEDGE NEEDED:

Students need to know how to calculate the probability of two events occurring and, if doing the advanced version of this activity, students need to know how to do hypothesis testing.

CLASSROOM USE:

1. Show students the full clip.
2. Provide students with the name statistics mentioned earlier and ask them

to calculate the probability of two females born between 1990 and 1999 both being named Julie.

3. Ask students to list five female friends around their age. Make a tally on the board of how many occurrences there are of each name. Since their friends most likely come from the same pool (students in their school), be careful not to count the same person twice. Count how many total names there are, then take names from the top ten and see if the probabilities match the statistics mentioned earlier. For example, if Emma is a name on the class list and it occurred once on a list of 125 names, then it came up .8 percent of the time. According to the statistics, Emma should occur with .89 percent probability (181,055 out of 20,285,168). In an advanced-placement statistics class, students can take this a step further and use hypothesis testing to see if their sample had the probability that was expected.

CONNECTION TO COMMON CORE:

In this activity, students are modeling with mathematics by applying mathematics to an everyday problem.

What Are the Odds? Part 2

In the television series *Suits*, Mike has a photographic memory and can calculate quickly in his head. In one episode (season 2, episode 15), Mike is talking to a fellow lawyer, Katrina, about the statistics needed for a gender-discrimination case. In a food service company there are 1.7 percent female executives. Mike says they need the probability of that ratio being chance across 22 divisions and 45 states, and they both say "1 in 8.3 billion" at the same time. Mike asked how she knew that, and Katrina says that she checked with a statistician. Mike says that he is wrong because he didn't adjust for outliers, which takes it to 1 in 6.4 billion. Katrina asks how Mike knew that and he said he did it in his head because that's what he does.

This probability would be difficult to calculate without additional information, but this clip can be used an introduction to the idea of outliers.

PRIOR KNOWLEDGE NEEDED:

No prior knowledge is needed for this activity.

CLASSROOM USE:

1. Show the clip to students.

2. Based on the clip and their prior knowledge (if they have any), ask students to come up with a definition of an outlier.
3. Find examples of data sets that have outliers and ask students to identify them.
4. For a possible connection with an English teacher, have students read *Outliers* by Malcolm Gladwell[13] at the same time they learn about outliers in a statistics class. This book is about people who can be considered outliers of the general population.

CONNECTION TO COMMON CORE:

In this activity students attend to precision as they come up with a definition for the term *outlier*.

Benford's Law

In 1881 an astronomer named Simon Newcomb was looking through logarithm tables and discovered that the beginning pages were more worn than the later pages. Newcomb published his results and proposed that the probability of n being the first digit of a number is $\log(n + 1) - \log(n)$. For

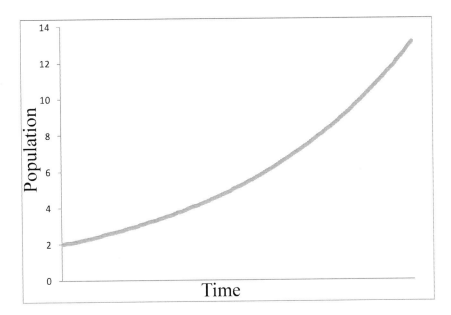

Fig. 38. Population growth over time.

example, plugging 1 into this equation yields log(1 + 1) - log(1) = .301. This means that 1 will be the leading digit about 30 percent of the time. In contrast, since log(8 + 1)-log(8) = .051, 8 will be the leading digit only about 5 percent of the time. In 1938 this idea was rediscovered by a physicist at General Electric named Frank Benford. He tested the formula on data from sources such as surface areas of rivers and numbers contained in *Reader's Digest*.

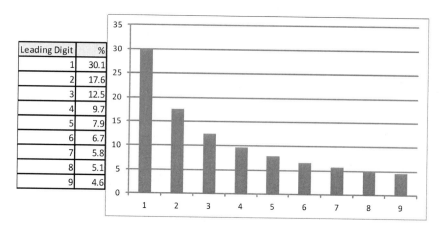

Leading Digit	%
1	30.1
2	17.6
3	12.5
4	9.7
5	7.9
6	6.7
7	5.8
8	5.1
9	4.6

Fig. 39. Frequency with which each digit appears as a leading digit.

Most naturally occurring sets of data will follow this law. To see why this might be true, think about population growth. The formula for population growth is starting population multiplied by e^{rt}, where r = rate of growth and t = time. Figure 38 shows an example in which the starting population is 2 and growth rate is .2.

The graph shows that numbers that follow an exponential growth pattern similar to this will spend more time at the lower numbers and then increase quickly to get to the higher numbers. This means that lower digits are more likely to occur than the higher digits. The leading-digit distribution is shown in figure 39.

Benford's law has been used by the IRS to uncover fraud in accounting numbers, since most people assume that each digit is equally likely to appear. There is a Web site that has examples testing to see if some databases, such as most common iPhone passcodes, follow the law.[14]

In an episode of *Numb3rs* (season 2, episode 15), Charlie and Larry use Benford's Law when looking at a set of robberies. They use the law to help predict where the next robbery will take place. Charlie and Larry discuss the phenomenon noticed by Newcomb, that the beginning pages of logarithm tables are used the most. They then hypothesize that a thief will rob a place he knows.

PRIOR KNOWLEDGE NEEDED:

No prior knowledge is needed.

CLASSROOM USE:

1. Bring in a phone book and ask each student to open it to a random page, choose a person, write down the first digit of their address, and then pass the book to the next person. As the book is going around ask them to think about how the numbers will be distributed and have some of the students explain their reasoning.
2. Compile the numbers and calculate the percentage of occurrence for each digit. The teacher can quickly make a bar chart in Excel and see if it matches Benford's Law.
3. Show the clip to explain the results.

CONNECTION TO COMMON CORE:

When students explain their reasoning, they are constructing viable arguments.

Correlation

In *The Mindy Project* (season 2, episode 14), we learn that Danny's dad abandoned him as a child. Mindy claims that that has left him emotionally closed off and completely immune to tickling. Danny says there is no scientific correlation between being emotionally closed off and being ticklish.

In an episode of *The Big Bang Theory* (season 3, episode 1), Sheldon is speaking to his mother on the phone after returning from a research trip at the North Pole. His mother thinks that the reason he returned home safely is because her church group prayed for his safe return. Sheldon disagrees and says that she is committing the logical fallacy called *post hoc, ergo propter hoc.* This Latin phrase translates to "after this, therefore because of this." The fallacy lies in believing that if a second event occurs after a first event, the first event caused the second event to occur. This is another way of saying that correlation implies causation, and it is faulty logic. Since correlation does not imply causation, Sheldon thinks that his mother is arriving at a faulty conclusion.

It is important for students to understand that correlation does not imply causation. Many times the media generates stories in which two things have a correlation and it seems plausible that one could have caused the other. For example, *Time* magazine printed an article on how getting straight A's in high school leads to better health.[15] They reported that the higher a person's class rank in high school, the more likely they were to say their health was excellent or very good in their sixties. This doesn't seem like an outrageous claim. Maybe the smarter a person is the more likely they are to earn more money and be able to afford better healthcare. The problem is that we have no idea what all the other factors involved are and what is really causing these people to report good health. One way to get this point across is by showing examples of two things that are highly correlated but completely unrelated. This Web site[16] gives examples of bizarre correlations. For example, they show that the correlation between the consumption of mozzarella cheese and the number of civil engineering doctorates awarded is .958648. It should be pretty obvious that eating mozzarella cheese doesn't cause people to get civil engineering degrees and that there are other factors involved.

PRIOR KNOWLEDGE NEEDED:

Students should know what correlation is and how to calculate the correlation coefficient either by hand or using technology such as a calculator or Excel.

CLASSROOM USE:

1. Show students these clips. After *The Big Bang Theory* clip, explain what the Latin phrase means and go through examples such as those above.
2. Ask students to brainstorm two seemingly unconnected events.
3. For homework, have students pick two events from the class discussion, get data over a specified time range, create line graphs, and calculate the correlation coefficient. The next day students can share their results.

CONNECTION TO COMMON CORE:

In this activity, students model with mathematics when they obtain data and create graphs for their chosen events.

How Not to Calculate Percentages

There are also examples in movies and television shows of mathematical ignorance and error. The following examples show characters making mistakes when they calculate a percentage, or their inability to do so.

In an episode of *Modern Family* (season 4, episode 2), Phil talks about a book he wrote called *Phil's-osophy Book*. One part of the book says success is 1 percent inspiration, 98 percent perspiration, and 2 percent attention to detail.

In *Charlie and the Chocolate Factory*, one of Charlie's teachers has his students calculate percentages based on opening chocolate bars to look for a golden ticket. He says to suppose there are 1,000 Wonka Bars in the world and they each opened a certain percentage of them. He then asks around the room to find how many Wonka Bars the students opened. Madeline opened 100 and there are 10 hundreds in 1,000, so she opened 10 percent. Peter opened 150. The teacher notes that this is one and a half times what Madeline opened, which means Peter opened 15 percent of the bars. Charlie only opened two bars. The teacher is unable to compute the percentage for 2, so he pretends Charlie opened 200.

In another scene Willy Wonka is in the invention room leading a tour for the golden-ticket winners and their parents. He says that invention is 93 percent perspiration, 6 percent electricity, 4 percent evaporation, and 2 percent butterscotch filling. One of the mothers says that is 105 percent.

PRIOR KNOWLEDGE NEEDED:

Students need to know that percentages range from 0 to 100 and how to calculate a percentage.

CLASSROOM USE:

Show one or more of these clips to students. Depending on the clip(s) shown, either ask them to figure out the mistake made or find the correct solution that Charlie's teacher was unable to calculate.

CONNECTION TO COMMON CORE:

In this activity, students critique the reasoning of others when they have to follow the reasoning that these characters made and then make corrections.

Standard Deviation

In an episode of *Everybody Loves Raymond* (season 1, episode 4), Robert gives Ray and Deborah an IQ test. Ray scores 100, which is average, and Deborah scores 115, which is one standard deviation higher. When Robert tells them their scores, Ray asks what it means to be a standard deviation away, and Robert says it means that Deborah is in a higher class of brains.

PRIOR KNOWLEDGE NEEDED:

For this activity students should know how to calculate the mean of a data set.

CLASSROOM USE:

1. Have students measure the length of their left thumbnail and record it on a chart.
2. Ask students to calculate the mean of these measurements.
3. Next tell students they should come up with a measurement for how far away each piece of data is from the mean. Take suggestions from the class or tell them that the most obvious approach is to find the mean of the distances each one is from the mean. Then ask them to calculate this.
4. Once students see that this comes out to be zero, ask them why this happened. Eventually they should realize that they should only care about the distance from the mean and not whether it is smaller or larger than the mean. There are two ways to get around this. One is to take the absolute value of each deviation and the other is to square each deviation. Finding the mean of the absolute value of each deviation is called the mean deviation. However, this measure is rarely used. Finding the mean of the squares of each deviation and then taking the square root of this value gives what is called the standard deviation. There has been some debate on which measure is better, but for various reasons, such as the fact that computations with absolute values are difficult to manipulate, the standard deviation is what is now commonly used.[17]
5. Have students calculate the standard deviation of left thumbnails for the class.
6. Give follow-up questions such as these (see Appendix B):
   a. What can be concluded if the standard deviation for the left thumbnail of the entire class is zero?
   b. A new student joins the class and her left thumbnail length is equal to the average left thumbnail length for the class. What impact will this addition have to the standard deviation and mean for the class?
   c. If everyone cut one hundredth of an inch off of their left thumbnail, what would happen to the standard deviation and mean for the class?
   d. If everyone's left thumbnail length doubled, what would happen to the standard deviation and mean for the class?
7. Show this clip to students.
8. Ask students to explain what it means for Deborah to be one standard deviation higher than Ray.

CONNECTION TO COMMON CORE:

In this activity, students reason abstractly and quantitatively when they figure out the formula for standard deviation, calculate the standard deviation for fingernail length, and answer additional questions that test their understanding of this concept.

The Normal Distribution

In an episode of *Dilbert* (season 2, episode 12), some of the employees invent a person named Todd who they say works at the company so that they can claim an empty cubicle to store obsolete computer equipment. The evil head of human resources wants to punish these employees in the form of a new policy, so he declares that they must have a normal distribution of performance reviews. Since Todd took the top spot, Wally was moved down to the lowest ranking.

PRIOR KNOWLEDGE NEEDED:

In this activity, students need to know how to draw a histogram.

CLASSROOM USE:

1. Draw the normal curve on the board and ask students to name some variables that will have a normal distribution. They may think of the height of adult females in the United States or grades on a test.
2. One that they may not come up with is popcorn popping in a microwave. To demonstrate this, there needs be access to a microwave. Alternatively, students can listen to a recording of popcorn popping. Have students make a chart recording the time over a two-minute interval, split into groups of five seconds, along with the number of kernels popping in that interval. One student can be assigned to be the timer to let everyone know when each five seconds is over.
3. Have students draw a histogram to represent their results and notice that it has the same shape as the normal curve.
4. Show this clip to students.
5. Ask students to explain how the example given in the clip works.

CONNECTION TO COMMON CORE:

Students model with mathematics when they apply it to this real-world problem. Students also make sense of the problem when they first think about what variables fit a normal curve and then persevere in solving it when they show how popcorn popping follows a normal curve.

Game Shows

Just as the Monty Hall Problem came from a game show, other game shows can be examined for probability and statistics examples.

Wheel of Fortune

Solving puzzles in *Wheel of Fortune* depends heavily on letter choices. The writers of the *Oxford English Dictionary* performed an analysis to see how frequently different letters appeared in the main entries of their 2004 edition.[18] The letter distribution is shown in figure 40.

On a side note, something interesting to have students think about is that the distribution of letter frequencies changes for different languages. For example, in Turkish the letter y comes up with a frequency of 3.336 percent[19] versus the 1.78 percent seen in English.

In 1988 the final bonus round in *Wheel of Fortune* was changed. Originally players got to choose five consonants and one vowel. Now, players are given the letters R, S, T, L, N, and E. The players then choose three more con-

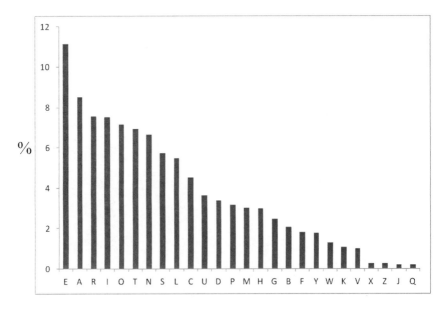

Fig. 40. Frequency of letters in the *Oxford English Dictionary*.

sonants and one more vowel. The show producers want some people to win the bonus round so that the audience joins in the excitement and doesn't feel like the game is impossible. On the other hand, they don't want too many people to win, because then they are giving away a lot of money. It has been found that 37.76 percent of contestants solve the bonus-round puzzle.[20]

Was this change of giving contestants the more popular letters beneficial to the player? From figure 40 one can see that players are given the top vowel and the top five consonants. Whoever makes the puzzles for wheel of fortune has to keep in mind that some puzzles become too easy once R, S, T, L, N, and E are filled in. Try solving this one with the clue "movie": slee_less _n se_ ttle. Before the change in 1988, most contestants chose those letters anyway, so perhaps the producers were already mindful of picking phrases that did not have an overabundance of the popular letters. In fact, one analysis shows that from 2007 to January 2014 there is a large difference in the letter distribution of the main game versus the letter distribution in the bonus round. The letter E went from being in the main game 11.32 percent of the time to being in the bonus round only 7.87 percent of the time.[21] The next most frequently chosen letters are C, M, D, and A. The producers are also aware of this, and these letters are underrepresented in the bonus-round puzzles as well.

PRIOR KNOWLEDGE NEEDED:

Students should know how to calculate basic probabilities. For the second activity, students also need to know how to do hypothesis testing.

CLASSROOM USE:

Various activities are presented for different skill levels.

Activity #1

1. The wheel in *Wheel of Fortune* has twenty-four spaces. However, in one of the rounds one of the spaces is split into three parts, with a "bankrupt" on the two ends and "$1,000,000" in the middle. This makes calculating the probability of landing on a "bankrupt" space a little more challenging than if all spaces were the same size. Ask students to calculate the probability of landing on "bankrupt" on a single spin. (See Appendix B.)
2. For homework have students watch an episode of *Wheel of Fortune* and keep track of how many total spins there were in the game and how many of them landed on "bankrupt." Did this match their calculated probability?

CONNECTION TO COMMON CORE:

In this activity, students are modeling with mathematics.

Activity #2

1. Ask students to take the first paragraph of their favorite book and tally how many times each letter is used. This activity can also be used as an introduction to or practice with Excel.
2. Combine everyone's results to get a larger data set. Compare the results with the letter distribution in the *Oxford English Dictionary*. Run a Chi-Square Goodness of Fit test to see if the results match what was expected. (See Appendix B.)
3. As an additional component of or a variation on this activity, students can also use bonus-round answers as their data set. A collection of *Wheel of Fortune* answers starting in 2003 is available online.[22] Before going through the letter tallies, have students hypothesize whether the results will match or not.
4. As a follow-up, have students think about how letter frequencies affect the way a keyboard is set up. Keyboards have the same design as typewriters. Typewriters initially had their letters arranged in alphabetical order, but the keys jammed because people would type too fast. To solve this problem it was decided that the best tactic would be to slow down the typist. The QWERTY keyboard (look at the top row of letters to see why it is called that) is what we use today, and the letters that get used frequently are spaced out so that most words you have to type make your fingers cover a lot of distance on the keyboard.

Connection to Common Core:

Students have to use appropriate tools to do this activity. They can use either a calculator or Excel. Students also model and construct viable arguments during this activity.

Activity #3

Is there a new group of letters that contestants always choose in the bonus round? Based on the letter frequency given above, the letters C, D, P, and A would be the most logical choices. Have students watch *Wheel of Fortune* for a week and calculate the percentages that these letters are chosen in the bonus round. One analysis suggests choosing the letters P, H, O, and G.[23]

Jeopardy!

On February 14 through 16 in 2011, Watson, a computer designed by IBM, competed on *Jeopardy!* against two human contestants and won. The algorithm Watson used to pick a wager for daily doubles is very involved and complicated, but students can try to come up with a simplified version.

PRIOR KNOWLEDGE NEEDED:

Students need to understand what regression is and how to use Excel to get a regression equation.

CLASSROOM USE:

This could be a long-term project for a statistics unit.

1. Show a clip of Watson wagering on a daily double.
2. Have students come up with a list of factors to consider when deciding how much to wager on a daily double. These can include how much is left on the board, how much money each player has, the contestant's level of confidence in the category, or how much the clue was worth, for example.
3. Have students collect data using the factors that they consider important and put the data into Excel. A lot of information can be found online.[24] Every game since 1985 is listed, with information such as where on the board the daily double was, how much the wager was for, who landed on the daily double, the scores after each question, when the daily double was revealed, and overall daily double statistics for each season.
4. Next, have students run a regression analysis on the data to come up with a possible equation that would predict how much a contestant should wager on the daily double.
5. Finally, have students test the formula out on a *Jeopardy!* show.

CONNECTION TO COMMON CORE:

Students have to make sense of the problem when they think about what factors to consider for the daily double wager. They are modeling with mathematics and using appropriate tools when answering this question.

The Price Is Right

Once a contestant wins the first round in *The Price Is Right*, he or she gets to play a pricing game. One of the pricing games is called "Pick-a-Number." In this game there is a prize with most of the numbers in the price shown except for one missing digit. The contestant has to choose the correct digit from among three choices.

The top three winners of the pricing games get a chance to spin the wheel. The numbers on the wheel are all multiples of 5 and range from 5 to 100. Each contestant gets two spins to get as close to 100 as possible, but can stop after one spin. If the spin or spins reach 100 the contestant gets $1,000 and a bonus spin. If the bonus spin lands on 100 the contestant gets $10,000 or if it lands on the 5 or 15, the numbers above and below the 100, the contestant gets $5000. The order for the numbers on the wheel is as follows: 100, 5, 90, 25, 70, 45, 10, 65, 30, 85, 50, 95, 55, 75, 40, 20, 60, 35, 80, and 15. The "Pick-a-Number" game and the wheel spins lend themselves to activities in probability.

Prior knowledge needed:

Students need to know how to calculate probabilities, particularly the probabilities of the union and intersection of events.

Classroom use:

1. Show a clip of a contestant playing "Pick-a-Number." Ask students to calculate the probability of guessing the correct number. (See Appendix B.)
2. Show a clip of a contestant spinning the wheel and landing on 100. Ask students to calculate this event's probability. (See Appendix B.)
3. Show a clip of a contestant spinning the wheel twice and getting a sum of 100. Ask students to calculate the probability of this happening. Then have them calculate the probability of a contestant getting 100 on either one or two spins. Finally, have the students calculate the probability of a contestant getting 100 in one or two spins and then landing on 100 during the bonus spin. (See Appendix B.)

Connection to Common Core:

Students reason abstractly when they think about the possibilities for getting 100 over two different turns.

Deal or No Deal

There has been some debate—among mathematicians at least—on what formula is used to calculate the banker's offer in *Deal or No Deal*. While the official formula has not been released or decoded, students can use the idea of expected value to approximate a formula, or at least use it to make an informed decision about whether to accept the offer or not. These are the dollar values at the start of the game:

$0.01	$1,000
$1	$5,000
$5	$10,000
$10	$25,000
$25	$50,000
$50	$75,000
$75	$100,000
$100	$200,000
$200	$300,000
$300	$400,000
$400	$500,000
$500	$750,000
$750	$1,000,000

PRIOR KNOWLEDGE NEEDED:

Students should know how to calculate an expected value, or this activity can be used to teach them how to calculate expected values. For the advanced activity, students need to know how to perform a regression.

CLASSROOM USE:

Activity #1

1. Ask students to calculate the expected value at the start of a game (see Appendix B).
2. Pick a televised game to use as an example and show the first round; or to save time, just show what the contestant is left with at the end of the first round and have students calculate the expected value at that point. Show what the banker's offer is and see how that compares to the expected value. Ask students if they would choose deal or no deal and to explain why. (See Appendix B.)
3. Repeat this process for additional rounds.
4. A few other questions for students to think about (see Appendix B):
   • What is the probability that a contestant chooses the million-dollar case?
   • If the contestant makes it all the way to the end, with only the original chosen case and a final case remaining, the contestant has the choice of keeping the original case or switching to the remaining case. Should the contestant switch? How does this compare to the Monty Hall Problem?

Connection to Common Core:

In this activity, students reason quantitatively and construct viable arguments when they decide if the banker's offer is fair.

Activity #2

This activity is similar to the one described for *Jeopardy!*

1. Have students think of any factors that could affect the banker's offer. These may include the expected value, the highest value left on the board, and the number of cases left.
2. Collect data for any factors that were considered important.
3. Run a regression analysis to get a formula that predicts what the banker's offer will be.

Connection to Common Core:

Students have to make sense of the problem when they think about what factors to consider for the banker's offer. They are modeling with mathematics and using appropriate tools, such as Excel, by answering this question.

CHAPTER EIGHT

Outside the Classroom

Once students are introduced to the idea of mathematics being embedded into popular culture, the next logical step is for them to look for examples on their own, independent of the classroom. In this way students make the leap from student to independent learner. They develop not only mathematical skills but also psychological skills to learn how to learn on their own. They mature as they realize that not all of education involves school and not all of their learning has to come from a teacher. Suggestions on how to help students make that leap will be discussed in this chapter. Additionally, other ideas for uses outside the classroom will be discussed, such as the sort of exercises that can be done in home schooling, tutoring, and self-study. In all these cases, there is an effort made to bring mathematics from the classroom to the real world in which students live, to make them see that it is important to learn not just for a test or to please the teacher. They need to learn for self-development and to improve their own confidence in handling mathematical problems. In an ideal situation, the students will master the subject and develop such self-confidence that they will feel prepared to teach the skills they have acquired to others.

Showing these clips and having students do activities based on these clips will make students more aware of mathematics outside of the classroom. These are the types of activities that students will talk about with their parents because the motivation of the movie or television show will get them excited and interested in the math. Additionally, the activities give a good way in for parents who aren't good at math. Normally these parents would not be able to understand the math that their child is learning in high school, but at least they can see the connection with the movie or television show and can have a mathematical conversation with their child. For example, students who learned the Monty Hall example in Chapter Seven may be excited to explain

189

the scenario to their parents and ask if they would switch doors or stick with their original door. Parents will probably find this example interesting because they may remember when *Let's Make a Deal* was on television and have fond memories of it. Even if parents are not familiar with the show, they can easily understand the situation and play along without any advanced mathematical knowledge. When the student explains the solution to their parents, he or she reinforces the math they learned. In fact, one of the best ways to learn something is to teach it.[1]

It has been found that the amount of time mothers spend modeling math behavior is related to their child's interest in mathematics.[2] Additionally, parental involvement in school has been found to increase school success.[3] Thus, it is important for parents to show interest in math and participate in math behaviors, such as discussions with their child. Children can become their parents' teachers, but in a way parents can enjoy. It was, for example, a common phenomenon among new immigrants to America for children to learn English in school and teach it to their parents at home. Similarly, parents can acquire a new understanding of and appreciation for the role of mathematics in their own life and in American popular culture through these activities.

Once students are excited about the math they are learning in the classroom, they will be more likely to think about math outside of the classroom. Once students see the connection between math and popular culture (through doing some of the activities in this book) they may want to look for math in the movies and television shows they watch. Students who can do this will feel empowered and proud of themselves. As a result, they may perform better in school and in life. If students express an interest in finding their own examples but don't know where to start, there are some television shows that regularly feature math. These include *The Simpsons*, *Futurama*, and *The Big Bang Theory*. Many of the examples in this book were found in a similar manner because they were taken from movies and television shows that were watched for entertainment and the math topic was found by chance.

Looking for math shown in movies and television shows is something that students can do with their parents and siblings; this, again, is a way for parents who are not confident in their math abilities to participate in a math-related activity with their child. Just having students aware of and thinking about math at times outside of the classroom can make them more interested in the subject.

Teachers can keep interest levels up by encouraging students to look for their own examples. Then, as students report their findings, the teacher can have a dialogue with them about the math they found. There are many ways to accomplish this. One way is to encourage students to keep a journal in which they jot down ideas, list programs they plan to watch, and write out any math example they see as they watch the movie or show. They can then share any math they find in movies and television shows with classmates. Every Monday there can be five minutes dedicated to students sharing what they found. This can also be done in extra help sessions or as a math club activity. Ideally these examples should raise questions about math topics that students have not encountered yet, so teachers should be prepared to guide students interested in learning more.

Home-schooling parents can use this book as enrichment in addition to the textbook. This is especially useful if the parent has a weakness in math. Including popular media as a basis for a lesson will be extra motivation for both the parent and the student. The activities based on Mr. Collins from *The Wonder Years* (Chapter Three) are good activities for engaging parents because this is a television show that many of them watched. Additionally, these activities go beyond the mathematics in them because they also portray a relationship between the main character and his math teacher. Sharing the results with other home-schooling parents will be appreciated. It can also lead to a network of people who enjoy watching the same shows and learning how math is used in them.

This book is also useful for tutors. Tutors can use this book as a way of getting students excited about the subject. Additionally, the activities in this book provide another way of learning a topic, using a different methodology than the one their teacher employed. Tutors can search the book by subject to find a topic that the student is studying and use the corresponding activity. Tutors also have a closer relationship with the student since they are working one on one, so it is more likely that a tutor will know the student's interests. Therefore, the tutor can also search the book for movies or television shows that match the student's interests. For example, if the tutor knows that the student likes *Star Trek*, then he or she can find an example in the book based on this television show and share it with the student. Some of the activities in this book that use group work will need to be adjusted for a single student.

This book can also be used by a student interested in self-study. This book will be very useful for this purpose because it covers topics in a way that is more interesting than how they are typically seen in the classroom. The activities are explained in enough detail that a student should be able to follow along. If students find an example that they are unable to follow, they will likely be inspired to seek out more information on that topic, either through their teacher or through further reading. Students may also find some of the historical and background descriptions interesting, such as in the randomness activity in Chapter Seven where students learn about the "Texas Sharpshooter Fallacy" and its famous example comparing the deaths of Abraham Lincoln and John F. Kennedy. Since this book is arranged by Common Core subject strands, students can easily find the mathematical topics they are currently studying to deepen their understanding or find topics they are interested in learning about.

Using the activities in this book may also inspire students to think about ways that they can apply mathematics outside of the classroom and in their future professions. One job students may become interested in is being a script writer who introduces math ideas into movies and television shows. Arguably the most mathematical television show out there is *The Simpsons*. This is because many of the writers have degrees in mathematics and computer science. There is a long tradition of writers for this show having advanced degrees in mathematics from prestigious schools such as Harvard University.[4] On the flip side, there are some movies and television shows that could really use a mathematically proficient writer. The movie *Ice Princess* is an unfortunate example of this because the main character Casey is a high school physics nerd who does a science project on using physics to become a better ice skater. It is stressed over and over how brilliant she is in physics. Yet, most of the times she talks about physics and math she says incorrect things. In one scene, Casey, who works in the concession booth at an ice skating rink, is serving three girls. When telling them the food prices Casey says that they cost $1.65, $2.35, and $3.35 and she adds them in her head to get a total of $7.30. The total should actually be $7.35. In another scene Casey is at a party where a guy ziplines down a flight of stairs. She says that he will go through the window because momentum times velocity equals acceleration. This is not a valid formula. Finally, Casey says that if a skater pulls her arms in tight while spinning she will increase her moment of inertia. Actually, the exact opposite is true; her moment of inertia is decreased when she pulls her arms in closer. Seeing the mathematical mistakes made in movies and television shows mentioned here and throughout this book may motivate students to be writers or consultants.

Other activities in the book may inspire other job choices. Learning about the *Moneyball* example (Chapter Seven) may inspire students to be sports coaches or analysts so that they can apply statistics to form winning teams. Others may be inspired to become math teachers based on positive interactions in the "Mr. Collins" activity in Chapter Three or the "Perfect Student" activity in Chapter Six. Doing the "Kayak Math" example in Chapter Three may inspire students to be math savvy when starting a business. The "Quadrilaterals" example (Chapter Six) and the "Find the Target" example

(Chapter Three) may encourage students to use math in law enforcement. Students aspiring to be doctors or nurses will be interested in the "Drip Rate" activity in Chapter Five, where they learn to calculate a medication's drip rate.

Other activities in this book may inspire the use of mathematics in students' hobbies and interests. Students learn how to send and decode secret messages in the cryptography example in Chapter Two. In Chapter Seven students learn successful strategies for various game shows. In Chapter Four students learn how interest rates work. Students can use this to help them find the best bank account to save their money in.

Overall, the activities in this book are meant to make math interesting to students so that they will want to involve friends and family members in mathematical discussions. This interest will then motivate students to learn about math on their own. Additionally, students will be inspired to think about careers involving mathematics. They may even learn that math is used in some unexpected careers.

Appendix A:
The Euclidean Algorithm

The Euclidean algorithm is a method for finding the greatest common divisor (GCD) of two positive integers. First take the larger of the two integers and calculate how many times the second integer divides into it plus what the remainder is. For example, to find the GCD of 172 and 20, we find that 20 goes into 172 eight times with 12 left over. We would write this as $172 = 20(8) + 12$. Next, repeat the same process for the 20 and the 12, getting $20 = 12(1) + 8$. Keep repeating this until there is no remainder left. In this example it becomes $12 = 8(1) + 4$ and $8 = 4(2)$. The GCD of 172 and 20 is the last remainder written, which in this case is 4. Here is another example written out, finding the GCD of 2,415 and 3,289:

$$3289 = 2415(1) + 874$$
$$2415 = 874(2) + 667$$
$$874 = 667(1) + 207$$
$$667 = 207(3) + 46$$
$$207 = 46(4) + 23$$
$$46 = 23(2)$$

This means that the GCD of 2,415 and 3,289 is 23.

Appendix B:
Selected Solutions

Solutions from Chapter Two:
Number and Quantity

Prime Numbers

Shown here is the Sieve of Eratosthenes with the numbers 1 through 100. All the numbers that are shaded in gray are crossed off for being a multiple of another number. The number 1 is also shaded since by definition it is not prime.

1	2	3	4	5	6	7	8	9	10
11	12	13	14	15	16	17	18	19	20
21	22	23	24	25	26	27	28	29	30
31	32	33	34	35	36	37	38	39	40
41	42	43	44	45	46	47	48	49	50
51	52	53	54	55	56	57	58	59	60
61	62	63	64	65	66	67	68	69	70
71	72	73	74	75	76	77	78	79	80
81	82	83	84	85	86	87	88	89	90
91	92	93	94	95	96	97	98	99	100

Multiplication by Nines

Proof for why the multiplication by nines trick works:

Since this trick only works for multiplying 9 by 1 through 10, we will first prove that in these cases the sum of the digits of these multiples is exactly 9. Let's start with the example of 9 times 8 is 72. This can be written as $9 \cdot 8 = 70 + 2 = 7 \cdot 10 + 2$. This checks out since $7 + 2 = 9$. If we think more generally by letting the 8 be represented by n, then the tens digit will be $n - 1$. We can write this as $9(n) = (n - 1)(10) +$ (ones digit). Since the two sides have to be equal and $(n - 1)(10) = 10n - 10$, the ones digit must be $10 - n$. Thus, the sum of the digits is $n - 1 + 10 - n = 9$. This is exactly what we wanted to get. Also notice that the tens digit is $n - 1$, one less than the number that is multiplying 9. This proves what we want, because we hold down the finger of whatever number we multiply 9 by (n), which leaves the number of fingers to the left as one less than the held-down finger $(n - 1)$. This was proved to be the tens digit of the product. Additionally, since the sum of the digits is 9, the number of fingers to the right must be $9 - (n - 1) = 9 - n + 1 = 10 - n$. This is the same value we proved was in the ones digit of the product.

Finding the Day of the Week

3a. If today is Tuesday, what day of the week will it be 1,000 days from today?

$1000 = 7 \cdot 142 + 6$. The "+ 6" indicates that one less day than a full week elapsed. Therefore, the day of the week will be the weekday prior to today, a Monday.

3b. If today is Friday, then what day will it be a year from today (if this year and next year are not leap years)?

There are 365 days in a year and there are 7 days in a week. We can write $365 = 7 \cdot 52 + 1$. So next year it will 52 weeks and 1 day later. Since today is Friday, that would make one year from today a Saturday.

3c. Jan. 1, 2000, was a Saturday, and 2000 was a leap year. What day of the week will Jan. 1, 2050, be?

Since 2000 is a leap year and leap years occur every four years, we know that there will be 13 leap years from 2000 to 2049. This gives a total of $365 \cdot 50 + 13 = 18,263$ days. Since $18,263 = 7 \cdot 2,609 + 0$, it will be a Saturday.

Solutions from Chapter Three: Algebra

Mr. Collins: Activity #1: Absolute Value

1. Here is a sample chart with the celebrity's age, a guess for how old he or she is, and the difference between the two.

NAME	AGE GUESS	ACTUAL AGE	DIFFERENCE
Person A	26	32	6
Person B	15	16	1

Person C	56	60	4
Person D	28	25	3
		Total	14

2. What matters here is the distance. In this example the student who guessed 58 is two years off from the celebrity's actual age, just as is the student who guessed 54. In either case, two will be added to the total score.

Mr. Collins: Activity #2: Completing the Square

3. The missing numbers and signs have been filled in:

$$(x + 1)^2 = x^2 + 2x + 1$$

$$(x - 3)^2 = x^2 - 6x + 9$$

$$(x + \tfrac{1}{2})^2 = x^2 + x + \tfrac{1}{4}$$

$$(x - \tfrac{3}{4})^2 = x^2 - \tfrac{3}{2}x + \tfrac{9}{16}$$

$$(x - \tfrac{2}{3})^2 = x^2 - \tfrac{4}{3}x + \tfrac{4}{9}$$

$$(x + \tfrac{5}{6})^2 = x^2 + \tfrac{5}{3}x + \tfrac{25}{36}$$

5. The blanks are filled in to get a squared term on the left:

$$x^2 - 8x + 17 = 0$$

$$x^2 - 8x + 16 = -17 + 16$$

$$(x - 4)^2 = -1$$

6. Students can manipulate the following equations to get a squared term on the left:

$$x^2 - 10x + 23 = 0 \text{ and } x^2 + \tfrac{2}{3}x - \tfrac{10}{9} = 0.$$

$$x^2 - 10x + 23 = 0 \qquad\qquad x^2 + \tfrac{2}{3}x - \tfrac{10}{9} = 0$$

$$x^2 - 10x + 25 = -23 + 25 \qquad\qquad x^2 + \frac{2}{3}x + \frac{1}{9} = \frac{10}{9} + \frac{1}{9}$$

$$(x - 5)^2 = 2 \qquad\qquad\qquad\qquad (x + \frac{1}{3})^2 = \frac{11}{9}$$

Where Does the 1 Go?

2. Ask students to use a graphing calculator to graph both $x = \frac{1+w^3}{\pi}$ and $x = 1 + \frac{w^3}{\pi}$ and to describe the differences between the two equations.

   The easiest observations are that the two graphs cross the x and y axes at different points. Students who have studied the rules for polynomial transformations will know that the addition of a number to the polynomial will make the graph shift up by that value. Therefore, the first graph will shift up a distance of $\frac{1}{\pi}$ while the second graph will shift up 1.

Find the Target

Place all three transparency sheets on top of each other and over the given map. Locate a possible target for the blackouts.

All of the inequalities are plotted in the following diagram and the enclosed region is shaded. The final solution where all three areas are shaded is the pentagonal shape outlined in bold.

Word Problems, Part 1

Intersection of the inequalities.

4. Ask students to create a general solution to the problem that works if there are three painters.

   Let's assume that Sam can paint $1/m$ of a house in an hour, Joe can paint $1/n$ of a house in an hour, and Beth can paint $1/p$ of a house in an hour. Then their combined hourly rate is $\frac{1}{m} + \frac{1}{n} + \frac{1}{p} = \frac{np+mp+mn}{nmp}$. Next we want to solve the equation $\frac{np+mp+mn}{nmp} x = 1$. This gives us $\frac{nmp}{np+mp+mn}$.

Solutions from Chapter Four: Functions

Secondary Trigonometry Ratios

2. Ask students which one of the prince's answers was correct and what the secondary trigonometry functions actually are.

   The secondary trigonometry functions are secant, cotangent, and cosecant.

3. Ask students to explain how they can get the values of each secondary trigonometry function, given the value of the primary trigonometry functions.

   Taking the reciprocal of each main trigonometry function will result in a secondary trigonometry function. The reciprocal of sine is cosecant, the reciprocal of cosine is secant, and the reciprocal of tangent is cotangent.

4. Ask students what other trigonometry values they can get, given only a sine value.

   All of the remaining trigonometry functions can be found. Since the sine value is the same as opposite side over hypotenuse of a right triangle, the adjacent side can be found using the Pythagorean Theorem. Then the cosine value will be adjacent over hypotenuse and tangent will be opposite over adjacent. The secondary trigonometry functions can be found by taking the reciprocals of each of these.

SOHCAHTOA

2. The chart is filled out below:

TRIANGLE	OPPOSITE	ADJACENT	HYPOTENUSE	OPPOSITE HYPOTENUSE	ADJACENT HYPOTENUSE	OPPOSITE ADJACENT
A	1	1.7	2	.5	.85	.59
B	2	3.5	4	.5	.88	.57
C	3	5.2	6	.5	.87	.58

3. Ask students what they might conclude from this chart. Ask them what they would expect to be in the last three columns if they did the same for a triangle with a 60-degree angle.

   The triangles are all similar, so the ratios come out to around the same value. They are not exact, because the adjacent side was rounded, and this made the last two calculations a little off. The exact values in the adjacent column should be $\sqrt{3}$, $2\sqrt{3}$, and $3\sqrt{3}$. This means that sin(30) is .5, cos(30) is around .87, and tan(30) is around .58. Repeating this chart for the 60-

degree angle will be similar, but the roles of the opposite side and the adjacent side switch. This means that sin(60) is the same as cos(30), cos(60) is the same as sin(30), and tan(60) is the reciprocal of tan(30).

The Pigeonhole Principle

3. John has *m* keys and *n* locks, but he has forgotten which keys open which locks.

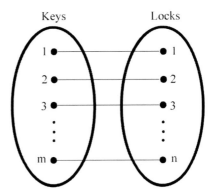

Arrow diagram for the function "open."

a) Assume that each key can open one and only one lock.

i) Think about this problem in terms of functions. Let the function "open" go from the set of keys to the set of locks. Draw an arrow diagram for this situation.

ii) Let *m* = 6 and *n* = 8, can all of the locks be opened?
Not all of the locks can be opened, because each key can only open one lock. Once the sixth lock has been opened there are no more keys left to open the remaining locks.

iii) Again letting *m* = 6 and *n* = 8, is this function one-to-one? Onto? Why or why not?
This function is one-to-one because each key opens one and only one lock, meaning every key is mapped to a lock (making it a function) and no two keys are mapped to the same lock (making it one-to-one). This function is not onto because, as stated in part ii, there are two locks that cannot be opened. This means that not all of the *y* values have an arrow pointing at them, and the function is not onto.

iv) What needs to be true about *m* and *n* to ensure that every lock gets opened?
To open every lock *m* has to be equal to *n*. When *m* is equal to *n*, each key opens exactly one lock and all of the locks will be opened. When *m* is greater than *n* this situation will not work, because every key has to open exactly one lock, but there are more keys than locks. If *n* is greater than *m* then there would be extra locks that don't get opened.

b) Now assume that there are two keys that open the same lock, while the rest of the keys open one and only one lock.

i) Draw an arrow diagram for this situation.

ii) Let $m = 6$ and $n = 5$. Can John open all of the locks?

He can open all of the locks because two of the keys will open one lock and then the remaining four keys will open the remaining four locks.

iii) Again letting $m = 6$ and $n = 5$, is this function one-to-one? Onto? Why or why not?

This function will not be one-to-one because two keys open the same lock, meaning two x values are mapped to the same y value. This function is onto because all of the locks will be opened, meaning all y values have arrows pointing at them.

iv) What is the minimum number of keys needed to open n locks?

Because two keys open the same lock there has to be one extra key. Therefore, to open n locks there has to be $n + 1$ keys.

c) Now assume that there is one key that opens exactly two locks while the other keys open one and only one lock.

ii) In this case is "open" a function? Why or why not?

This is not a function because one x value is mapped to two different y values.

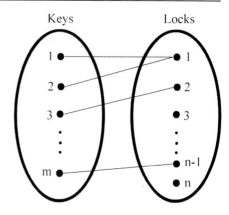

Keys   Locks

Arrow diagram for the modified function "open."

Solutions from Chapter Five: Modeling

Rocket Motion

2. The formulas for vertical and horizontal displacement can be given as parametric equations with $x = (v_0 cos\theta)t$ and $y = (v_0 sin\theta)t - \frac{1}{2}at^2$. Have students prove that the path given by these equations is parabolic by eliminating the t parameter and showing that the resulting equation is a parabola.

Start by solving the first equation for t to get $t = \frac{x}{v_0 cos\theta}$. Plug this into the t values in the second equation to get $y = (v_0 sin\theta)\left(\frac{x}{v_0 cos\theta}\right) - \frac{1}{2}a\left(\frac{x}{v_0 cos\theta}\right)^2$. At this point the equation can be recognized as a parabola or it can be worked on further to get it into the standard form for a parabola. In this case the equation becomes

$$y = \left(\frac{x\sin\theta}{\cos\theta}\right) - \frac{ax^2}{2(v_0\cos\theta)^2} = \frac{2xv_0^2\cos\theta\sin\theta - ax^2}{2(v_0\cos\theta)^2} = \frac{xv_0^2\cos2\theta - ax^2}{2(v_0\cos\theta)^2} = \frac{-a\left(x^2 - \frac{xv_0^2\cos2\theta}{a}\right)}{2(v_0\cos\theta)^2} =$$

$$\frac{-a\left(x^2 - \frac{xv_0^2\cos2\theta}{a} + \frac{v_0^4\cos^2 2\theta}{4a^2}\right) + \frac{v_0^4\cos^2 2\theta}{4a}}{2(v_0\cos\theta)^2} = \frac{-a\left(x - \frac{v_0^2\cos2\theta}{2a}\right)^2 + \frac{v_0^4\cos^2 2\theta}{4a}}{2(v_0\cos\theta)^2} = -\frac{a}{2(v_0\cos\theta)^2}\left(x - \frac{v_0^2\cos2\theta}{2a}\right)^2 + \frac{v_0^4\cos^2 2\theta}{4a(2(v_0\cos\theta)^2)} =$$

$$-\frac{a}{2(v_0\cos\theta)^2}\left(x - \frac{v_0^2\cos2\theta}{2a}\right)^2 + \frac{v_0^2 4\cos^2\theta\sin^2\theta}{4a(2(\cos\theta)^2)} = -\frac{a}{2(v_0\cos\theta)^2}\left(x - \frac{v_0^2\cos2\theta}{2a}\right)^2 + \frac{v_0^2\sin^2\theta}{2a}.$$

Solutions from Chapter Six: Geometry

Quadrilaterals

Can You Stop the Crime?

The police in upstate New York are stumped, so you are called in as a math special agent. So far there have been two murders (shown in the map as point A and point B), and the killer left notes at each location implying there will be a third and final murder. Your job is to figure out where the final crime will occur so the police can get to the scene beforehand and prevent it. This is a map of the first two crimes.

At the first crime the following clue was found:

> Unlike its salmon
> When I cross and climb Bear Mountain
> My bridges will be burned
> For I will not return.
> There will be three dead by the third night.
> Say what you will, I am always RIGHT.

And on the second night this clue was found:

> The north better be armed
> For the third time won't be a charm.
> My crime spree will be terminated
> Thirty degrees northwest of where I originated.

The first clue says that the murderer will not go back across Bear Mountain. Also, since we know there will be three murders, they will form a triangle. The first clue tells us that it will be a right triangle. The second clue says that the next murder will be in the north and it will be 30 degrees northwest of point A. Figure 44 shows the right triangle that is formed and that the third murder will take place at Orrs Mills.

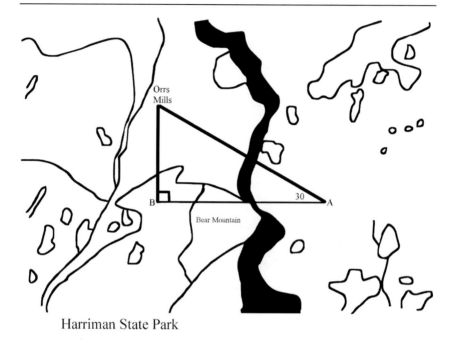

Harriman State Park

Map of upstate New York with solution.

Solutions from Chapter Seven:
Statistics and Probability

The Birthday Problem

3. The probability that at least two people share a birthday in a group of four people is $1 - \frac{365 \cdot 364 \cdot 363 \cdot 362}{365^4} = .016$. In a group of n people the probability is $\frac{(_{365}P_n)}{365^n}$. Note that $_mP_n$ is the permutation formula and is equal to $\frac{m!}{(m-n)!}$.

4. (Extra Credit) Come up with a formula that includes the leap day.
   We will assume that a leap year occurs once every four years, even though there are some exceptions. Then the probability of a person being born on leap day is $.25/365.25$ and the probability of a person being born any other day is $1/365.25$. To find the probability that n people have different birthdays, we will split this into the probability that all n people were born on different days, not including leap day, and the probability that all n people were born on different days, with one of them being born on leap day. The first probability is similar to the previous problem but with the denominator of 365.25. This probability is $\frac{(_{365}P_n)}{365.25^n}$. The second probability needs

to include the leap day as a birthday. Let's think about two people. One will have a leap day birthday ($p = .25/365.25$) and one will have any other birthday ($p = 365/365.25$). But there are two different ways that this can occur, because the leap day birthday can be the first person or the second person. The probability is $\frac{.25(365)+365(.25)}{365.25^2} = \frac{.25(365)(2)}{365.25^2}$. For three people it works similarly. One person has a leap-day birthday and the other two have non-leap day but different birthdays. There are three ways that this can occur, with the leap day birthday being the first, second, or third person. The probability is $\frac{.25(365)(364)(3)}{365.25^3}$. In general, for n people the probability is $\frac{.25(365 P_{n-1})(n)}{365.25^n}$. We can sum these two probabilities because they are mutually exclusive. Then the probability that n people have different birthdays is $\frac{(365 P_n)+.25(365 P_{n-1})(n)}{365.25^n}$. Thus the probability that there is at least one birthday match with n people is $1 - \frac{(365 P_n)+.25(365 P_{n-1})(n)}{365.25^n}$. Plugging in different values for n shows that the probabilities are slightly lower, but pretty similar to the probabilities in the original birthday problem. It is interesting to note that the solution is the same; in a group of 23 people there is a slightly higher than 50 percent chance that two people share a birthday.

Standard Deviation

6. Give follow-up questions such as these:
   a. What can be concluded if the standard deviation for the left thumbnail of the entire class is zero?
   A standard deviation of zero means that everybody's thumbnail is the same length.
   b. A new student joins the class and her left thumbnail length is equal to the average left thumbnail length for the class. What impact will this addition have to the standard deviation and mean for the class?
   The mean will remain the same. If the mean $= \frac{\sum_{i=1}^{n} x_i}{n}$ then the new mean with the new student added is $\frac{\sum_{i=1}^{n} x_i + \frac{\sum_{i=1}^{n} x_i}{n}}{n+1} = \frac{\frac{n \sum_{i=1}^{n} x_i + \sum_{i=1}^{n} x_i}{n}}{n+1} = \frac{\frac{\sum_{i=1}^{n} x_i(n+1)}{n}}{n+1} = \frac{\sum_{i=1}^{n} x_i}{n} =$ old mean. The standard deviation will move towards zero. This happens because the new student's deviation from the mean is zero, which will keep the numerator in the standard deviation formula the same. However, the denominator will increase with the increase in the number of data values.
   c. If everyone cut one hundredth of an inch off of their left thumbnail, what would happen to the standard deviation and mean for the class?
   The mean will also be reduced by one hundredth. If the mean $= \frac{\sum_{i=1}^{n} x_i}{n}$ then the new mean is $\frac{\sum_{i=1}^{n}(x_i-.01)}{n} = \frac{\sum_{i=1}^{n} x_i}{n} - \frac{\sum_{i=1}^{n} .01}{n} = \frac{\sum_{i=1}^{n} x_i}{n} - \frac{.01(n)}{n} = \frac{\sum_{i=1}^{n} x_i}{n} - .01$ $=$ old mean $- .01$. The standard deviation will remain the same. The

numerator of the new variance formula becomes $\sum_{i=1}^{n}[(x_i - .01) - (\bar{x} - .01)]^2 = \sum_{i=1}^{n}[x_i - .01 - \bar{x} + .01]^2 = \sum_{i=1}^{n}[x_i - \bar{x}]^2 = $ the numerator of the old variance formula.

d. If everyone's left thumbnail length doubled, what would happen to the standard deviation and mean for the class?

If everybody's value doubles then the mean will also double. If the mean $= \frac{\sum_{i=1}^{n} x_i}{n}$ then the new mean will be $\frac{\sum_{i=1}^{n} 2x_i}{n} = \frac{2\sum_{i=1}^{n} x_i}{n} = 2$ times the old mean. The standard deviation will also double. If the old variance is $\frac{\sum_{i=1}^{n}(x_i-\bar{x})^2}{n-1}$ then the doubled values turns it into $\frac{\sum_{i=1}^{n}(2x_i-2\bar{x})^2}{n-1} = \frac{\sum_{i=1}^{n} 4(x_i-\bar{x})^2}{n-1} = \frac{4\sum_{i=1}^{n}(x_i-\bar{x})^2}{n-1} = 4$ times the old variance. Take a square root to get the result that the standard deviation is 2 times the old standard deviation.

Wheel of Fortune Activity #1

1. The wheel in *Wheel of Fortune* has 24 spaces. However, in one of the rounds one of the spaces is split into 3 parts, with a "bankrupt" on the two ends and "$1,000,000" in the middle. This makes calculating the probability of landing on a "bankrupt" space a little more challenging than if all spaces were the same size. Ask students to calculate the probability of landing on bankrupt on a single spin.

One way to think about this is to imagine all of the 24 spaces split into 3 pieces. This will give a total of 72 pieces. The bankrupt spaces are 2 of those 72 pieces, so the probability of landing on it is 2/72.

Wheel of Fortune Activity #2

2. An example table is shown here with the letters listed in order of popularity. The frequency with which each letter is expected to appear, based on the *Oxford English Dictionary* letter analysis, is in the second column. Next is the number of observed letters in a sample paragraph, with the total number of letter summed at the bottom. The fourth column has the number of expected for each letter based on the percentage expected multiplied by the total number of letters (188). Finally, the Chi-Square values are calculated using the formula . These values are summed to get the test statistic of approximately 19.33. Using a .05 significance level and degrees of freedom of 26–1 = 25, the critical value on the Chi-Square chart is 36.42. Since the test statistic is less than the critical value, we do not reject the null hypothesis. This means that there is a good chance that the observed values match the expected values, meaning that the letter distribution of

this sample paragraph fits with what was found by the writers of the *Oxford English Dictionary.*

LETTER	% EXPECTED	# OBSERVED	# EXPECTED	CHI-SQUARE
E	11.16	26	20.9808	1.2007344
A	8.5	20	15.98	1.0112891
R	7.58	13	14.2504	0.1097162
I	7.54	9	14.1752	1.8894051
O	7.16	17	13.4608	0.9305492
T	6.95	13	13.066	0.0003334
N	6.65	12	12.502	0.0201571
S	5.74	7	10.7912	1.3319369
L	5.49	12	10.3212	0.2730661
C	4.54	8	8.5352	0.0335597
U	3.63	3	6.8244	2.1431973
D	3.38	8	6.3544	0.4261613
P	3.17	3	5.9596	1.4697685
M	3.01	6	5.6588	0.0205728
H	3	8	5.64	0.9875177
G	2.47	2	4.6436	1.5050006
B	2.07	3	3.8916	0.2042735
F	1.81	6	3.4028	1.9823227
Y	1.78	3	3.3464	0.0358573
W	1.29	3	2.4252	0.1362341
K	1.1	4	2.068	1.8049439
V	1.01	2	1.8988	0.0053936
X	0.29	0	0.5452	0.5452
Z	0.27	0	0.5076	0.5076
J	0.2	0	0.376	0.376
Q	0.2	0	0.376	0.376
	Total	188		19.326791

The Price Is Right

1. Show a clip of a contestant playing "Pick-a-Number." Ask students to calculate the probability of guessing the correct number.
   Assuming that the contestant is randomly guessing the missing number, then the probability is 1/3.

2. Show a clip of a contestant spinning the wheel and landing on 100. Ask students to calculate this event's probability.

There are 20 numbers on the wheel (each occurring once), so the probability of getting 100 is 1/20.

3. Show a clip of a contestant spinning the wheel twice and getting a sum of 100. Ask students to calculate the probability of this happening. Then have them calculate the probability of a contestant getting 100 on either one or two spins. Finally, have the students calculate the probability of a contestant getting 100 in one or two spins and then landing on 100 during the bonus spin.

When spinning the wheel twice there are $20 \times 20 = 400$ possible outcomes. Out of these 400 outcomes, there are 20 of them that will sum to 100. Therefore, the probability of a contestant spinning the wheel twice and getting a sum of 100 is $20/400 = 1/20$. To find the probability of a contestant getting 100 on either one or two spins we can use the formula $P(A \cup B) = P(A) + P(B) - P(A \cap B)$. These two events are mutually exclusive (i.e., they have no intersection), because if a contestant got a 100 on the first spin he or she would not spin again. This means we can just sum the probabilities to get $1/20 + 1/20 = 1/10$. Getting 100 in one or two spins and landing on 100 during the bonus spin are independent events, because each spin is independent. To find the probability of this occurring we can find $P[(A \cap B) \cap C] = P(A \cap B)P(C) = (1/10)(1/20) = 1/200$.

Deal or No Deal Activity #1

1. Ask students to calculate the expected value at the start of a game.
   There are 26 suitcases, so the probability of each value is 1/26. Let x_i be the value of the ith suitcase. The expected value is then $E[X] = \sum_{i=1}^{26} x_i P(x_i) = \sum_{i=1}^{26} x_i(\frac{1}{26}) = \frac{1}{26}\sum_{i=1}^{26} x_i = \frac{1}{26}(.01 + 1 + 5 + \cdots + 1000000) = 131{,}477.54$.

2. Pick a televised game to use as an example and show the first round; or to save time, just show what the contestant is left with at the end of the first round and have students calculate the expected value at that point. Show what the banker's offer is and see how that compares to the expected value. Ask students if they would choose deal or no deal and to explain why. For example, if the values left on the board are 50, 300, 750, 100,000, and 400,000 then the expected value is $(50 + 300 + 750 + 100{,}000 + 400{,}000) \cdot \frac{1}{5} = \frac{(501,100)}{5} = 100{,}220$. If the banker's offer is any bigger than the expected value then the contestant should accept it.

4. A few other questions for students to think about:
   - What is the probability that a contestant chooses the million-dollar case? The probability is 1/26.

- If the contestant makes it all the way to the end, with only the original chosen case and a final case remaining, the contestant has the choice of keeping the original case or switching to the remaining case. Should the contestant switch? How does this compare to the Monty Hall Problem? It does not matter if the contestant switches, because they both have a 50 percent probability of containing the higher number. The difference between this situation and the Monty Hall Problem is that the host does not know what values are contained in the suitcases. Additionally, it is not the host that is opening the cases, it is the contestant.

Appendix C:
Game Theory

The activities in this appendix don't fit into the Common Core Curriculum. However, interested students and teachers can use them for an extra challenge.

Common Knowledge

One concept used in game theory is called common knowledge. This means that information is known to all players, all players know that it is known to all players, all players know that all players know that it is known to all players, and so on.

An example of common knowledge is given in *The Princess Bride*. Westley and Vizzini compete in a battle of wits. There are two glasses of wine with poison in one of the glasses. Vizzini is shown going through various arguments to decide which glass has the poison. He says that a clever man would put poison in his own cup because he knows only a fool would drink from the cup placed before him. Vizzini says that he is not a fool so he cannot drink from Westley's cup. However, Westley must know that he is not a fool so he also cannot drink from his own cup. Basically, he is saying that anything he can deduce, Westley can also deduce. Vizzini goes on with similar arguments until he finally drinks from his own cup. Westley says that he guessed incorrectly, but Vizzini says not really because he actually switched cups when Westley wasn't looking. As it turns out, both cups were poisoned and Westley had built up an immunity to the poison, so Vizzini dies.

The idea of a player being rational in the context of game theory means that the player is trying to maximize his or her payoff. Assuming rationality and common knowledge can lead to a surprising paradox.[1] Suppose that a teacher announces on the first day of class that there will be a surprise quiz one day during the school year. The rational student knows that the surprise quiz cannot be on the last day of class because by then they would have gone through all the previous classes without the quiz. In this case, the night before the last class, students would know there was a quiz and it wouldn't be a surprise. Likewise, the quiz cannot be on the second to last day. The same argument can be used for each previous day going backwards to the first day. But that means that it is impossible to give a surprise quiz.

A popular example that uses logic and illustrates an argument similar to that of the surprise quiz is the brown-eyed native problem. In this problem, there is an island where n natives have blue eyes and the rest have brown eyes. There are no reflective surfaces on the island and nobody discusses eye color. This means that none of the natives know their own eye color. The natives gather together each night. One night a person visiting the island says at least one of them has blue eyes (this is now common knowledge). Any natives that discover they have blue eyes must leave the island immediately. How do they figure out who has blue eyes?

To get the solution let's first think about $n = 1$. This means that one of the natives has blue eyes and the rest have brown eyes. On the first day the blue-eyed native will leave because he can see that everybody else has brown eyes. Since at least one of them has blue eyes, he must have blue eyes. Next consider $n = 2$. On the first day nobody will leave because they all look out and see at least one blue-eyed person. The brown-eyed people will see two blue-eyed people, and the blue-eyed people will see one blue-eyed person. Since nobody left the first day, all of the natives know that there are at least two people with blue eyes. This is common knowledge because they themselves all know this is true, plus they know that everybody else knows that this is true, and so on. On the second day the two blue-eyed people will look out and see only one other blue-eyed person. At this point they will both leave because they know there are at least two blue-eyed people. The same methodology can be used for any n value. Thus, by day n the natives will know who has blue eyes.

PRIOR KNOWLEDGE NEEDED:

No specific prior knowledge in needed for this activity.

CLASSROOM USE:

1. Go over the basics of game theory and give the definitions of common knowledge and rational.

2. Show the clip from *The Princess Bride*.
3. Ask students to explain the use of common knowledge in this clip.
4. Guide students through the surprise-quiz example.
5. Have students solve the brown-eyed native problem in groups or have the class act it out by assigning eye color to students by putting a sticker on their back. This way students will be able to see everyone's eye color except their own.

CONNECTION TO COMMON CORE:

In this activity students make sense of problems and persevere in solving them when they draw conclusions by comparing complex scenarios with similar simpler forms of the brown-eyed native problem.

The Prisoner's Dilemma

The Prisoner's Dilemma is a popular example in game theory. There are two people who get arrested for a crime. They cannot communicate with each other in any way. The police don't have enough evidence to convict them of the larger crime, but can convict them of a smaller crime giving each one year in prison. The prisoners can either keep silent or accuse the other of doing the crime. If both prisoners accuse each other, then they both get two years in prison. If one betrays the other while the second prisoner remains silent, then the accused gets three years in prison and the accuser gets set free. If they both remain silent then they each go to prison for one year. It is in each prisoner's best interest to accuse the other, thus leading to the outcome of each prisoner getting two years in jail. This outcome occurs even though, if they cooperated by remaining silent, they would both be better off with only one year in jail.

To help students understand how the Prisoner's Dilemma really works, McPherson and Nieswiadomy suggest performing a class experiment by giving students a chance to earn extra credit.[2] For this experiment students cannot communicate with each other in any way. Each student can choose two points or eight points. If all students choose two points, then everybody gets two points extra credit on a quiz or test. If most students choose two points but a few choose eight (they suggest two people choosing eight in a class smaller than 100) then those who chose eight get eight points extra credit and those who chose two get nothing. Finally, if more than a few people choose eight then nobody gets extra credit. McPherson and Nieswiadomy ran this experiment with twenty-one classes and only one of those classes received extra credit.

In an episode of *Dilbert* (season 2, episode 12), Dilbert and his friends are taken in for questioning at the police station after their boss accuses them of killing Todd, an employee that they invented. An officer tries to get Dilbert to confess, but Dilbert says it won't work because he knows about the Prisoner's Dilemma. The police have no evidence, so someone can be convicted only if someone else rats them out. Since they all know this, nobody will talk and they will soon be free. Unfortunately, not all of Dilbert's friends understand this.

PRIOR KNOWLEDGE NEEDED:

No specific prior knowledge is needed for this activity.

CLASSROOM USE:

1. Perform the extra credit experiment and then ask some students to share their strategies.
2. Explain what the Prisoner's Dilemma is.
3. Show the clip from *Dilbert*.
4. Ask students to explain how the extra credit experiment relates to the Prisoner's Dilemma.

CONNECTION TO COMMON CORE:

In this activity, students construct viable arguments when they use logic to come up with a strategy.

Chicken

Another popular game theory game is called chicken. In this game there are two drivers coming from opposite directions, heading towards a single-lane bridge. If neither of the drivers swerve then they crash into each other. If one driver swerves then he is called a chicken. The best outcome for each driver is to continue driving while the other driver swerves. Again, if both drivers choose in their best interest then they do not end up with the best result.

An example of chicken is shown in *Stand By Me*. Two groups of teenagers are each in their cars driving down a highway. They are going in the same direction, but Ace pulls his car into the wrong lane so that they are driving side by side. A truck is coming towards Ace from the other direction. Ace's friends tell him to swerve, but he keeps going and the truck ends up swerving.

Then Ace says he wins. He did indeed win the game of chicken, even though the truck driver was not aware that he was playing.

A real life example of chicken occurred in 2013 when there was a government shutdown. The Republicans and Democrats couldn't agree on a spending bill concerning the Affordable Care Act (also known as Obamacare). Each side could give in or they could remain firm. If either side gave in, then the shutdown would be avoided. If both sides remained firm then there would be a shutdown. If both sides gave in then, presumably, they would reach a compromise. In this example both sides remained firm and the government shut down for sixteen days. In terms of the chicken game, both sides did not swerve and there was a crash.

PRIOR KNOWLEDGE NEEDED:

No specific prior knowledge is needed for this activity.

CLASSROOM USE:

1. Explain the game of chicken.
2. Show students the clip from *Stand By Me*.
3. Give students an article about the government shutdown and ask them to explain how this relates to the game of chicken.

CONNECTION TO COMMON CORE:

In this activity, students model with mathematics when they apply game theory to a real world problem.

The Stable Marriage and Stable Roommates Problems

The Stable Marriage Problem involves a group of n men and n women. Each male ranks each female in preference order from 1 to n and each female does likewise for the males. The men and women are married together. The marriages are considered stable if there are no males or females who would both prefer each other over their current partner. Here's an example with three men and three women. Ann prefers Arnie, Bob, and then Carl. Beth prefers Bob, Carl, and then Arnie. Cindy prefers Arnie, Carl, and then Bob. Arnie prefers Ann, Beth, and then Cindy. Bob prefers Beth, Cindy, and then Ann. Carl prefers Cindy, Beth, and then Ann. Then an example of a stable set of marriages is Arnie with Ann, Bob with Beth, and Carl with Cindy. This is stable because Ann and Arnie each get their first choice so they don't want any other partner. Bob, Beth, and Carl also get their first choices. The only person who didn't get her first choice is Cindy, who would prefer Arnie. However, Arnie does not prefer Cindy over his partner Ann. This means that there are no males or females who would both prefer each other over their current partner.

David Gale and Lloyd Shapely proved that there is always a solution to this problem.[3] They also developed an algorithm to solve it called the male-proposing algorithm. Each male proposes to their top female choice. Females automatically accept their first proposition, but later if a more preferred male proposes she will reject the first male in order to accept her more preferred choice. As an example, let's suppose males are represented by letters and females are represented by numbers. For men, A's preference list is 1342, B's preference list is 2341, C's preference list is 2134, and D's preference list is 1432. For women, 1's preference list is DCAB, 2's preference list is CDBA, 3's preference list is ACDB, and 4's preference list is BDCA. By the male proposing algorithm, A and 1 get engaged. Then B and 2 get engaged. Next, C proposes to 2. Since 2 prefers C over B, C and 2 are now engaged. B moves on to his next choice, 3. D proposes to 1 and 1 prefers D, so she accepts. Then A proposes to 3. 3 prefers A, so they are engaged and B proposes to 4. We end up with A and 3 engaged, B and 4 engaged, C and 2 engaged, and D and 1 engaged.

There is a strategy for outsmarting this algorithm. There is an incentive for women to be dishonest about their preference list. It has been proven that men have no incentive to be dishonest.

The most famous application of the Stable Marriage Problem is the National Resident Matching Program. This is a non-profit organization that matches medical students with residency programs.

A variation of the Stable Marriage Problem is the Stable Roommates Problem. The difference between these two problems is that the roommates problem doesn't have two separate lists such as males and females; any two people can be matched from the set. A stable matching may not exist. Robert Irving developed an algorithm to either show there is no stable solution or, if there is one, to find it.[4] The way his algorithm works is to have each person propose to their top choice. If a person is proposed to a second time, he or she will reject the proposal lowest on the preference list. The rejected person then proposes to his or her next choice. Once a person is rejected, the pairing of these two people is crossed off both preference lists. After this phase the same process is repeated with the new preference lists. This continues until one of two conclusions is reached. First, if someone is rejected by everyone else, there is no stable solution. Second, the process ends with each person paired to one other person (this is the stable solution).

An example of the Stable Roommates Problem with four people is as follows: The preference list for 1 is 2, 4, 3. The preference list for 2 is 1, 3, 4. The preference list for 3 is 2, 1, 4. The preference list for 4 is 3, 1, 2. Initially, 1 is matched with 2, 2 is matched with 1, and 3 is matched with 2. Now two people are matched to 2, so we look at 2's preference list and see that 1 is higher than 3. This means that 3 is rejected and 2 and 3 are crossed off for the next round. 3 moves on to 1. Again, there are two people matched with 1 and we see 2 is higher on 1's preference list. This means that 3 is rejected again, and 1 and 3 are crossed off for the next round. 3 moves on to 4. Then 4 is matched to 3. The new preference list for 1 is 2, 4. The new preference list for 2 is 1, 4. The new preference list for 3 is 4. The preference list for 4 remains the same as 3, 1, 2. Now the process is repeated. 1 is matched to 2. 2 is matched to 1. 3 is matched to 4. 4 is matched to 3. This is a stable solution since 1, 2, and 4 are with their top choices, and even though 3 prefers 1 and 2 to his partner, it is not mutual.

The Stable Roommates Problem is featured in an episode of *Community* (season 3, episode 4). There are seven main characters in the show. In their biology class the teacher has them work in pairs on a project. They bring in another student named Todd to make an even eight. The group tries to figure out a fair way to divide into partners. Jeff suggests they each write down their preferences in order, and Abed will figure out the best way to partner them. Abed's method for solving the problem begins by ranking everyone according to how popular they are on everyone's ballot. Then, he will pair the most popular with the least popular.

PRIOR KNOWLEDGE NEEDED:

No prior knowledge is needed for this activity.

CLASSROOM USE:

1. Explain the Stable Marriage Problem and how Gale and Shapely's algorithm works.
2. There is a Web site that illustrates the Stable Marriage Problem through examples.[5] Players can choose to have 4, 5, or 6 pairs and whether the men or the women propose. Each male and female is displayed along with his or her preference list. Players can see the solution worked out in steps or go directly to the final solution. Have students go through some examples until they understand how the algorithm works.

3. Have students get into groups. Then, have each group make up their own example of the Stable Marriage Problem. Lastly, have the groups exchange problems, solving the new problem they receive.
4. Show the *Community* clip to students.
5. Explain what the Stable Roommates Problem is and how Irving's algorithm works.
6. We don't get to see everyone's preference list on the show, but students can come up with their own. Have students work in groups, with each group making up their own preference list for each of the eight characters.
7. Have each group of students go through the algorithm, using their preference list, to see if they can get a stable solution.
8. Have each group share and explain their results with the class.

CONNECTION TO COMMON CORE:

In this activity, students model with mathematics when they apply logic and game theory to real-world problems. They also use appropriate tools when they understand the Stable Marriage Problem through the use of the Stable Marriage Problem Web site.

Chapter Notes

Preface

1. Oliver Knill, "Mathematics in the Movies," *Harvard University*, last updated March 2013, http://www.math.harvard. edu/~knill/mathmovies; Burkard Polster and Marty Ross, *Math Goes to the Movies* (Baltimore: Johns Hopkins University Press, 2012); Luis Sobrecueva and Jose Luis, "Subzin: Find Quotes in Movies and Series," *Subzin*, last accessed August 29, 2014, http:// www.subzin.com.

Introduction

1. Martin E. Ford, *Motivating Humans: Goals Emotions, and Personal Agency Beliefs* (Newbury Park: Sage, 1992), 3.

2. James A. Middleton and Photini A. Spanias, "Motivation for Achievement in Mathematics: Findings, Generalizations, and Criticisms of the Research," *Journal for Research in Mathematics Education* 30, no. 1 (1999): 66.

3. Brett D. Jones, Lida J. Uribe-Florez, and Jesse L.M. Wilkins, "Motivating Mathematics Students with Manipulatives: Using Self-Determination Theory to Intrinsically Motivate Students," in *Motivation and Disposition: Pathways to Learning Mathematics*, ed. Daniel J. Brahier and William R. Speer (Reston, VA: National Council of Teachers of Mathematics, 2011), 216.

4. Kou Murayama, Reinhard Pekrun, Stephanie Lichtenfeld, and Rudolf vom Hofe, "Predicting Long-Term Growth in Students' Mathematics Achievement: The Unique Contributions of Motivation and Cognitive Strategies," *Child Development* 84, no. 4 (2013): 1485.

5. Jones, Uribe-Florez, and Wilkins, "Motivating Mathematics Students with Manipulatives," 216.

6. Middleton and Spanias, "Motivation for Achievement," 69.

7. Richard M. Ryan and Edward L. Deci, "Intrinsic and Extrinsic Motivations: Classic Definitions and New Directions," *Contemporary Educational Psychology* 25, no. 1 (2000): 57.

8. Jones, Uribe-Florez, and Wilkins, "Motivating Mathematics Students with Manipulatives," 216.

9. Jennifer M. Deitte and Michael Howe, "Motivating Students to Study Mathematics," *Mathematics Teacher* 96, no. 4 (2003): 278.

10. Ryan and Deci, "Intrinsic and Extrinsic Motivation," 56.

11. Middleton and Spanias, "Motivation for Achievement," 69.

12. Ibid.

13. Ibid., 75.

14. Ibid., 82.

15. Ibid., 81.

16. Keith Devlin, "Bringing Cool into School," in *Motivation and Disposition: Pathways to Learning Mathematics*, ed. Daniel J. Brahier and William R. Speer (Reston, VA: National Council of Teachers of Mathematics, 2011), 242.

17. Charlene E. Beckmann, Denisse R. Thompson, and Richard A. Austin, "Exploring Proportional Reasoning Through Movies and Literature," *Mathematics Thinking in the Middle School* 9, no. 5 (2004): 261.

18. Michaele F. Chappell and Denisse R. Thompson, *Activities to Engage Middle School Students Through Film, Literature, and the Internet* (Portsmouth, NH: Heinemann, 2009), 5.

19. Steven M. Ross, "Increasing the Meaningfulness of Quantitative Material by Adapting Context to Student Background," *Journal of Educational Psychology* 75, no. 4 (1983): 519.

20. Angeline Stoll Lillard, *Montessori: The Science Behind the Genius* (Oxford: Oxford University Press, 2005), 229.

21. Sarah J. Greenwald and Andrew Nestler, "r dr r: Engaging Students with Significant Mathematical Content from the Simpsons," *PRIMUS: Problems, Resources, and Issues in Mathematics Undergraduate Studies* 14, no. 1 (2004): 30–1.

22. Ibid., 31–2.

23. Ibid., 32–5.

24. Ibid., 36–7.

25. Ibid., 37.

26. William T. Butterworth and Paul R. Coe, "Come On Down…. The Prize Is Right in Your Classroom," *PRIMUS: Problems, Resources, and Issues in Mathematics Undergraduate Studies* 14, no. 1 (2004): 18.

27. Ibid.

28. Nirmala Naresh and Bridget Royce, "Dropping In on the Game of Plinko," *Mathematics Teaching in the Middle School* 19, no. 4 (2013): 216–7.

29. "What Is Project Look Sharp?" *Ithaca College*, accessed August 28, 2014, http://www.projectlooksharp.org.

30. Cynthia L. Scheibe, "A Deeper Sense of Literacy: Curriculum-Driven Approaches to Media Literacy in the K–12 Classroom," *American Behavioral Scientist* 48, no. 1 (2004): 60.

31. Ibid., 61–2.

32. Andy Maillet, "Numb3rs Activities," *Have Your Pi and Eat It Too: Musings of a Math Coach*, last modified December 2, 2013, http://mathstrategies.wordpress.com/numb3rs-activities.

33. Brian Hopkins, "Kevin Bacon and Graph Theory," *PRIMUS: Problems, Resources, and Issues in Mathematics Undergraduate Studies* 14, no. 1 (2004): 10.

34. Keith Devlin and Gary Lorden, *The Numbers Behind Numb3rs: Solving Crime with Mathematics* (New York: Plume, 2007), 6.

35. Chappell and Thompson, *Activities to Engage Middle School Students*, 23.

36. James Frieden and Deborah W. Elliott, "Supplement Lesson Plans in Mathematics Using Movies and Film," *Teach with Movies*, accessed August 28, 2014, http://www.teachwithmovies.org/math-subject-list.htm.

37. Timothy P. Chartier, "Using the Force: *Star Wars* in the Classroom," *PRIMUS: Problems, Resources, and Issues in Mathematics Undergraduate Studies* 17, no. 1 (2007): 8.

38. Tony DeRose, "Pixar: The Math Behind the Movies," *TED-Ed Lessons Worth Sharing*, accessed August 29, 2014, http://ed.ted.com/lessons/pixar-the-math-behind-the-movies-tony-derose.

39. Philip Munz, Ioan Hudea, Joe Imad, and Robert J. Smith, "When Zombies Attack!: Mathematical Modelling of an Outbreak of Zombie Infection," in *Infectious Disease Modelling Research Progress*, ed. Jean Michel Tchuenche and Christinah Chiyaka (Hauppauge, NY: Nova, 2009), 133.

40. Kristine Larsen, "'You Never Said Anything About Math': Math Phobia and Math Fanaticism in the World of *Lost*," in *Mathematics in Popular Culture: Essays on Appearances in Film, Fiction, Games, Television, and Other Media*, ed. Jessica K. Sklar and Elizabeth S. Sklar (Jefferson, NC: McFarland, 2012), 27–41.

41. Kris Green, "What's in a Name? *The Matrix* as an Introduction to Mathematics," in *Mathematics in Popular Culture: Essays on Appearances in Film, Fiction, Games, Television, and Other Media*, ed. Jessica K. Sklar and Elizabeth S. Sklar (Jefferson, NC: McFarland, 2012), 44–52.

42. Matthew Lane, "Counting with the Sharks: Math-Savvy Gamblers in Popular Culture," in *Mathematics in Popular Culture: Essays on Appearances in Film, Fiction, Games, Television, and Other Media*, ed. Jessica K. Sklar and Elizabeth S. Sklar (Jefferson, NC: McFarland, 2012), 149–60.

Chapter One

1. Thomas L. Friedman, *The World Is Flat: A Brief History of the Twenty-first Century* (New York: Farrar, Straus and Giroux, 2005).

2. National Center for Education Statistics, "Mathematics Literacy Performance of 15-Year-Olds," *Program for International Student Assessment*, accessed July 8, 2013,

http://nces.ed.gov/surveys/pisa/pisa2009hi
ghlights_3.asp.

3. National Governors Association Center for Best Practices, Council of Chief State School Officers, "Frequently Asked Questions," *Common Core State Standards Mathematics*, accessed July 8, 2013, http://www.corestandards.org/resources/frequently-asked-questions.

4. National Center for Education Statistics, "First-Year Undergraduate Remedial Coursetaking: 1999–2000, 2003–04, 2007–08," *National Center for Education Statistics*, accessed July 8, 2013, http://nces.ed.gov/pubs2013/2013013.pdf.

5. National Governors Association Center for Best Practices, Council of Chief State School Officers, "Frequently Asked Questions," *Common Core State Standards Mathematics*, accessed July 8, 2013, http://www.corestandards.org/resources/frequently-asked-questions.

6. Judy Nichols Douglass, "Which States Have the Highest Standards for Students," *Christian Science Monitor*, October 30, 2009, http://www.csmonitor.com/USA/2009/1030/p02s07-usgn.html.

7. National Governors Association Center for Best Practices, Council of Chief State School Officers, *Common Core State Standards Mathematics* (Washington, D.C.: National Governors Association Center for Best Practices, Council of Chief State School Officers, 2010).

Chapter Two

1. Mary Gray, "Sophie Germain," in *Women of Mathematics: A Bibliographic Sourcebook*, ed. Louise S. Grinstein and Paul J. Campbell (New York: Greenwood Press, 1987), 52.

2. Arthur Benjamin, *The Secrets of Mental Math* (Chantilly, VA: Great Courses, 2011), 1.

3. Anthony Ralston, "Let's Abolish Pencil-and-Paper Arithmetic," *The Journal of Computers in Mathematics and Science Teaching* 18, no. 2 (1999): 183.

4. Arthur Benjamin and Michael Shermer, *Secrets of Mental Math: The Mathemagician's Guide to Lightning Calculation and Amazing Math Tricks* (New York: Three Rivers, 2006).

5. Greg Tang, "BreakApart," *Greg Tang's World of Math*, last modified May 24, 2012, http://gregtangmath.com/Games/Break Apart.

6. Greg Tang, "Kakooma," *Greg Tang's World of Math*, last modified May 24, 2012, http://gregtangmath.com/Kakooma.

7. Laurence Sigler, *Fibonacci's Liber Abaci* (New York: Springer, 2002), 404.

8. Karl Grammer and Randy Thornhill, "Human (Homo sapiens) Facial Attractiveness and Sexual Selection: The Role of Symmetry and Averageness," *Journal of Comparative Psychology* 108, no. 3 (1994): 240.

9. "Cryptography and Ciphers," *Shodor*, accessed January 3, 2013, http://www.shodor.org/interactivate/discussions/CryptographyCipher.

10. Andrej Cherkaev and Elena Cherkaev, "Mathematical Humor," *Math Jokes*, accessed January 3, 2013, http://www.math.utah.edu/~cherk/mathjokes.html.

11. Daniel T. Willingham, *Why Don't Students Like School?* (San Francisco: Jossey-Bass, 2009), 19.

12. Dudley Underwood, *Numerology: Or, What Pythagoras Wrought* (Washington, D.C.: Mathematical Association of America, 1997), 2.

13. David Burton, *History of Mathematics: An Introduction* (New York: McGraw-Hill, 2010), 90.

14. Annie Heese and Adam Banks, "Numerology," *Cafe Astrology*, accessed January 3, 2013, http://www.cafeastrology.com/numerology.html.

15. Tracy Wilson, "How Numerology Works," *How Stuff Works*, last modified March 28, 2007, http://science.howstuffworks.com/science-vs-myth/extrasensory-perceptions/numerology.htm.

16. Elaine Young, "Palindrome Numbers," *Youngzones*, accessed January 3, 2013, http://math.youngzones.org/palindrome.html.

17. Martin Gardner, *Mathematical Circus: More Puzzles, Games, Paradoxes and Other Mathematical Entertainments from Scientific American* (New York: Knopf, 1979), 242–45.

18. Ken Bigelow, "What Do Your HTML Pages Look Like?" *Play-Hookey*, accessed June 15, 2014, http://www.play-hookey.com/htmltest.

19. Alex Bello, "Dozenalists of the World Unite! Rise Up Against the Tyranny of Ten!" *Alex's Adventures in Numberland*, last

updated December 12, 2012, http://www.theguardian.com/science/alexs-adventures-in-numberland/2012/dec/12/dozenalists-world-unite-tyranny-ten.

20. "The Duodecimal Bulletin Archive Index," *The Dozenal Society of America*, last updated September 3, 2011, http://www.dozenal.org/archive/archive.html.

21. Sidney J. Kolpas, "Let Your Fingers Do the Multiplying," *Mathematics Teacher* 95, no. 4 (2002): 246.

22. Elizabeth Green, "(New Math)—(New Teaching) = Failure," *The New York Times Magazine*, July 23, 2014, 25.

23. Paul J. Nahin, *An Imaginary Tale: The Story of* (Princeton: Princeton University Press, 2010), 4.

24. John J. O'Conner and Edmund F. Robertson, "The Fundamental Theorem of Algebra," *The MacTutor History of Mathematics Archive*, last modified May 1996, http://www-history.mcs.st-and.ac.uk/history/HistTopics/Fund_theorem_of_algebra.html.

25. John J. O'Conner and Edmund F. Robertson, "Rafael Bombelli," *The MacTutor History of Mathematics Archive*, last modified January 2000, http://www-history.mcs.st-andrews.ac.uk/Biographies/Bombelli.html.

26. O'Conner and Robertson, "The Fundamental Theorem of Algebra."

Chapter Four

1. Stefanie Olsen, "Google Recruits Eggheads with Mystery Billboard," *CNET*, July 9, 2004, http://news.cnet.com/Google-recruits-eggheads-with-mystery-billboard/2100-1023_3-5263941.html.

2. Keith Devlin, "Finding Musical Beauty in Euler's Identity," *Mathematical Association of America*, April 2007, http://www.maa.org/external_archive/devlin/devlin_04_07.html.

3. "Stadium Comparison," *The New York Yankees*, accessed July 25, 2014, http://newyork.yankees.mlb.com/nyy/ballpark/new_stadium_comparison.jsp.

4. Robert Milson, "Cantor's Diagonal Argument," *Planetmath.org*, last updated March 21, 2013, http://planetmath.org/cantorsdiagonalargument.

5. John Green, "Questions About the Fault in Our Stars (SPOILERS!)," *John Green Books*, accessed October 30, 2014, http://

johngreenbooks.com/questions-about-the-fault-in-our-stars-spoilers/#hazel.

6. Kate Nowak, "Speed Dating," *Function of Time Blog*, last modified October 6, 2009, http://function-of-time.blogspot.com/search?q=speed+dating.

Chapter Five

1. "The San Francisco/Oakland Bay Bridge," *California Department of Transportation*, accessed July 11, 2014, http://www.dot.ca.gov/hq/esc/tollbridge/SFOBB/Sfobbfacts.html.

2. Wesley C. Salmon, *Zeno's Paradoxes* (Indianapolis: Hackett, 2001), 7.

3. E.T. Bell, *Men of Mathematics: The Lives and Achievements of the Great Mathematicians from Zeno to Poincare* (New York: Simon & Schuster, 1986), 24.

4. "Earthquake Triangulation Activity," *Scripps Institution of Oceanography*, last modified 2007–2008, http://earthguide.ucsd.edu/eoc/teachers/t_tectonics/swf_earthquake_triangulation/p_activity_eqtriangulation.html.

5. Nancy S. Todd, "Exploring Meteorite Mysteries: Lesson 2—Following the Falling Meteorite," *NASA*, last modified April 29, 2011, http://curator.jsc.nasa.gov/outreach/expmetmys/Lesson2.pdf.

6. "War Machines of Tomorrow," *PBS*, last modified April 2004, http://www.pbs.org/wgbh/nova/education/activities/2305_warmachi.html.

7. Florian Cajorl, "History of Determinations of the Heights of Mountains," *Isis* 12, no. 3 (1929): 482.

8. David Austen and Will Dickinson, "Spherical Easel," *Grand Valley State University*, last modified 2002–2009, http://merganser.math.gvsu.edu/easel.

9. "The Millennium Prize Problems," *Clay Mathematics Institute*, last modified July 11, 2014, http://www.claymath.org/millennium-problems/millennium-prize-problems.

10. Nelson King, "Six Degrees: Psychologist Stanley Milgram Theorized That Every Person Is Only Six Connections Away, at Most, from Anyone Else on This Planet," *PC Magazine* 22, no. 6 (2003), 122.

11. Brian Hopkins, "Kevin Bacon and Graph Theory," *PRIMUS: Problems, Resources, and Issues in Mathematics Undergraduate Studies* 14, no. 1 (2004): 5.

12. Patrick Reynolds, "Find the Link from Actor A to Actor B," *The Oracle of Bacon*, last modified 1999–2013, http://oracleofbacon.org.

13. Susanna Epp, *Discrete Mathematics with Applications* (Boston: Brooks/Cole Cengage Learning, 2004), 656.

14. Gabriel Costa, Michael Huber, and John Saccoman, "Cumulative Home Run Frequency and the Recent Home Run Explosion," *Baseball Research Journal* 34 (2005): 39–41.

15. "Baseball Reference," *Sports Reference, LLC,* last modified July 12, 2014, http://www.baseball-reference.com.

16. Costa, Huber, and Saccoman, "Cumulative Home Run Frequency," 39–41.

17. J.K. Rowling, *Harry Potter and the Sorcerer's Stone* (New York: Scholastic, 1998), 285.

18. "Logic Puzzle," Mathbitswww, accessed October 19, 2014, http://mathbits.com/MathBits/MathMovies/HarryPotter.pdf.

Chapter Six

1. "Euclid's Construction of a Regular Dodecahedron (XIII.17)," *Wolfram Demonstrations Project,* accessed January 28, 2014, http://demonstrations.wolfram.com/EuclidsConstructionOfARegularDodecahedronXIII17.

2. "Dodecahedron Model," *Math Is Fun,* accessed January 28, 2014, http://www.mathsisfun.com/geometry/dodecahedron-model.html.

3. "Flatland (first edition)," *Wikisource,* last modified February 27, 2012, http://en.wikisource.org/wiki/Flatland_(first_edition).

4. Key Curriculum Press, *The Geometer's Sketchpad Dynamic Geometry Software for Exploring Mathematics* (Berkeley: Key Curriculum, 2001).

5. "Volume of a Sphere Explained," *YouTube,* last modified April 4, 2012, http://youtu.be/hjcUpeK-4A0.

6. Donald J. Albers, Constance Reid, and George B. Dantzig, "An Interview with George B. Dantzig: The Father of Linear Programming," *The College Mathematics Journal* 17, no. 4 (1986): 301.

7. J.V. Field, *Piero della Francesca: A Mathematician's Art* (New Haven: Yale University Press, 2005), 373.

8. Bertrand Russell, *Autobiography* (London: Routledge Classics, 2010), 138.

9. Eric W. Weisstein, "Catalogue Paradox," *MathWorld—A Wolfram Web Resource,* accessed January 28, 2014, http://mathworld.wolfram.com/CatalogueParadox.html.

Chapter Seven

1. Marilyn Vos Savant, "Game Show Problem," *Marilyn Vos Savant Online Headquarters,* accessed January 3, 2013, http://marilynvossavant.com/game-show-problem.

2. Webster West, "The Let's Make a Deal Applet," *Texas A&M University Department of Statistics,* accessed January 3, 2013, http://www.stat.tamu.edu/~west/applets/LetsMakeaDeal.html.

3. John Tierney, "Behind Monty Hall's Doors: Puzzle, Debate, and Answer?" *New York Times,* July 21, 1991.

4. Edward Neukrug, "Galton's Board," *Old Dominion University,* September 11, 2013, http://ww2.odu.edu/~eneukrug/galton.htm.

5. "Why People Think They Can Win the Lottery," *CBS DC,* last modified December 17, 2013, http://washington.cbslocal.com/2013/12/17/why-people-think-they-can-win-the-lottery.

6. Jacque Wilson, "Why You Keep Playing the Lottery," CNNwww, last modified May 17, 2013, http://www.cnn.com/2012/08/15/health/psychology-playing-lottery-powerball.

7. "What Are the Odds of Being Struck by Lightening?" DiscoverTheOddswww, last modified October 8, 2012, http://discovertheodds.com/what-are-the-odds-of-being-struck-by-lightning.

8. "10 Things More Likely to Happen Than Winning the Mega Millions Lottery," *Bay News 9,* last modified February 19, 2014, http://www.baynews9.com/content/news/baynews9/news/article.html/content/news/articles/cfn/2013/12/17/mega_millions_odds.html?cid=rss.

9. Nigel Turner and Roger Horbay, "How Do Slot Machines and Other Electronic Gambling Machines Actually Work?" *Journal of Gambling Issues* 11 (2004): 10–50, http://jgi.camh.net/loi/jgi.

10. Dan Brown, *The Da Vinci Code* (New York: Anchor, 2003), 199.

11. "Top Names of the 2000s," *The Official Website of the U.S. Social Security Administration*, last modified May 14, 2012, http://www.ssa.gov/oact/babynames/decades/names2000s.html.

12. "How Many of Me," *How Many of Me*, accessed January 3, 2013, http://howmanyofme.com.

13. Malcolm Gladwell, *Outliers: The Story of Success* (New York: Little, Brown, 2008).

14. Jason Long and Bryce Thornton, "Testing Benford's Law," *Testing Benford's Law*, accessed January 3, 2013, http://testingbenfordslaw.com.

15. "Straight A's in High School May Mean Better Health Later in Life," www.Time.com, December 9, 2010, http://content.time.com/time/health/article/0,8599,2036232,00.html.

16. Tyler Vigen, "Spurious Correlations," *Spurious Correlations*, accessed July 29, 2014, http://www.tylervigen.com/.

17. Stephen Gorard, "Revisiting a 90-Year-Old Debate: The Advantages of the Mean Deviation" (presentation, British Educational Research Association Annual Conference, University of Manchester, September 16–18, 2004).

18. "What Is the Frequency of the Letters of the Alphabet in English?" *Oxford Dictionaries*, accessed January 3, 2013, http://oxforddictionaries.com/words/what-is-the-frequency-of-the-letters-of-the-alphabet-in-english.

19. Sefik Ilkin Serengil and Murat Akin, "Attacking Turkish Texts Encrypted by Homophonic Cipher," *World Scientific and Engineering Academy and Society*, accessed July 29, 2014, http://www.wseas.us/e-library/conferences/2011/Cambridge/NEHIPISIC/NEHIPISIC-20.pdf.

20. William Spaniel, "How to Win at 'Wheel of Fortune,'" newrepublicwww, last updated February 25, 2014, http://www.newrepublic.com/article/116732/wheel-fortune-strategy-how-win-gameshow.

21. Ibid.

22. "Wheel," *The Evil Petting Zoo*, last modified January 3, 2013, http://evilpettingzoo.com/wheel.

23. Spaniel, "How to Win."

24. "J! Archive," *J! Archive*, last modified January 2, 2013, http://j-archive.com.

Chapter Eight

1. Goéry Delacôte, "Putting Science in the Hands of the Public," *Science* 280, no. 5372 (1998): 2054.

2. Janis E. Jacobs and Martha M. Bleeker, "Girls' and Boys' Developing Interests in Math and Science: Do Parents Matter?" *New Directions for Child and Adolescent Development* 2004, no. 106 (2004): 17.

3. Wenfan Yan and Qiuyun Lin, "Parent Involvement and Mathematics Achievement: Contrast Across Racial and Ethnic Groups," *The Journal of Educational Research* 99, no. 2 (2005): 116.

4. Simon Sing, *The Simpsons and Their Mathematical Secrets* (London: Bloomsbury, 2013), 3.

Appendix C

1. Mike Shor, "Common Knowledge and Rationality: The Surprise Quiz," Vanderbilt University, last updated 2008, http://www2.owen.vanderbuilt.edu/mike.shor/Courses/game-theory/docs/lecture02/surprise.html.

2. Michael A. McPherson and Michael L. Nieswiadomy, "Teaching the Prisoner's Dilemma More Effectively: Engaging the Students," University of North Texas, last updated December 2012, http://www.cas.unt.edu/~mcpherson/papers/mcpherson_nieswiadomy_JEE.pdf.

3. David Gale and Lloyd Shapely, "College Admissions and the Stability of Marriage," *American Mathematical Monthly* 69, no. 1 (1962): 12–13.

4. Robert W. Irving, "An Efficient Algorithm for the 'Stable Roommates' Problem," *Journal of Algorithms* 6, no. 4 (1985):579–80.

5. David Gale and John Potapenko, "Stable Marriage Problem," *MathSite*, accessed October 7, 2104, http://mathsite.math.berkeley.edu/smp/smp.html.

Bibliography

Albers, Donald J., Constance Reid, and George B. Dantzig. "An Interview with George B. Dantzig: The Father of Linear Programming." *The College Mathematics Journal* 17, no. 4 (1986): 293–314.

Austen, David, and Will Dickinson. "Spherical Easel." *Grand Valley State University*. Last modified 2002–2009. http://mergan ser.math.gvsu.edu/easel.

"Baseball Reference." *Sports Reference, LLC.* Last modified July 12, 2014. http://www. baseball-reference.com.

Beckmann, Charlene E., Denisse R. Thompson, and Richard A. Austin. "Exploring Proportional Reasoning Through Movies and Literature." *Mathematics Thinking in the Middle School* 9, no. 5 (2004): 256–62.

Bell, E.T. *Men of Mathematics: The Lives and Achievements of the Great Mathematicians from Zeno to Poincare.* New York: Simon & Schuster, 1986.

Bello, Alex. "Dozenalists of the World Unite! Rise Up Against the Tyranny of Ten!" *Alex's Adventures in Numberland.* Last updated December 12, 2012. http://www. theguardian.com/science/alexs-adven tures-in-numberland/2012/dec/12/dozen alists-world-unite-tyranny-ten.

Benjamin, Arthur. *The Secrets of Mental Math.* Chantilly, VA: Great Courses, 2011.

Benjamin, Arthur, and Michael Shermer. *Secrets of Mental Math: The Mathemagician's Guide to Lightning Calculation and Amazing Math Tricks.* New York: Three Rivers, 2006.

Bigelow, Ken. "What Do Your HTML Pages Look Like?" *Play-Hookey.* Accessed June 15, 2014. http://www.play-hookey.com/ htmltest.

Brown, Dan. *The Da Vinci Code.* New York: Anchor, 2003.

Burton, David. *History of Mathematics: An Introduction.* New York: McGraw-Hill, 2010.

Butterworth, William T., and Paul R. Coe. "Come On Down....The Prize Is Right in Your Classroom." *PRIMUS: Problems, Resources, and Issues in Mathematics Undergraduate Studies* 14, no. 1 (2004): 12–28.

Cajorl, Florian. "History of Determinations of the Heights of Mountains." *Isis* 12, no. 3 (1929): 482–514.

Chappell, Michaele F., and Denisse R. Thompson. *Activities to Engage Middle School Students Through Film, Literature, and the Internet.* Portsmouth, NH: Heinemann, 2009.

Chartier, Timothy P. "Using the Force: *Star Wars* in the Classroom." *PRIMUS: Problems, Resources, and Issues in Mathematics Undergraduate Studies* 17, no. 1 (2007): 8–23.

Cherkaev, Andrej, and Elena Cherkaev. "Mathematical Humor." *Math Jokes.* Accessed January 3, 2013. http://www. math.utah.edu/~cherk/mathjokes.html.

Costa, Gabriel, Michael Huber, and John Saccoman. "Cumulative Home Run Frequency and the Recent Home Run Explosion." *Baseball Research Journal* 34 (2005): 37–41.

"Cryptography and Ciphers." *Shodor.* Accessed January 3, 2013. http://www. shodor.org/interactivate/discussions/ CryptographyCipher.

Deitte, Jennifer M., and Michael Howe,

"Motivating Students to Study Mathematics." *Mathematics Teacher* 96, no. 4 (2003), 278–80.

Delacôte, Goéry. "Putting Science in the Hands of the Public." *Science* 280, no. 5372 (1998): 2054–55.

DeRose, Tony. "Pixar: The Math Behind the Movies." *TED-Ed Lessons Worth Sharing.* Accessed August 29, 2014. http://ed.ted.com/lessons/pixar-the-math-behind-the-movies-tony-derose.

Devlin, Keith. "Bringing Cool into School." In *Motivation and Disposition: Pathways to Learning Mathematics*, ed. Daniel J. Brahier and William R. Speer, 241–9. Reston, VA: The National Council of Teachers of Mathematics, 2011.

_____. "Finding Musical Beauty in Euler's Identity." *Mathematical Association of America.* April 2007. http://www.maa.org/external_archive/devlin/devlin_04_07.html.

Devlin, Keith, and Gary Lorden. *The Numbers Behind Numb3rs: Solving Crime with Mathematics.* New York: Plume, 2007.

"Dodecahedron Model." *Math Is Fun.* Accessed January 28, 2014. http://www.mathsisfun.com/geometry/dodecahedron-model.html.

Douglass, Judy Nichols. "Which States Have the Highest Standards for Students." *Christian Science Monitor*, October 30, 2009. http://www.csmonitor.com/USA/2009/1030/p02s07-usgn.html.

"The Duodecimal Bulletin Archive Index." *The Dozenal Society of America.* Last updated September 3, 2011. http://www.dozenal.org/archive/archive.html.

"Earthquake Triangulation Activity." *Scripps Institution of Oceanography.* Last modified 2007–2008. http://earthguide.ucsd.edu/eoc/teachers/t_tectonics/swf_earthquake_triangulation/p_activity_eqtriangulation.html.

Epp, Susanna. *Discrete Mathematics with Applications.* Boston: Brooks/Cole Cengage Learning, 2004.

"Euclid's Construction of a Regular Dodecahedron (XIII.17)." *Wolfram Demonstrations Project.* Accessed January 28, 2014. http://demonstrations.wolfram.com/EuclidsConstructionOfARegularDodecahedronXIII17.

Field, J.V. *Piero della Francesca: A Mathematician's Art.* New Haven: Yale University Press, 2005.

"Flatland (first edition)." *Wikisource.* Last modified February 27, 2012. http://en.wikisource.org/wiki/Flatland_(first_edition).

Ford, Martin E. *Motivating Humans: Goals, Emotions, and Personal Agency Beliefs.* Newbury Park: Sage, 1992.

Frieden, James, and Deborah W. Elliott. "Supplement Lesson Plans in Mathematics Using Movies and Film." *Teach with Movies.* Accessed August 28, 2014. http://www.teachwithmovies.org/math-subject-list.htm.

Friedman, Thomas L. *The World Is Flat: A Brief History of the Twenty-first Century.* New York: Farrar, Straus and Giroux, 2005.

Gale, David, and John Potapenko. "Stable Marriage Problem." *MathSite.* Accessed October 7, 2014. http://mathsite.math.berkeley.edu/smp/smp.html.

Gale, David, and Lloyd Shapley. "College Admissions and the Stability of Marriage." *American Mathematical Monthly* 69, no. 1 (1962): 9–15.

Gardner, Martin. *Mathematical Circus: More Puzzles, Games, Paradoxes and Other Mathematical Entertainments from Scientific American.* New York: Knopf, 1979.

Gladwell, Malcolm. *Outliers: The Story of Success.* New York: Little, Brown, 2008.

Gorard, Stephen. "Revisiting a 90-Year-Old Debate: The Advantages of the Mean Deviation." Presentation at the British Educational Research Association Annual Conference, University of Manchester, September 16–18, 2004.

Grammer, Karl, and Randy Thornhill. "Human (Homo sapiens) Facial Attractiveness and Sexual Selection: The Role of Symmetry and Averageness." *Journal of Comparative Psychology* 108, no. 3 (1994): 233–42.

Gray, Mary. "Sophie Germain." In *Women of Mathematics: A Bibliographic Sourcebook*, ed. Louise S. Grinstein and Paul J. Campbell, 68–75. New York: Greenwood Press, 1987.

Green, Elizabeth. "(New Math)—(New Teaching) = Failure." *The New York Times Magazine*, July 23, 2014.

Green, John. "Questions About the Fault in Our Stars (SPOILERS!)." *John Green Books.* Accessed October 30, 2014. http://johngreenbooks.com/questions-about-the-fault-in-our-stars-spoilers/#hazel.

Green, Kris. "What's in a Name? *The Matrix* as an Introduction to Mathematics." In *Mathematics in Popular Culture: Essays on Appearances in Film, Fiction, Games, Television, and Other Media*, ed. Jessica K. Sklar and Elizabeth S. Sklar, 44–54. Jefferson, NC: McFarland, 2012.

Greenwald, Sarah J., and Andrew Nestler. "ʳdr r: Engaging Students with Significant Mathematical Content from The Simpson." *PRIMUS: Problems, Resources, and Issues in Mathematics Undergraduate Studies* 14, no. 1 (2004): 29–39.

Heese, Annie, and Adam Banks. "Numerology." *Cafe Astrology*. Accessed January 3, 2013. http://www.cafeastrology.com/numerology.html.

Hopkins, Brian. "Kevin Bacon and Graph Theory." *PRIMUS: Problems, Resources, and Issues in Mathematics Undergraduate Studies* 14, no. 1 (2004): 5–11.

"How Many of Me." *How Many of Me*. Accessed January 3, 2013. http://howmanyofme.com.

Irving, Robert W. "An Efficient Algorithm for the 'Stable Roommates' Problem." *Journal of Algorithms* 6, no. 4 (1985): 577–95.

"J! Archive." *J! Archive*. Last modified January 2, 2013. http://j-archive.com.

Jacobs, Janis E., and Martha M. Bleeker. "Girls' and Boys' Developing Interests in Math and Science: Do Parents Matter?" *New Directions for Child and Adolescent Development* 2004, no. 106 (2004): 5–21.

Jones, Brett D., Lida J. Uribe-Florez, and Jesse L.M. Wilkins. "Motivating Mathematics Students with Manipulatives: Using Self-Determination Theory to Intrinsically Motivate Students." In *Motivation and Disposition: Pathways to Learning Mathematics*, ed. Daniel J. Brahier and William R. Speer. 215–27. Reston, VA: The National Council of Teachers of Mathematics, 2011.

Key Curriculum Press. *The Geometer's Sketchpad Dynamic Geometry Software for Exploring Mathematics*. Berkeley: Key Curriculum, 2001.

King, Nelson. "Six Degrees; Psychologist Stanley Milgram Theorized That Every Person Is Only Six Connections Away, at Most, from Anyone Else on This Planet." *PC Magazine* 22, no. 6 (2003): 122–23.

Kolpas, Sidney J. "Let Your Fingers Do the Multiplying." *Mathematics Teacher* 95, no. 4 (2002): 246–51.

Lane, Matthew. "Counting with the Sharks: Math-Savvy Gamblers in Popular Culture." In *Mathematics in Popular Culture: Essays on Appearances in Film, Fiction, Games, Television, and Other Media*, ed. Jessica K. Sklar and Elizabeth S. Sklar, 148–62. Jefferson, NC: McFarland, 2012.

Larsen, Kristine. "'You Never Said Anything About Math': Math Phobia and Math Fanaticism in the World of *Lost*." In *Mathematics in Popular Culture: Essays on Appearances in Film, Fiction, Games, Television, and Other Media*, ed. Jessica K. Sklar and Elizabeth S. Sklar, 27–43. Jefferson, NC: McFarland, 2012.

Lillard, Angeline Stoll. *Montessori: The Science Behind the Genius*. Oxford: Oxford University Press, 2005.

"Logic Puzzle." Mathbitswww. Accessed October 19, 2014. http://mathbits.com/MathBits/MathMovies/HarryPotter.pdf.

Long, Jason, and Bryce Thornton. "Testing Benford's Law." *Testing Benford's Law*. Accessed January 3, 2013. http://testingbenfordslaw.com.

Maillet, Andy. "Numb3rs Activities." *Have Your Pi and Eat It Too: Musings of a Math Coach*. Last modified December 2, 2013. http://mathstrategies.wordpress.com/numb3rs-activities.

McPherson, Michael A., and Michael L. Nieswiadomy. "Teaching the Prisoner's Dilemma More Effectively: Engaging the Students." *University of North Texas*. Last updated December 2012. http://www.cas.unt.edu/~mcpherson/papers/mcpherson_nieswiadomy_JEE.pdf.

Middleton, James A., and Photini A. Spanias. "Motivation for Achievement in Mathematics: Findings, Generalizations, and Criticisms of the Research." *Journal for Research in Mathematics Education* 30, no. 1 (1999): 65–88.

"The Millennium Prize Problems." *Clay Mathematics Institute*. Last modified July 11, 2014. http://www.claymath.org/millennium-problems/millennium-prize-problems.

Milson, Robert. "Cantor's Diagonal Argument." *Planetmath.org*. Last updated March 21, 2013. http://planetmath.org/cantorsdiagonalargument.

Munz, Philip, Ioan Hudea, Joe Imad, and Robert J Smith? "When Zombies Attack!: Mathematical Modelling of an Outbreak of Zombie Infection." In *Infectious Dis-*

ease Modelling Research Progress, ed. Jean Michel Tchuenche and Christinah Chiyaka, 133–50. Hauppauge, NY: Nova, 2009.

Murayama, Kou, Reinhard Pekrun, Stephanie Lichtenfeld, and Rudolf vom Hofe. "Predicting Long-Term Growth in Students' Mathematics Achievement: The Unique Contributions of Motivation and Cognitive Strategies." *Child Development* 84, no. 4 (2013): 1475–90.

Nahin, Paul J. *An Imaginary Tale: The Story of √−1*. Princeton: Princeton University Press, 2010.

Naresh, Nirmala, and Bridget Royce. "Dropping in on the Game of Plinko." *Mathematics Teaching in the Middle School* 19, no. 4 (2013): 214–21.

National Center for Education Statistics. "First-Year Undergraduate Remedial Coursetaking: 1999–2000, 2003–04, 2007–08." *National Center for Education Statistics*. Accessed July 8, 2013. http://nces.ed.gov/pubs2013/2013013.pdf.

_____. "Mathematics Literacy Performance of 15-Year-Olds." *Program for International Student Assessment*. Accessed July 8, 2013. http://nces.ed.gov/surveys/pisa/pisa2009highlights_3.asp.

National Governors Association Center for Best Practices, Council of Chief State School Officers. *Common Core State Standards Mathematics*. Washington, D.C.: National Governors Association Center for Best Practices, Council of Chief State School Officers, 2010.

_____. "Frequently Asked Questions." *Common Core State Standards Mathematics*. Accessed July 8, 2013. http://www.corestandards.org/resources/frequently-asked-questions.

Neukrug, Edward. "Galton's Board." *Old Dominion University*. Last modified September 11, 2013. http://ww2.odu.edu/~eneukrug/galton.htm.

Nowak, Kate. "Speed Dating." *Function of Time Blog*. Last modified October 6, 2009. http://function-of-time.blogspot.com/search?q=speed+dating.

O'Conner, John J., and Edmund F. Robertson. "The Fundamental Theorem of Algebra." *The MacTutor History of Mathematics Archive*. Last modified May 1996. http://www-history.mcs.st-and.ac.uk/history/HistTopics/Fund_theorem_of_algebra.html.

_____. "Rafael Bombelli." *The MacTutor History of Mathematics Archive*. Last modified January 2000. http://www-history.mcs.st-andrews.ac.uk/Biographies/Bombelli.html.

Olsen, Stefanie. "Google Recruits Eggheads with Mystery Billboard." *CNET*. July 9, 2004. http://news.cnet.com/Google-recruits-eggheads-with-mystery-billboard/2100-1023_3-5263941.html.

Ralston, Anthony. "Let's Abolish Pencil-and-Paper Arithmetic." *The Journal of Computers in Mathematics and Science Teaching* 18, no. 2 (1999): 173–94.

Reynolds, Patrick. "Find the Link from Actor A to Actor B." *The Oracle of Bacon*. Last modified 1999–2013, http://oracleofbacon.org.

Ross, Steven M. "Increasing the Meaningfulness of Quantitative Material by Adapting Context to Student Background." *Journal of Educational Psychology* 75, no. 4 (1983): 519–29.

Rowling, J.K. *Harry Potter and the Sorcerer's Stone*. New York: Scholastic, 1998.

Russell, Bertrand. *Autobiography*. London: Routledge Classics, 2010.

Ryan, Richard M., and Edward L. Deci, "Intrinsic and Extrinsic Motivations: Classic Definitions and New Directions." *Contemporary Educational Psychology* 25, no. 1 (2000): 54–67.

Salmon, Wesley C. *Zeno's Paradoxes*. Indianapolis: Hackett, 2001.

"The San Francisco/Oakland Bay Bridge." *California Department of Transportation*. Accessed July 11, 2014. http://www.dot.ca.gov/hq/esc/tollbridge/SFOBB/Sfobbfacts.html.

Serengil, Sefik Ilkin, and Murat Akin. "Attacking Turkish Texts Encrypted by Homophonic Cipher." *World Scientific and Engineering Academy and Society*. Accessed July 29, 2014. http://www.wseas.us/e-library/conferences/2011/Cambridge/NEHIPISIC/NEHIPISIC-20.pdf.

Scheibe, Cynthia L. "A Deeper Sense of Literacy: Curriculum-Driven Approaches to Media Literacy in the K-12 Classroom." *American Behavioral Scientist* 48, no. 1 (2004): 60–8.

Shor, Mike. "Common Knowledge and Rationality: The Surprise Quiz." Vanderbilt University. Last updated 2008. http://www2.owen.vanderbilt.edu/mike.shor/Courses/game-theory/docs/lecture02/surprise.html.

Sigler, Laurence. *Fibonacci's Liber Abaci.* New York: Springer, 2002.

Sing, Simon. *The Simpsons and Their Mathematical Secrets.* London: Bloomsbury, 2013.

Spaniel, William. "How to Win at 'Wheel of Fortune.'" Newrepublicwww. Last updated February 25, 2014. http://www.newrepublic.com/article/116732/wheel-fortune-strategy-how-win-gameshow.

"Stadium Comparison." *The New York Yankees.* Accessed July 25, 2014. http://newyork.yankees.mlb.com/nyy/ballpark/new_stadium_comparison.jsp.

"Straight A's in High School May Mean Better Health Later in Life." Timewww. December 9, 2010. http://content.time.com/time/health/article/0,8599,2036232,00.html.

Tang, Greg. "BreakApart." *Greg Tang's World of Math.* Last modified May 24, 2012. http://gregtangmath.com/Games/BreakApart.

_____. "Kakooma." *Greg Tang's World of Math.* Last modified May 24, 2012. http://gregtangmath.com/Kakooma.

"10 Things More Likely to Happen Than Winning the Mega Millions Lottery." *Bay News 9.* Last modified February 19, 2014. http://www.baynews9.com/content/news/baynews9/news/article.html/content/news/articles/cfn/2013/12/17/mega_millions_odds.html?cid=rss.

Tierney, John. "Behind Monty Hall's Doors: Puzzle, Debate, and Answer?" *New York Times,* July 21, 1991.

Todd, Nancy S. "Exploring Meteorite Mysteries: Lesson 2—Following the Falling Meteorite." *NASA.* Last modified April 29, 2011. http://curator.jsc.nasa.gov/outreach/expmetmys/Lesson2.pdf.

"Top Names of the 2000s." *The Official Website of the U.S. Social Security Administration.* Last modified May 14, 2012. http://www.ssa.gov/oact/babynames/decades/names2000s.html.

Turner, Nigel, and Roger Horbay. "How Do Slot Machines and Other Electronic Gambling Machines Actually Work?" *Journal of Gambling Issues,* 11 (2004) 10–50. http://jgi.camh.net/loi/jgi.

Underwood, Dudley. *Numerology: Or, What Pythagoras Wrought.* Washington, D.C.: The Mathematical Association of America, 1997.

Vigen, Tyler. "Spurious Correlations." *Spurious Correlations.* Accessed July 29, 2014. http://www.tylervigen.com.

"Volume of a Sphere Explained." *Youtube.* Last modified April 4, 2012. http://youtu.be/hjcUpeK-4A0.

Vos Savant, Marilyn. "Game Show Problem." *Marilyn Vos Savant Online Headquarters.* Accessed January 3, 2013. http://marilynvossavant.com/game-show-problem.

"War Machines of Tomorrow." *PBS.* Last modified April 2004. http://www.pbs.org/wgbh/nova/education/activities/2305_warmachi.html.

Weisstein, Eric W. "Catalogue Paradox." *MathWorld: A Wolfram Web Resource.* Accessed January 28, 2014. http://mathworld.wolfram.com/CatalogueParadox.html.

West, Webster. "The Let's Make a Deal Applet." *Texas A&M University Department of Statistics.* Accessed January 3, 2013. http://www.stat.tamu.edu/~west/applets/LetsMakeaDeal.html.

"What Are the Odds of Being Struck by Lightening?" DiscoverTheOddswww. Last modified October 8, 2012. http://discovertheodds.com/what-are-the-odds-of-being-struck-by-lightning.

"What Is Project Look Sharp?" *Ithaca College.* Accessed August 28, 2014. http://www.projectlooksharp.org.

"What Is the Frequency of the Letters of the Alphabet in English?" *Oxford Dictionaries.* Accessed January 3, 2013. http://oxforddictionaries.com/words/what-is-the-frequency-of-the-letters-of-the-alphabet-in-english.

"Wheel." *The Evil Petting Zoo.* Last modified January 3, 2013. http://evilpettingzoo.com/wheel.

"Why People Think They Can Win the Lottery." *CBS DC.* Last modified December 17, 2013. http://washington.cbslocal.com/2013/12/17/why-people-think-they-can-win-the-lottery.

Willingham, Daniel T. *Why Don't Students Like School?* San Francisco: Jossey-Bass, 2009.

Wilson, Jacque. "Why You Keep Playing the Lottery." CNNwww. Last modified May 17, 2013. http://www.cnn.com/2012/08/15/health/psychology-playing-lottery-powerball.

Wilson, Tracy. "How Numerology Works." *How Stuff Works.* Last modified March

28, 2007. http://science.howstuffworks. com/science-vs-myth/extrasensory-perceptions/numerology.htm.

Yan, Wenfan, and Qiuyun Lin. "Parent Involvement and Mathematics Achievement: Contrast Across Racial and Ethnic Groups." *The Journal of Educational Research* 99, no. 2, (2005): 116–127.

Young, Elaine. "Palindrome Numbers." *Youngzones.* Accessed January 3, 2013. http://math.youngzones.org/palindrome. html.

Index